THE PALACE
LADY'S
SUMMERHOUSE

THE PALACE LADY'S SUMMERHOUSE

And other
INSIDE STORIES FROM A
VANISHING TURKEY

PATRICIA DAUNT

FOREWORD BY
JOHN JULIUS NORWICH

Photographs
Fritz von der Schulenburg, Simon Upton
Cemal Emden, Jean-Marie del Moral

CORNUCOPIA

At the author's request,
proceeds from this book will be given to
the Friends of Aphrodisias Trust,
a British charity dedicated to supporting excavations
and research at the ancient city of Aphrodisias,
disseminating the findings and raising
awareness of the site's importance.
www.aphrodisias.org.uk

To Timothy

A Cornucopia Book

Published in 2017 by
Caique Publishing Ltd,
1 Rutland Square,
Edinburgh EH3 3AY, in
association with Kayık
Yayıncılık Ltd, Valikonağı
Caddesi 64, Nişantaşı,
34367 Istanbul

ISBN 978-0-9957566-0-1
ISBN 978-605-83080-3-9

Text © Patricia Daunt 2017

Patricia Daunt has asserted
her right to be identified
as the author of this work.

PROJECT EDITORS
John Scott, Berrin Torolsan

DESIGN Clive Crook

TEXT EDITORS Susana Raby,
Hilary Stafford-Clark,
Tony Barrell

Printed and bound in Turkey
by Ofset Yapımevi, Istanbul
www.ofset.com

Cornucopia Books
PO Box 13311,
Hawick TD9 7YF, Scotland
www.cornucopia.net

CONTENTS

Foreword 6

PALACES OF DIPLOMACY   1   The Winter Palaces *The Pera Embassies* 10

WINDOW   2   Boating with Billy 34
ON THE BOSPHORUS   3   The Summer Palaces *The Bosphorus Embassies* 40
   4   The Jewel Box *The Çürüksulu Mehmet Pasha Yalı* 56
   5   The Vizier's Retreat *The Kıbrıslı Yalı* 68
   6   A Room for the Books *Ahmed Vefik Pasha's Library* 78
   7   Water's Edge *The Hekimbaşı Yalı* 86
   8   The Talk of the Bosphorus *The Zeki Pasha Yalı* 96
   9   Some Enchanted Evenings *The Ratip Efendi Yalı* 106
   10 The House that Came out of the Blue *The Germen Yalı* 114
   11 In the Spirit's Wake *Sumahan on the Water* 126
   12 The Palace Lady's Summerhouse *The Ethem Pertev Yalı* 134

TRAVELS IN ANATOLIA   13 The Country Houses that Ride the Storm 150
   14 The Lake that Time Forgot 166
   15 Sublime Portals *The Great Mosque and Hospital of Divriği* 182

SECRET ANKARA   16 A Brave New World *The Embassies' Big Move to Ankara* 194
   17 Fly in the Face of Fashion *Ankara's Hidden Assets* 236

PARIS À LA TURQUE   18 Treasures of a Lost Dynasty 256
   19 From Lunacy to Diplomacy 276

APHRODISIAS REBORN   20 City of Aphrodite 286

   Acknowledgements and glossary 298
   Index 300

John Julius Norwich

One morning a few years ago I received an email. It was from my son Jason, who was doing a tour of the Caucasus on his motorbike. Did I, he asked, know of anywhere in central Anatolia where he could safely leave his machine for the winter? Now Jason has always been an optimist but this time, I felt, he was carrying optimism too far. It was a good thirty years since I had been in the region, and even then I should have been unable to make the vaguest recommendation. I was just about to tell him so when I had a brainwave. I telephoned Patricia Daunt. She instantly asked me for his email address, which I gave her. Half an hour later she had discussed the matter with a riding stable near Kayseri, and Jason was on his way.

That's Patricia. No one is happier or readier to help – she had never met Jason in her life, though they are now firm friends – and no one knows Turkey better than she. Moreover, to the delight of us all, she has incorporated a small but vitally important part of her knowledge in a series of articles written in recent years for *Cornucopia*. And *Cornucopia* is another miracle – one of the most beautifully produced magazines in existence anywhere. Most readers of this book will know it already; those who don't should subscribe at once.

For the magnificent volume that you now hold in your hands is a rare treasure indeed: *Cornucopia*'s flair and know-how with Patricia's knowledge and wit, all dazzlingly combined. From it you will learn of another, semi-secret Turkey, a Turkey far removed from that of Haghia Sophia and Kariye Camii, of the Blue Mosque and the Grand Bazaar. For Patricia is not only a passionate Turcophile and a most impressive scholar; she is also a former ambassadress, who over many years has been able to penetrate far more deeply than most of us into the life and customs of what we must, alas, describe as a vanishing Turkey.

Her diplomatic experience comes into play with the very first article, 'Palaces of Diplomacy', those magnificent erstwhile embassies whose glory was stolen away when the capital was moved to Ankara in 1923. From these, however, we soon move down to the Bosphorus and those enchanting yalıs (how I enjoy that undotted i), in one of which I can still remember, after more than half a century, the reflected water making wonderful designs like golden wire-netting on the ceiling in the evening sun.

At last we leave Istanbul, travelling in turn to deepest Anatolia and the little town of Divriği (which boasts the most astonishing – though not, perhaps, the most beautiful – mosque in all Turkey), and thence to Ankara and Paris, where the Turkish Embassy occupies the old home of that most intimate friend of Marie Antoinette the Princesse de Lamballe, who is said to have been so sensitive that she once fainted dead away at the sight of an oil painting of a lobster.

And, finally, to Aphrodisias, to many of us the loveliest classical site in all Turkey and the one to which Patricia has for the past thirty-odd years dedicated her life. It is, thank God, relatively inaccessible, which means that it is not thronged with tourists like Ephesus and the other sites along the coast. And it is yielding up more glorious sculptures every year than all the rest put together. Of course it is a concerted effort: the names of the late and much-lamented Kenan Erim, of Professor Bert Smith and of Trevor Proudfoot can never be forgotten; but to me it will always mean Patricia, and I am more than happy that she has been able to use it as the grand finale to this glorious book. If, in Aphrodisias, you would see her monument, look around.

London, July 2017

Previous pages
'Istanbul', 1918, by
Ahmet Ziya Akbulut
(1869–1938). A timeless
view of the Bosphorus,
perhaps from the
village of Kandilli on
the Asian side. The
painting now hangs
in the Sakıp Sabancı
Museum in Emirgan on
the European shore

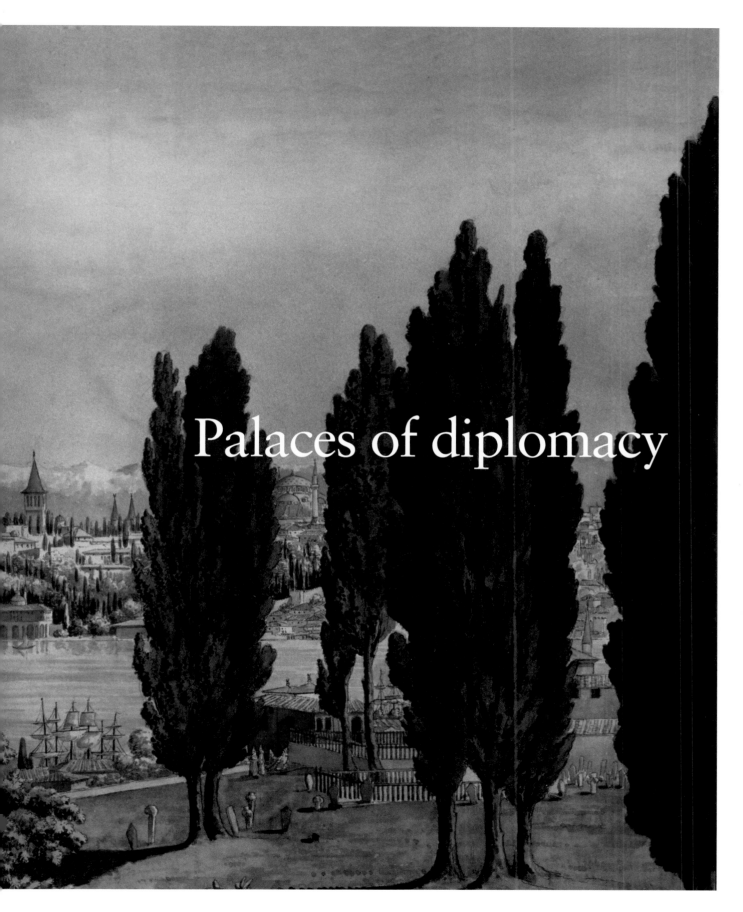

Palaces of diplomacy

THE WINTER PALACES

THE FORMER WINTER EMBASSIES OF ISTANBUL ARE CLUSTERED
IN PERA, THE OLD EUROPEAN QUARTER, LIKE OPULENT COUNTRY
HOUSES IN NATIONAL COSTUME. THEY HAVE MORE OF A CONSULAR
ROLE TODAY, BUT THEIR VAST CHAMBERS STILL EVOKE THE
DIPLOMATIC RITUALS OF THEIR OTTOMAN PRIME

*The Dutch had set up
their embassy among
the vineyards of Pera as
early as 1612. This
residence of the Dutch
ambassador was built
in 1850 after fire
destroyed the earlier
wooden palace*

*Previous pages
The Topkapı from the
Swedish Embassy in
Pera by Carl Gustaf
Löwenhielm, envoy
from 1824 to 1827.
'The view from the
garden kiosk heals
the spirits,' wrote
his predecessor, Nils
Gustaf Palin*

Cosmopolitan, trendsetting, with distractions to suit almost every taste, modern Beyoğlu – the Pera of old – holds an unusual extra to whet the enthusiasm of even the most jaded tourist: the pleasure of seeking out the 'winter embassies' so relished by the ambassadors and envoys to the Ottoman Porte. They are the grandest diplomatic buildings of any imperial capital in the world and, with the exception of the Italian, are all more-or-less nineteenth-century contemporaries. Extravagantly built, referred to as 'palaces', once endowed with prisons, chapels and throne rooms, they stand in their own grounds protected by high walls and fine gates. Demoted to consulates when the embassies removed to Ankara after it became the new Republic's capital in 1923, all but the German palace are within a stone's throw of the Grand' Rue de Pera – or İstiklâl Caddesi, as it became in the 1920s.

Trade with the Ottoman Empire, the raison d'être of the foreign community of Constantinople, had brought diplomatic missions in its wake. The first embassies were established near their traders' factories around the docks of Galata on the Golden Horn, jostling the Genoese, Anconite, Ragusan, Pisan and Florentine merchants and at the mercy of Hebrew moneylenders, Armenian dragomans (interpreters) and Greek jacks-of-all-trades. It was the constant danger of fire, the risk of bubonic plague and the discomfort of overcrowding that led them to follow the richer Franks, as Europeans were known, away from the port into a garden suburb, known as 'les vignes de Péra', the site of present-day Beyoğlu.

Venice had been represented since 1082 by a succession of *bailos*, envoys nominated by the Doge. The first Russian emissary arrived at the Porte in 1492. France's first resident ambassador arrived in Istanbul in 1535, and a treaty full of substantial privileges was signed in 1536. The French alliance with Turkey arose from expediency. François I would have allied with the Devil if the latter had fought against the Emperor Charles V; he found the Great Turk a reliable substitute.

The English, then indisposed to form a trading company in seas infested with African pirates, contented themselves with trading their wool and cloth for rhubarb and 'trash-berries' (currants) under the French flag. During the 1570s, Queen Elizabeth I decided on an embassy, but English overtures were vigorously opposed by both France and Venice, by now the favoured claimants of Ottoman privilege and Levantine commerce. The English nonetheless received their first official capitulations (trading and diplomatic concessions) in 1578.

Sweden was no stranger to the Levant, having made use of the Russian rivers to trade with the Byzantines as early as 860. In 1631 the Swedes combined with the Dutch, who had received their first capitulations in 1612, to conclude a treaty of friendship, not only to promote trade but also to co-operate with the Ottomans against the enemy emperors in Vienna and St Petersburg.

From the harbour at Galata, a steep rise flattened into an avenue leading through Pera. Known as the Grand' Rue, it ran along the spine of the hill commanding magnificent views of both the Golden Horn and the Bosphorus. At its most elevated point, near Galatasaray, the area was called the Heights of Pera. Tucked into the folds of the vine-clad hills running east to the Bosphorus, modest wood and plaster villas clung to the steep slopes. By 1517 the Venetian *bailo* was renting such a villa – paper-thin and impossibly cold, or so he complained.

The French in 1581 acquired the estate next door, enjoying the same idyllic view looking over the seraglio of Topkapı Palace to the islands in the Sea of Marmara beyond. The English soon followed, taking a 'faire house within a large field and pleasant gardens compassed with a wall' near the Venetians and the French. Though this rented house nearly burned down twice, they would stay here until 1801, when the Sultan gave them a piece of land on the Heights of Pera in thanks for the part they played in the expulsion of the French from Egypt. The Dutch established themselves on Tophane Hill, near the Ottoman palace at Galatasaray, probably on the site they occupy to this day.

Diplomatic life in seventeenth-century Pera was conducted in some style and was expensive. The first Dutch ambassador housed a staff of close to two dozen, among them a steward, a clerk, a messenger, a tailor, a cellar-master/butler, a doorkeeper, an under-cook, a stableman, two valets, three dragomans, an apprentice dragoman, an apothecary, a painter, a Turkish scribe and, finally, two Janissary guards allotted by the Sublime Porte at the ambassador's expense.

The sedan chair was introduced by an English ambassador in 1674. It was initially frowned on by the Turks, the grand vizier threatening to 'break that cage' on the ambassador's head. Once adopted, however, it lingered on in Turkey long after it had disappeared elsewhere. As late as 1875 it was still in common use. The British ambassador's step-daughter was painted being conveyed in a sedan chair to her wedding in 1896, and the Italian ambassador's residence still has one standing in its entrance hall.

Rivalries among the foreigners were intense. The Catholic Latins generally considered the Protestant northerners of no consequence. The Frenchman became apoplectic at the thought that an Englishman might be given precedence, and the Venetian threatened war when a Dutchman entered a door before him.

The finest eighteenth-century embassy was that of the Swedes, which stood on the Grand' Rue and was completed, some say, with monies collected as Sunday church offerings by the Protestant faithful for the buying and freeing of slaves. During the mid-eighteenth century the Russians also acquired a piece of land on the Grand' Rue. It is said that a shipload of sacred Russian earth was brought in at the command of Catherine the Great so that her embassy 'should stand on Russian soil'. The first embassy was wooden and burned down in 1767. It was the general belief of Turks and foreigners alike that fires such as this, which were frequent, were spread by red-hot nails catapulted with explosive force over great distances from burning timbers.

The palace of the Venetian *bailo*, now the Italian ambassador's Istanbul residence, was transformed in the 1750s from a wooden structure into the fine brick and stone palace we know today. But it did not satisfy the *bailo* Andrea Memmo: in the late 1770s he found the place both 'insufficiently spaced' and 'unhealthily tucked into the hill'. He wanted to sell it to the Armenian Patriarch and build a new and even grander palace. The Senate would have none of it, but it did find the funds for a major refurbishment.

With the end of the Venetian Republic in 1797, the great palace of the *bailos* passed from hand to hand with the ebb and flow of European military fortunes. The French and Austrians each in turn won and lost it. It was sumptuously refurbished by Baron Karl von Bruck during his term as Austrian ambassador. When he inaugurated the newly renovated rooms by holding a splendid ball on the night of 6 February 1854, 'full-grown orange and lemon trees lined the walls of every room'. The scent of the blossom and the sight of the fruit enchanted the people of Pera, who 'after the departure of the Sultan, danced until six in the morning', congratulating their host on the fact that the sherbet never ran out.

A series of fires at the beginning of the nineteenth century left Pera in ruins. 'More than thirty-eight outbreaks in less than two months of the new Vizier's administration,' wrote the Swedish ambassador Nils Gustaf Palin the day after Sweden's embassy burned down during the night of 25 March 1818. It was a devastating blaze which left only the foundations of the building, the mutilated walls of the stables, laundry and outbuildings and, alone and untouched, a garden kiosk in which the minister and his family sheltered. Though the archives and his famous collection of antiquities were safe in one of the fireproof magazines, everything else that the Palins possessed was lost, including his completed memoirs. 'Whatever the shock,' he wrote, 'the view from the garden kiosk heals the spirits and for a moment numbs the senses into forgetting the reality of the ruin and desolation around.'

A severe earthquake set the bells of Pera tolling a week after another catastrophic fire which engulfed the Russian Embassy 'in an amphitheatre of flames'. Then, during the morning of 22 August 1831, the worst of all the fires to ravage Pera destroyed the Dutch, British and French Embassies but miraculously missed the Venetian. The flames reached its gates but a freak lull in the wind, followed by a particularly fierce blast, lifted them over the roof to continue down the hillside, leaving havoc in their wake. It was said that more than a thousand houses were destroyed in six hours, and the heat was so intense that even fireproof magazines were melted.

Only in 1837 did work on the new Russian Embassy begin. Plans for an imposing Neoclassical palace were prepared by a young Swiss-Italian architect, Gaspare Fossati, who had won his spurs in St Petersburg as court architect to the Tsar, and worked in Istanbul with his brother, Giuseppe. The best Russian craftsmen were brought in; the iron gates, imperial arms and window grilles were specially cast at the famous Russian ironworks at Lugansk, and a team of Italian artists was commissioned to paint the ceilings and walls. A palace of no uncertain grandeur rose from the ashes of its wooden predecessors; the height of the ceiling in the columned ballroom was thirteen metres, with the adjacent loggia commodious enough to receive all Pera in comfort.

A year after the great fire of 1831, the French minister of foreign affairs wrote to his new ambassador, Admiral Roussin, of the advantages of a stay in Constantinople, emphasising the pleasure of living in a residence as

The Swedish Embassy,
now the consulate
general, was constructed
in 1870 to designs by
the Austrian Domenico
Pulgher, with rooms
radiating from a central
hall. The previous
building was destroyed
by fire in 1818 along
with the memoirs of
Nils Gustaf Palin, the
Swedish minister. A
garden kiosk became a
temporary base

Centre The medallion
of the aristocrat Nils
Silfverschiöld on the
staircase is by the royal
sculptor Johan Tobias
Sergel (1753–1813)

Bottom The griffins
on the sofa arms are
a recurrent symbol on
Gustavian furniture

agreeable as the Palais de France. Admiral Roussin's problem on arrival was how it should be rebuilt. On a new site away from the city? In stone or in wood? He invited the archaeologist Charles Texier, in Istanbul for his first mission in Asia Minor, to draw up plans for a stone building resistant to fire. But the credits did not cover the cost of even a wooden edifice.

The Parisian architect Pierre Laurecisque produced designs for a charming and innovative building that would enable the ambassador to live, entertain and work under the same roof. He grossly underestimated the cost in order to win the contract. The French Romantic poet Gérard de Nerval, passing through in 1843, noted that the palace was 'costing millions of francs' and that it was not yet finished. Building had indeed halted, and the Maltese stonemasons who had been working on the fire-resistant white stone had been laid off while funds were awaited.

Four years later the palace was standing on a raised terrace, on the levelled rubble of its predecessor. Its only decorations were the busts of François I and Henri IV above the west doorway, and the monogram LP, for Louis-Philippe, traced onto the wings of the southern side of the house.

A magnificent stairway sweeps up to the ambassador's apartment on the second floor, which houses a fine collection of portraits of kings of France and sultans of Turkey, history paintings, *firmans* (Ottoman decrees) and rare furniture. The columned drawing room is hung with tapestries bearing the arms of France and Navarre, specially woven for the palace by the Gobelin workshops. The panelled ballroom is decorated with a carved frieze of alternating swans and musical instruments. Both empire-blue boudoirs are lined with Louis XVI furniture and porcelain from the factory at Sèvres. The dining room, giving onto a terrace overlooking the garden, is hung with tapestries based on cartoons by Le Brun. In the wonderful gardens there is still a chapel and the disused sixteenth-century prison, a reminder of the powers of the foreign representatives in Ottoman times.

AEDES LEGATIONIS ANGLICANAE AEDIFICATAE VICTORIA REGNANTE ANNO DOMINI MDCCCXLIV (The Palace of the English Legation, built in the Reign of Queen Victoria 1849) is how the British Embassy, 'a monument of lavish expenditure of public money combined with false economy', proclaims itself along the top of its southern façade. The violently Turcophile Queen Victoria, who had to be reminded by her prime minister Benjamin Disraeli that he was not her grand vizier, never saw her palace at Constantinople. How gratified she would have been by her initials intertwined on the pillars in her drawing room, and her bust carved into the marble mantelpiece in her ballroom. In the race for palace rebuilding, Britain finished last. After the fire the British ambassador was comfortable up the Bosphorus at Tarabya and shelved all plans to return to the squalor of 'the dirty quarter of town'.

When the arrival of Sir Stratford Canning as the new ambassador became imminent, a decision had to be made. Known both in Turkey and in Britain as 'the Great Elchi', or Great Envoy – and from 1852 as Lord Stratford de Redcliffe – he was no stranger to the old palace, which he remembered for the bats that were in the habit of hovering over the dining table. They created a disturbance during evening parties, their sooty wings and foul odour suggestive of the Harpies. He had witnessed the Auspicious Event – the dissolution of the Janissaries – from his seat at table commanding a view of Stamboul beyond the Golden Horn: '…I had scarcely taken my place when I observed columns of smoke rising above the opposite horizon. What could they mean? I asked, and the reply informed me that the Sultan's people had fired on the barracks of the Janissaries…'

Only in July 1844 was it finally decided in London to begin building on the foundations of the old palace. Thomas Smith, a disciple of Sir Charles Barry's Renaissance Revival, designed a rectangular Anglo-Italian structure. An important feature was a fine marble staircase. Alleys of trees would border the garden on three sides, secluding a southerly terrace; some of the mastic trees that had been brought from the Aegean had survived the fire, but there would be new plantings of pines, Judas, magnolia, persimmon, chestnut, bay and *Albizia julibrissin* (*gül ibrişim*). They remain to this day.

The most pressing problem was that the building of Dolmabahçe Palace was by then under way on the shore of the Bosphorus and all the best quarries and workmen had been commandeered for it. The price of stone had doubled. A quarry was found, five hours' journey by horse westward from the city, but doubts were expressed about the durability of the fine limestone. It was difficult to get stone cut to the required size and presents had to be made to the Sultan's director of kilns in order to obtain lime. The foundations were found to be too soft and had to be dug to a depth of twenty feet and filled in with hard stone. Smith was asked by the Sultan's chief physician to make plans for a school of medicine. Permission was granted so long as it did not interfere with his embassy work, but the British authorities began to suspect that their architect was doing a thriving trade building for Turks while drawing his salary from the Office of Works.

By 1846 half the roof was in place, and by October 1848 the ambassador had moved in to occupy the second floor. The costs had escalated. The architect was in disgrace. Canning objected to the glazed iron roof planned to cover the central courtyard. He raged over the painting, papering and bell-hanging. Thomas Smith returned to London in the summer of 1853 and, even in the spring of 1855, by which time it had been under construction for over ten years, the embassy was not complete and the roof was leaking in some sixty or seventy places. But on 25 December 1855 the Great Elchi's palace was ready enough for a Christmas Day ball. Florence Nightingale, much weakened by her recent illness, spent the evening on a sofa in the new ballroom beside a blazing fire. Lady Hornby found the palace 'very beautiful, its spacious white stone corridors, richly and warmly carpeted... an air of perfectness was very striking'.

The following year Sultan Abdülmecid attended a fancy-dress ball, escorted from Galata to the embassy by a company of English Lancers, every man carrying a torch. Lord Stratford met him at the carriage door and, as he alighted, 'a communication by means of galvanic wires was made to the fleet, who saluted him with prolonged salvos of cannon'. It was reported that the Sultan was gratified by this splendid ball, not least by the Highlanders and Lancers who lined the grand staircase, one on each step, and by the Light Dragoons and Royals who presented arms to him in the hall.

The search for the site of the first German Embassy, behind Dolmabahçe Palace and overlooking the Bosphorus and the Sea of Marmara, began in 1870, and building started in 1874. It was completed in three years. Hubert Göbbels's neo-Renaissance celebration of German might dominated this district of wooden structures. 'The new palace impresses us more than it pleases our aesthetic senses... it is a mammoth lacking elegance, an unrelieved mass without architectural worth and stands out in this blessed place like a sore thumb,' wrote a contemporary Austrian correspondent. Today it is dwarfed by the new Park Hotel [the tower of which was later torn down], but perhaps the Austrian's judgement was not far from the mark.

The palace was certainly splendid. Marble lined the walls of the principal reception rooms and was used for columns, stairways and balconies. Stucco bas-reliefs decorated walls and ceilings. Ornamental marble and marquetry floors complemented the wall and ceiling paintings. Gas lighting and air-propelled heating lit and warmed the great interiors. It was, said a visitor, 'just like something out of the *Arabian Nights*'.

The establishment of the United States legation at the Porte came later, although American missionaries had been in the country since the 1830s and Robert College had been founded in 1863. It was not until the arrival in 1901 of John G.A. Leishman as minister of the legation that the present building was hired and later bought. It had been built by one of the 'last opulent Franks to move up the hill', Ignazio Corpi, a Genoese shipowner who had amassed a vast fortune since arriving in Turkey as a young man. It was a Neoclassical monument to prosperity on the western slopes of the Heights of Pera. Its Italian architect, Giacomo Leoni, had imported all the building materials from Italy – marble for the floors and mantelpieces from Carrara, rosewood for the window frames and doors from Piemonte – and a team of Italian painters had been specially commissioned to cover the walls and ceilings, even those of the bathrooms, with frescoes of heroic and bacchanalian scenes.

It is said that a soothsayer had foretold that on completion of the palace its owner was to die. During the night of its inauguration in 1882, Ignazio Corpi did indeed expire, allegedly in the arms of a mistress, his cousin, a liaison which was considered incestuous. The house stood abandoned and was fought over by his heirs, who were undecided whether to lease or to sell. The United States government bought it in 1907. The story goes that Leishman, unable to persuade his government to buy what was to become the first state-owned embassy in Europe, arranged for a game of poker between himself and those of the department concerned. If they won, Leishman bought it; if Leishman won, the government bought it. Leishman won.

With the move of emphasis to Atatürk's new capital in the 1920s, the old palaces were neglected. Only when trade with Turkey revived in the 1980s was the decay reversed – a fitting development, since it was trade that had brought the foreign powers to the shores of the Bosphorus and financed the palaces in the nineteenth century.

Turkey's economic miracle revived the Istanbul consulates. The Italians installed fourteen new marble bathrooms in 1989. The French carried out a major refurbishment ahead of Mitterrand's visit in 1992. The Germans are rumoured to have spent over two million dollars on the restoration of Kaiser Wilhelm II's palace to its original splendour. The Americans have started to peel off the grey-green paint used to cover the walls in 1937, and Corpi's fabled frescoes are again seeing the light of day [the fully restored Palazzo Corpi is now leased to the London club Soho House]. The Russians, celebrating the 500th anniversary of the first embassy in 1992, have already restored the ceiling in Fossati's palace, which shows pre-revolutionary St Petersburg – a rare record of how the city looked in the nineteenth century. The British have spilled into the old stable block and have painted their ballroom *bayrak* red, the bright red of the Turkish flag, perhaps in remembrance of Sir Stratford Canning, who was persuaded to hand over his household linen to Florence Nightingale for bandaging the wounded from the Crimean War.

Foreign flags fly in Ankara above utilitarian residences. In Istanbul high walls shelter the consulates as hidden oases in the hustle and bustle of Beyoğlu, but the flags once again flutter proudly over the extravagant architecture and lush gardens relished so much in the past by envoys to the Sultan.

Cornucopia Issue 5, 1993

The Heights of Pera: a view from the Palais de France. In the embassy grounds is the church of Saint-Louis-des-Français with its domed bell tower. Above the church, on the old Grand' Rue de Pera, is the white-painted Dutch palace. The large red building on the left is the Russian Embassy. Both were designed by the Swiss-Italian Fossati brothers, who also restored the Byzantine basilica of Haghia Sophia

The Great Elchi's palace

The British Embassy, designed by Thomas Smith in the spirit of Sir Charles Barry, took more than a decade to build, being completed in late 1855. Few embassies had greater pretensions. Pera House was ordered for Queen Victoria's ambassador, Sir Stratford Canning, known both in Turkey and in Britain as 'the Great Elchi' (the Great Envoy)

The splendid Palm Court. Canning objected to the plans for glassing in the roof, and it was still leaking when the building was finished

Above The ambassador's butler awaits guests on the marble staircase leading up to the state rooms

Right Polishing the ballroom's parquet. Florence Nightingale attended the first Christmas ball, in 1855, but did not venture far from the blazing fire

Miss Singleton, daughter of the poet Violet Fane and stepdaughter of the British ambassador Sir Philip Currie, crosses the garden of Pera House in a sedan chair on the way to her wedding in 1896, in a painting now hanging in the nearby Pera Museum. Currie asked Fausto Zonaro, Abdülhamid II's court painter, to include the view over the Golden Horn. The Sultan's wedding gift was a diamond bracelet

The sumptuous Palais de France

The most sumptuously furnished of the diplomatic buildings in Pera today is the Palais de France (right), rebuilt in 1839–47 by Pierre Laurecisque after the great Pera fire of 1831. Many of the rooms were redecorated for President Mitterrand's official visit in 1992

Left The airy dining room, which leads out to the embassy gardens Right The staircase hall, hung with a Gobelin tapestry designed by Charles Le Brun

A grandiose palace for the Tsar

This is the most imposing of the embassies viewed from the sea. Built between 1837 and 1845 by Gaspare and Giuseppe Fossati with hundreds of Russian craftsmen and Italian artists, it needed heavy restoration after the 1894 earthquake and a violent gale in 1905
Right The palm-fringed Neoclassical entrance
Below The columned ballroom
Opposite Classical divinities in the hallway

The Venetian palace

The Palazzo di Venezia, the residence of the Italian ambassador, was rebuilt in the 1750s, and with the demise of the Venetian Republic became a diplomatic base for France, Austria and then Italy. It survived the 1831 fire that ravaged the Dutch, British and French legations

Above The façade of the Palazzo di Venezia, still the Italian ambassador's residence (other former embassies have now become consulates)
Left A sedan chair in the hall
Opposite, top Freshly painted shutters dry in the loggia alongside a winged lion of St Mark, symbol of Venice. The pedestal records the year the palazzo became the Italian Embassy – 1919
Opposite, bottom Portrait of a doge in one of the reception rooms

The Palazzo Corpi

The Palazzo Corpi was built between 1873 and 1882 for Ignazio Corpi, a wealthy Genoese shipowner; he died on its completion, reputedly in the arms of his mistress. The building was bought for the United States government in 1907. It was the first diplomatic property to be owned by the United States on European soil

Top Palazzo Corpi in the days when the Stars and Stripes still flew over the house. In 2014 it was leased to the London club Soho House

Above A Renaissance figure on the staircase holds a newel light
Right Neptune has been restored to his full glory in this dramatic fresco on a hall ceiling

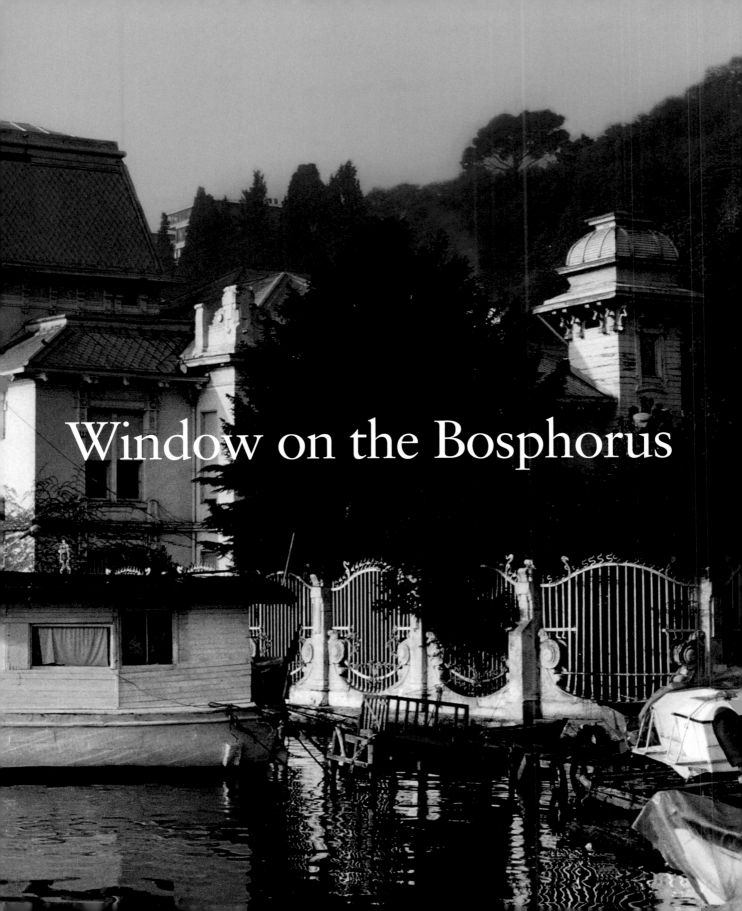

Window on the Bosphorus

2

UP AND DOWN THE BOSPHORUS

BOATING WITH BILLY

LOOKING BACK AFTER TWENTY-FIVE YEARS OF WRITING ABOUT
THE HISTORIC WATERSIDE HOUSES OF THE BOSPHORUS,
PATRICIA DAUNT TAKES TO THE WATER WITH A YOUNG GRANDSON
TO GIVE HIM A GUIDED TOUR OF HER FAVOURITE YALIS

*The historic Köprülü
Yalı on the Asian
shore is the oldest
surviving house on the
Bosphorus. It belonged
to Amcazade Hüseyin
Pasha, last of a line of
grand viziers from the
distinguished Köprülü
family, who signed the
Treaty of Karlowitz
with the Habsburgs
in the house on
26 January 1699*

*Previous pages A 1994
photograph of the
eclectic palace at Bebek
built in 1902 for the
mother of the Khedive
of Egypt (page 47)*

The Bosphorus story isn't all castles and royal palaces, I tell my eager grandson Billy: 'Half of it is about yalıs, the wooden summerhouses built on the water's edge by the great and the good of the Ottoman Empire, who were all in search of retreats away from the heat and overcrowding in the Old City. So today we're going to have a rest from mosques and palaces. We're taking a boat up the Bosphorus.' Aged ten, Billy has an insatiable thirst for knowledge, jotting down answers to his constant enquiries in a grubby pocket notebook.

The building of these wooden yalıs on the Bosphorus and the Golden Horn, I tell him, had actually begun fifty years before they became fashionable in the early eighteenth century, under Ahmed III. Viziers and pashas tended to choose the Asian shore, to be within sight of the Old City and to enjoy its sunsets and opportunities for good hunting. One of the earliest yalıs [opposite] was built near the castle of Anadolu Hisarı by the grand vizier Amcazade Hüseyin Pasha, whose family, the Köprülüs, governed the empire for much of the seventeenth century. The Greeks, Armenians, Levantines and diplomats preferred to build on the more protected European bank.

The first object of our voyage is the remains of a yalı at Kuzguncuk on the Asian shore, once gaily painted pink. Upstream from the Leander Tower, it is well within sight of the Old City, and was built in the mid-eighteenth century. A hundred years later it became known as the Fethi Ahmed Pasha Yalı. The pasha was once envoy to Vienna, and his marriage to Sultan Abdülmecid's youngest sister may have been the reason why he represented the Ottoman Empire at Queen Victoria's coronation.

The tall, elegant timber pillars supporting the wings of the first storey – and the way it is cantilevered over the water – had a direct influence on Le Corbusier, who visited Istanbul in 1911. He described the whole as 'an architectural masterpiece'. During the 1990s it was sold off by the pasha's descendants: two sisters who in the 1960s had agreed to disagree over its division. The two halves of this lovely building are now painted white, reunited, and owned by new money. Let's hope that new money will mean new care for the Bosphorus's treasured yalıs.

Moving north against a six-knot surface current, with Billy fidgeting excitedly at my side, we pass the flamboyant Dolmabahçe Palace on the European shore and Beylerbeyi Palace on the Asian side.

Averting our eyes from the mass of suburban development on both sides, we aim for the second-oldest yalı surviving on the Bosphorus. Today the Sadullah Pasha Yalı [opposite] bears the name of a late-nineteenth-century owner, a diplomat whose fall from grace and death in exile left a grief-stricken widow who is said to haunt it still. Built at the end of the seventeenth century and remodelled internally in the 1730s by a grand vizier at the court of Mustafa III, it stands within its garden on the Asian shore north of the First Bosphorus Bridge at Çengelköy. Its projecting bays and shuttered windows, uniformly painted in the traditional oxblood red, give no hint of its harem's exuberant, almost theatrical interior. The yalı was in genteel limbo in the 1980s when fortune came its way. History doesn't relate whether Le Corbusier noted the two corner rooms projecting over the water in order to catch the view.

Carrying on up the Asian shore, past all the yalıs hanging over the water in Kandilli, we reach another house painted in oxblood red. Thought to have been built around 1790 by an Italian architect, it is now owned by the collector Rahmi Koç. Still known locally as the Kont Ostrorog Yalı, after the Polish count who, as one of the Sultan's legal advisers, acquired it in the late nineteenth century, it was sold by his descendants in the nick of time, in the early years of the millennium.

This exceptionally lovely house, sandwiched between the coast road and the sea, stands within its own gardens, scented front and back by magnolia, pine and paulownia. It was badly dilapidated when Rahmi Bey bought it. Once the house had been refloated on its original piers, and the sea wall, boathouse and garden repaired, the fragile structure was carefully brought into the twenty-first century. The yalı retains the Ottoman arrangement of rooms grouped round a central hall on both the ground and upper floors, the

The Sadullah Pasha Yalı in Çengelköy is typical of the houses that lined the shores of the Bosphorus in the eighteenth century. Its austere façade, a faded oxblood red in 1983, when Fritz von der Schulenburg photographed it, belies an exuberant interior, with an elliptical dome painted to resemble a tent

two connected by perhaps the finest double staircase in all the Bosphorus. As in Venice, the halls stretch from the back to the front of the house.

The Kıbrıslı Yalı, the longest wooden house on the Bosphorus, is perfectly set on the northwest-facing shore, commanding a sweeping view of both Bosphorus fortresses [Chapter 5]. Painted white, it could fool anyone into thinking that it had been built in one piece. In fact, as I explain to Billy, its completion took over a hundred years. To the 1770 *selamlık* – men's quarters or reception rooms – a harem was added in the mid-nineteenth century on one side, and an orangery, in the 1870s, on the other. The Kıbrıslı family acquired it in the 1850s, when the future grand vizier Mehmet Emin Efendi was in straitened circumstances and looking for a retreat away from the debt collectors. I have not discovered much about the long-forgotten pasha who built this jewel, but it was at a time when the Ottoman Empire was enjoying a twenty-year peace before the need arose to confront Catherine the Great's Russia. It was the golden age of yalı-building.

Still on the Asian shore, there is one important yalı beneath the second Bosphorus bridge (the Fatih Sultan Mehmet Bridge, often simply the Fatih Bridge). It is the summerhouse and botanic garden of the last chief physician to

the Ottoman Court, Hekimbaşı Salih Efendi [Chapter 7]. It is but a fragment, having been divided among three sisters. During the 1950s one sister sold off the garden – now swallowed up by the piers of the bridge – and had the library to its north pulled down. Another sister sold off the *selamlık* for conversion to a bungalow. Only the harem, boathouse and waterside terrace bequeathed to the youngest sister survive. They appear as if built in a series of steps, fitting Miss Pardoe's observation in *The Beauties of the Bosphorus* in 1836, that yalıs have 'the appearance of being put together in fragments'. What, I wonder, would the Sultan's physician have made of the bridge?

Before crossing to the European shore at Kanlıca, we must find the 1860s Ethem Pertev Yalı, also known as the Palace Lady's Summerhouse, with its ornately carved balcony, brackets and bargeboards [Chapter 12]. Nothing is known for certain about the woman who built it except the year of her death, 1908. Most probably it was a gift made by Sultan Abdülmecid, the Tanzimat reformer, and the recipient was probably one of the Palace ladies, who enjoyed exceptional licence.

The story of the house would almost certainly have ended in tragedy – collapse into the sea – had it not been bought in 2000 by a couple prepared painstakingly to dismantle the tottering harem and *selamlık*, making a minute

record of every surviving feature so that craftsmen could make exact replicas.

We now make for Emirgan, on the European shore, with its unmissable Sakıp Sabancı Museum, near the landing stage. Billy will be enthralled when he sees it, but there is no time for museums today, so on to Yeniköy.

When the Italian architect Raimondo D'Aronco and his Levantine contemporary Alexandre Vallaury introduced Art Nouveau to the Bosphorus, they quickly became the avant-garde architects to the super-rich, who demanded yalıs of five storeys. Much of Yeniköy was transformed into a confusion of opulent flamboyance in both wood and stone: scrolls, swirling lines, geometric motifs, sculpted balconies... Out went pasted-on 'historical styles'. In came experiments with new materials.

Two of Yeniköy's most important yalıs contrast wildly. The mid-nineteenth-century Sait Halim Pasha Yalı, guarded by stone lions, is a near-perfect, albeit reconstructed, piece of French Empire classicism. The Afif Pasha Yalı, with its deep eaves, screened windows and turrets sporting elaborate onion domes, is eclectically cosmopolitan.

We pass close by the summer embassy of the Italians which, *per miracolo*, still stands in Tarabya [page 53]. Created by D'Aronco in 1906 as a Tyrolean-style wooden building, it is now so vulnerable that it is anyone's guess when it might collapse on a passing car. The French and the English are next door. Both have lost their summerhouses: the French by abandoning theirs to Marmara University twenty-five years ago, the English never rebuilding after a fire in 1911. The coastal road now runs between the sea and their overgrown gardens, which appear to be the last few stretches of undeveloped hillside left on the Bosphorus.

Diplomats moved early to the remote upper shore – difficult to imagine now, since the villages are all part of a mega-metropolis whose tentacles spread from the heart of old Stamboul. The two oldest surviving summerhouses of the ambassadors to the Ottoman Empire stand at the head of Büyükdere Bay. The Spanish one, on land once belonging to the Franciscans, was rebuilt after a fire in the 1860s and is impeccably kept. The 1840s Neoclassical wooden palace of the Tsars, eaten away by the elements, is at present under scaffolding and, we must hope, will be saved.

Kaiser Wilhelm I's summer embassy in the bay of Tarabya has all its purpose-built, cottage-style clapboard houses beautifully maintained. Its setting always was the most beautiful of all the embassy sites on the Bosphorus.

As we turn and head south, spotting many yalıs that we'd missed on our way upstream, there's plenty of time for the story of Jason navigating the swirling channel with his band of heroes on their way to Colchis in the fifty-oared *Argo*.

Cornucopia Issue 52, 2015

Sultan Abdülaziz's splendid summer palace at Beylerbeyi, on the Asian shore of the lower Bosphorus, built in the 1860s. The Empress Eugénie, wife of Napoleon III, stayed here on her way to the opening of the Suez Canal in 1869

3

THE SUMMER PALACES

WHEN THE SUMMER HEAT MADE COOL-HEADED DIPLOMACY
IMPOSSIBLE IN THE CITY, THE EUROPEAN AMBASSADORS TO
THE SUBLIME PORTE AND THE VICEROYS OF EGYPT RETIRED TO
REMARKABLE RESIDENCES LINING THE BOSPHORUS. TODAY, THESE
NOBLE MONUMENTS LANGUISH, WEATHERED AND OVERGROWN

*Faded glory: the
ambassadorial
gardens of Austria's
consulate general in
Yeniköy, formerly the
Austro-Hungarian
Embassy, were once
the Patriarch of
Jerusalem's vineyard*

It has been said that in the great age of diplomacy, when ambassadors
lived like princes, ambassadors to the Sublime Porte lived like kings.
Swaggering Circassians, resplendent in scarlet uniforms and armed
with swords and beltfuls of daggers, preceded them wherever they
went. The power of the ambassadors waxed as that of the Ottoman
Empire waned. They divided their year between winter embassies in Pera,
described by a seventeenth-century traveller as 'a kind of town where
Christian Ambassadors dwell', and summer retreats away from a thirsty city
prone to earthquake, disease, drought and fire.

By the close of the nineteenth century, all the embassies, as well as the
Khedive, or viceroy, of Egypt, had summer residences on the European
shore of the Bosphorus, 'the most lovely waterway that ever invited a sail'.
Some remain, and of some there are only vestiges: the Egyptian at Bebek, the
Austrian at Yeniköy, the German, French, Italian and British at Tarabya, the
Spanish and Russian at Büyükdere. The cosmopolitan architecture of those
that have survived and the overgrown grounds of those that have not are still
best viewed from the sea, though their gardens no longer run down to the
water and their landing stages and boathouses are cut off by the road.

The summer palaces of the Khedive of Egypt and his mother, and of
the Habsburgs, Hohenzollerns, Bourbons and Romanovs, now hide behind
protective walls, their existence betrayed by a lodge, a gate, a glimpse of a

drive, a suggestion of a parterre, a turret or a steep roof. Sharing a hillside are the remnants of the embassy houses of England and France, destroyed by fires in 1911 and 1913, separated by a valley thick with sycamore and plane and protected by a belt of ancient beech. Ragged avenues of limes lead up to these ill-fated buildings, overgrown now by box, ilex and yew, studded in spring with the magenta of the Judas tree and in summer with the blue trumpets of paulownia, and heavy with the scents of syringa, acacia and magnolia. The ruins of their fishponds, stables, kennels and carriage houses are smothered in rioting eglantine; they are alive with fireflies in summer and resound to the song of nightingales in late spring.

For two-and-a-half centuries after the Ottoman conquest in 1453, the sultan and his court would leave Istanbul in late spring to spend the summer months in his former capital at Edirne. There they either campaigned to push the frontiers of the empire deeper into Europe or enjoyed the pleasures of the chase. A few favoured envoys were invited to accompany the court, but in general they were ignored and the functions of an ambassador were not well understood. As late as the eighteenth century, one grand vizier regarded them as mere spies, advising the Divan, or council of ministers, to confine the whole lot to the Princes Islands in the Sea of Marmara, to be isolated like lepers and other infectious and unclean persons.

The Princes Islands were already the refuge of those ambassadors not privileged to be at Edirne, who avoided the summer heat there, but soon found the risk of being marooned by contrary winds too great an inconvenience. They joined the Frankish traders in the cool of the Belgrade Forest. Abounding with springs, this vast forest had supplied the capital with water since the Roman emperor Valens connected it to the city by an aqueduct in the fourth century. The forest itself was renamed after the Ottoman conquest of Belgrade in 1521, and workmen resettled to manage the waterworks designed by Sinan for Süleyman the Magnificent. The beauty of Sinan's new fountains, waterfalls and aqueducts transformed it into a veritable paradise. Lady Mary Wortley Montagu, driven there by summer heat in 1717, thought it 'a place which perfectly answers the description of the Elysian Fields'.

Today the village of Belgrade is no more. Its inhabitants were removed in 1898 for 'injuring the waterworks and the forest' – by all accounts a minor re-enactment of the expulsion of Adam and Eve. For all Lady Mary's recognition of a new heaven on earth, in her day the forest was already becoming a refuge for deserting Janissaries and marauding bands of disaffected mercenaries no longer in the employ of the sultan. It was not long before the authorities encircled the forest and set it alight in order to rid it of its 'vermin'. The diplomats had by then begun to move to the upper shores of the Bosphorus, and there was a renewed popularity for long, narrow, multi-oared caiques able to negotiate its currents. It was such a craft that the British envoy Lord Elgin later described in a letter home as 'a pinnacle of Oriental design' and brought back to Fife, where it finally mouldered away in the 1840s.

The principal landowners of the orchards tucked into the loops of the upper shores of the straits, particularly around the villages of Büyükdere and Tarabya, were the aristocratic Phanariot Greeks (whose name derived from the district of Fener on the Golden Horn). Believing themselves to be the embodiment of diplomatic skill, they rivalled the resident Europeans, 'sweet-water Franks', by serving two masters: the Ottoman Empire, as grand dragomans to the Divan, and the Holy Roman Empire, as chief dragomans to the Internuntii (the Habsburg ambassadors). It was the Greeks' red-roofed wooden villas, more window than frame and set on basements of stone, that the European embassies took for the summer.

The oldest surviving summer embassy is the Spanish house at Büyükdere. Apart from a year in the mid-1860s when it was being rebuilt after a fire, it has been inhabited by the Spaniards without interruption since 1783. That year, with the capital in the grip of a cholera epidemic and the death carts heard nightly crossing the water to the Muslim, Christian and Jewish cemeteries, King Charles III's envoy, Don Juan de Bouligny, fled up the Bosphorus to find refuge with Franciscan friars who had land in Büyükdere on which to cultivate their vines. With France and Naples already settled in Tarabya, Bouligny was anxious to purchase the property, idyllically set on a south-facing shore, commanding the straits and catching the summer breezes, yet sheltered from the winter wind off the Black Sea. Only in 1818 were the friars persuaded to part with it, together with its chapel, for 20,000 piastres.

It was probably in 1864 that the well-remembered but badly documented fire broke out in the Spanish residence. Miraculously, it was contained, and most of the furniture and all the paintings in the building were saved. The late Orthodox Patriarch Demetrius, when he last visited the house a few years ago, told the ambassador that it was under the protection of the local 'owl of good omen', which was painted into the signature of a scriptural text in the study. The painting and the owl had been carefully restored during refurbishment after the fire. The only major alteration evidently made at this time was the incorporation of the chapel within the house. The house itself, like many others in Büyükdere, has a central hall open both to the seaward and garden sides to catch the summer breezes.

The Spaniards had soon been joined by the Russians, thereby placing the embassy of 'the o'ergrown barbarian of the East' alongside that of 'the Most Catholic King'. So they remain to this day, though both lost their landing stages and gardens to the coastal road early in the twentieth century. In compensation, they acquired large and splendid parks on the landward side.

Whereas the upkeep of the Spanish Embassy is impeccable, the Russian building is collapsing, eaten away by salt, spray, decay and neglect. But the ghost of its most notorious incumbent, General Nikolai Ignatiev, is said to haunt it still. Amusing, ingratiating and perhaps the most dangerous of all the nineteenth-century envoys, he earned the name Menteur Pasha through his long years of intrigue at the Porte. His overriding ambition was to acquire for his country control, and preferably sovereignty, over the very waters onto which he looked. Although the house is now in poor condition, the site remains one of the best on the European shore.

 The French received the first of a series of gifts of embassies on the Bosphorus from the sultans to the rulers of the principal European powers. Eight years earlier, however, in 1799, the French were in neither Tarabya nor Istanbul itself. The Turks had confined them to the Yedikule prison in view of the outrage at their invasion of Egypt. The Elgins had taken over the French palace in Pera, and Lady Elgin apparently had no compunction about keeping the French ambassadress's canopy, as 'being of greater glory than that which we ourselves have brought out'.

 However, French fortunes in Turkey had changed by 1807. Selim III presented Napoleon Bonaparte with a permanent summer embassy at Tarabya, largely in recognition of the French role in saving Istanbul from naval bombardment by the British. The immediate beneficiary of the Sultan's munificence was the soldier-diplomat and Corsican arch-intriguer Horace-François Bastien Sébastiani, once destined for the priesthood, who would die a marshal of France. His ascendancy at the Porte unmatched, he was the first non-Muslim envoy ever permitted to wear a sword in the sultan's presence. The beautiful summerhouse given to the French had been confiscated the previous year from Prince Alexander Ypsilanti, the late Phanariot *voivode*, or governor, of the Danubian principality of Wallachia, who had been executed on suspicion of high treason. The British were temporarily occupying the yalı next door to the French. It was probably close observation of Sébastiani's methods that caused Sir Stratford Canning to remark that he found the French Embassy to contain 'the vilest scum that ever fell from the overboilings of the pot of imperial Jacobinism'.

 When the French writer Théophile Gautier was visiting Istanbul in 1853, he found the Ypsilanti yalı 'without architectural merit' though large, spacious, cool and set on one of the most beautiful promontories in the world. It had fallen into a bad state of repair. Its roof, beams, lath and plaster were collapsing, and it needed 100,000 piastres' worth of repair. The work was eventually put in hand, and a second traditional Turkish house was built for the secretaries and dragomans on the terraced cliff above.

 The second French house remains, still painted oxblood red. But the main house burned to the ground in 1913, and plans to rebuild it on its foundations were never realised. The kitchen walls, in which a massive fig is entwined, are its most easily recognisable traces. The bulk of the foundations now lies beneath the coastal road. The grounds and all but the secretaries' house, which is used by the French community, have since 1990 been made available to Marmara University for business courses.

The fire that broke out in Pera on 22 August 1831 reduced every winter embassy but for the Palazzo di Venezia to a pile of smouldering rubble. The diplomats had no choice but to stay on at Büyükdere and Tarabya. Rebuilding was so expensive and slow that it was a full ten years before anyone returned. The Russians were the first to do so.

In 1847 the British were still at Tarabya, their new embassy in Pera not yet even roofed. But with the Turkish minister to the Court of St James the idol of London society, and Sir Stratford Canning by now treated with exaggerated respect in Istanbul, it was the right moment for Abdülmecid I to make a gift of land, formerly the property of the Phanariot Dragoyannis family. A mantle of ilex now masks the view up the straits to the Black Sea from the granite monolith that stands as a monument to this gift, on the spur of the hill across the stream from the French summer embassy. An inscription, altered at a later date and still clear, acknowledges the Sultan's gift of the land in 1847. Beneath the monument, a modern cottage perches on top of the sprawling foundations of the embassy and of the adjoining secretaries' house.

Contemporary photographs show a fine three-storey clapboard mansion with prominent eaves and several turrets. This, and the 'awfully jolly' secretaries' house, crackled like holly leaves in a bonfire when they went up in flames in December 1911; they were never rebuilt. Gone are the fine rooms, the great corridors and the bow windows looking up and down the Bosphorus, whose clear waters reflected patterns between the slats of the wooden shutters onto the ceilings. Only the woodshed, which once served as the chapel, survives.

With Abdülhamid II angling for help from the Germans to modernise his army, Kaiser Wilhelm I's ambassador was summoned to Yıldız Palace in April 1880. There he was asked to implore His Imperial Highness to accept the Sultan's gift of a property on the southern outskirts of Tarabya, where Abdülhamid himself had spent his childhood summers. The Kaiser accepted. But his minister of works, having had his fingers burnt with overspending on the new embassy in Pera, would have none of the expense of building a second on the Bosphorus.

It was three years before the money was found, and the architect and archaeologist Dr Wilhelm Dörpfeld, Schliemann's architect at Troy, was invited to judge a competition for the design. The winner was the

Istanbul architect Alphonse Cingria, who completed the project in time for Kaiser Wilhelm II's state visit in 1889. The design was for a compound of purpose-built cottage-style clapboard houses with fashionable turrets and overhanging eaves, set in the most beautiful of all embassy sites on the Bosphorus.

The German ambassador's house, with its ornamental conservatory and covered way to the chancery building, was restored to its original state in 1990, together with the separate houses for the embassy secretaries and naval attachés, the chapel, cemetery, memorials, teahouse, bathhouse and boathouse and the wooded park surrounding the formal gardens. This meticulous restoration was not, however, the first. In 1952, when the property was returned to the Germans after its sequestration by the Allies in 1945, it was in a deplorable state. A scheme to demolish the houses and replace them with cement bungalows was considered but fortunately not implemented, and by 1955 an already resurgent Germany had the funds for restoration rather than demolition.

Tons of building materials and eighty workmen were brought in from the Federal Republic. They began by building a boundary wall and replacing the corroded iron gates. Before they were finished they had even replaced the bronze name tags in the cemetery. The stables were converted into garages; less predictably, great trouble was taken over the rechannelling of the water from the spring beside the chapel. The Byzantines had been the first to channel these waters, which were then hot and considered therapeutic – hence, almost certainly, the name of the village, which has passed from the Greek Therapia into modern Turkish as Tarabya. An earthquake in 1372 disturbed the spring, which hissed and bubbled into the Bosphorus. Some time thereafter, it lost both temperature and healing powers, becoming a cold-water source that dries out in times of drought.

In the cemetery 265 war graves surround a granite obelisk, overhung now with cypress and pine, recording Field Marshal Helmuth von Moltke's four years in the service of the Sultan's army. Until after the First World War the lime avenue separating the property from the summer gardens of the Sisters of Notre Dame de Sion was known as l'allée Alsace-Lorraine.

Apart from the embassy in London, the only diplomatic building belonging to the Austro-Hungarian Empire that passed to the Austrian Republic after the First World War was the Habsburg summer embassy on the Bosphorus. It had been presented to Emperor Franz Josef by Abdülhamid II in 1883 in a semi-ruinous condition, 'roof and second floor more or less lacking, central hall open to the skies'. For all that, it was, and still is, the most impressive of all buildings in Yeniköy, standing in parkland which was once a vineyard belonging to the Patriarch of Jerusalem. Probably constructed

Constructed by a wealthy tax-farmer, money-lender and early industrialist who had fallen dramatically from grace, the building lay empty for a number of years before the Habsburgs acquired it. It was extravagantly built, most unusually in brick, with newfangled steel beams used to support the top floor, as at the British residence in Pera. It had an elaborate Turkish bathhouse and extensive 'Ottoman gardens' behind, and a canal leading from a vaulted structure to the Bosphorus, allowing direct travel to the capital by boat.

It was ten years before Vienna found the funds to redesign it as a summer embassy, but by 1898 the splendid building had been restored and impeccably furnished. No reigning Habsburg was ever to stay in it, however. It has been suggested that despite the monogram FJI on every one of its pieces of Meissen porcelain and damask cloth, and the magnificence of its chandeliers, ironwork and stonework, the absence of even one bathroom within the building may have put them off.

At the end of the First World War almost the entire contents were sold on the orders of the last Austro-Hungarian ambassador, Count Pallavicini, known as 'the Cassandra of Pera'. Funds were needed to repatriate citizens of the former empire, be they Austrian, German or Hungarian.

The British high commissioners used the house in 1920, during the Allied occupation, before it passed to the Austro-Hungarian condominium and thence to the Austrian Republic. During the Second World War it was German property but was never used; the lack of sanitation may again have been the reason. Only in 1955 did it once more become the summer residence of ambassadors, having been considered fleetingly for conversion as a residence for the president of Turkey. Its restoration as an embassy residence recaptured much of the 1898 glory, particularly that of the *bel étage*, while making room for a girls' school run by nuns with dormitories on the top floor. The school has since moved, and further restoration this year has left the façade a radiant salmon pink.

The banner of Art Nouveau, which was to transform much of Pera and the Bosphorus, was raised by the north-Italian architect Raimondo D'Aronco, who was invited to Istanbul by Abdülhamid II in 1893 to design the venue for a great exhibition, and remained for sixteen years. His renunciation of pasted-on 'historical' styles, disregard for symmetry, and experiments with new materials and types of ornament were so enthusiastically received that D'Aronco became both court architect to the Sultan and avant-garde designer to the Levantine communities, rebuilding in the wake of the 1894 earthquake. The summer yalı in Bebek of the Khediva Mother, Princess Emine İlhami, and the summer palace of her son Abbas Hilmi II on the hills above Çubuklu are extravagant celebrations of this new art.

The Khediva Mother's yalı is now the Egyptian consulate general. Built in

The ghost of General Ignatiev

*At Büyükdere, on the
upper Bosphorus,
a pebble-mosaic path
leads from the sea
through a formal
garden up to the
wooden palace built
in 1840 for General
Nikolai Ignatiev.
The Tsar's envoy is
reputed to haunt the
building still. The
Bosphorus here is wide
enough for the Russian
fleet to have been able
to weigh anchor*

1902 by Antonio Lasciac, an Italian architect of Slovene descent who worked for many years in Egypt, it is a riot of flamboyance, surrounded by gardens and conveniently near the old landing stage for the village of Bebek. When the Khedive was deposed in 1914, the yalı became Egypt's first embassy. Today it accommodates the residence of the consul general in what was the harem, and consular offices occupy the *selamlık*.

The heavy mansard roof – the vogue in turn-of-the-century northern France – supports two turrets and is crowned by a rising sun, the Art Nouveau symbol of hope for the new century, and a vast satellite dish. The bay windows overlooking the sea, and seemingly fixed clumsily to the seaward elevation, are protected by Viennese Secessionist-type balconies formed by winding tendrils of exotic plants and wrought-iron foliage. A lamp crowns every fourth post of the sea railings, each section of which is embellished with a scrolled pedestal. The swirling lines and geometric motifs decorating the entrance gates are as original in style as the sculpted wrought-iron staircase balustrades leading up to the harem and the *selamlık*. As if to imitate the roof of an Art Deco railway station, the central court has an extensive skylight with asymmetric panes.

Still lived in by diplomats in the 1960s, D'Aronco's 1906 Tyrolean-style Italian Embassy in Tarabya may collapse unless it is restored soon. It is built in wood, while the Khediva Mother's palace is stone – perhaps a choice made for practical reasons, since the terrible fires that broke out during the month-long earthquake of July 1894 were fresh in everyone's mind when the Egyptian project was conceived. A charming wooden kiosk was, however, added on the summit of the hill behind the yalı. Refreshments were taken there by the owner and her guests when they walked up the hillside to admire one of the most spectacular panoramic views of the Bosphorus.

A burgeoning metropolis of some eleven million inhabitants, Istanbul has spread in every direction. The formerly remote villages of Bebek, Yeniköy, Tarabya and Büyükdere are now part of the conurbation, and are more easily reached by the new roads leading down from what is left of the Belgrade Forest than from the sea. The polo ground in the once-lush meadow at Büyükdere and the cricket pitch of the mad Englishmen, *deli İngiliz*, in the field behind Beykoz are now covered with houses. The Summer Palace Hotel at Tarabya, where American envoys spent the summers and invited their colleagues to tennis, has been replaced by a giant modern hotel which has swallowed up the old gardens and tennis courts. The dressed cornerstones of the Italian ambassadorial yalı beside it no longer protect the wooden building from the force of the Bosphorus water, but from the traffic on the coastal road. The old summer embassies are now emeralds on a riband of concrete.

Cornucopia Issue 6, 1995

A palace for the Habsburgs

A gift of Abdülhamid II to Franz Josef I, the
Austro-Hungarian palace in Yeniköy was
lavishly restored in 1898. The ballroom, with
its tall pier glasses and exuberant Murano
chandeliers, spans the length of the 'bel étage'

Top The rear façade, crowned by an imperial coat
of arms, seen from the 'Ottoman garden'
Above A central alcove overlooks the Bosphorus

طرابزه ده کأس صیفیلك تکلیز سفارتخانه‌سی

THE BRITISH SUMMER PALACE, TARABYA

Between woods and water

The waterside palace, where Elgar performed in 1905, burned down in 1911 and was not rebuilt. In the woods (right) a monument marks the Sultan's gift of the land

THE ITALIAN SUMMER PALACE, TARABYA

D'Aronco's masterpiece

Built in 1906 by the Sultan's architect Raimondo D'Aronco, this neglected wooden palace (opposite) stood next to the famous Summer Palace Hotel

Commander of the straits

The oldest surviving and best-kept ambassadorial residence on the Bosphorus is said to be protected by an 'owl of good fortune'. Charles III of Spain's envoy first leased the house from Franciscan friars in 1783
Left The south-facing seaside façade
Right Summer breezes cool the house, with its commanding views
Below Steps at the back of the embassy lead down to a garden of gently banked terraces where the friars once tended their vines

To Nessi with most sincere
admiration gratitude & affection
1979/Oct 1

4

THE ÇÜRÜKSULU MEHMET PASHA YALI

THE JEWEL BOX

ONCE HOME TO THE DIPLOMAT MUHARREM NURİ BİRGİ, THIS
IS THE YALI ON THE ASIAN SHORE WHERE ONLY FREYA STARK
WAS ALLOWED BREAKFAST IN BED AND THE ENTRANCING
BELKIS HANIM HELD COURT IN A CLOUD OF LILAC GAUZE

*A 1979 Renaissance-
style profile of the
diplomat Muharrem
Nuri Birgi by the
English portrait painter
Derek Hill, a regular
guest, who called the
yalı 'the most beautiful
house in Asia'*

A late-eighteenth-century yalı stands on the cliff above Salacak, the headland sandwiched between the ancient harbour of Chrysopolis, 'City of Gold', present-day Üsküdar, and Chalcedon, 'City of the Blind', present-day Kadıköy. It is a jewel box of a house, as exquisite in shape as it is in proportion. Its wooden frame is painted in the traditional dark-red *aşıboya*, the colour reserved for the most privileged of the Ottoman sultans' Turkish subjects.

The yalı could not have belonged to anyone but the late Muharrem Nuri Birgi, so infused is it with his personality. He was one of those distinguished Turkish diplomats educated as Ottomans. After the Second World War he was ambassador to London, then to Nato. His *art de vivre*, impeccable taste, acerbic wit and remarkable erudition were bywords in Europe and America. From 1970 much of his talent and energy was devoted to the restoration and adornment of the yalı. Now owned by his friends Selahattin and Ayşe Beyazıt, it is kept just as Nuri Bey left it.

From its dramatic site, the yalı looks across the confluence of the Bosphorus and the Sea of Marmara to the hilly promontory of Sarayburnu on which Topkapı Palace was built. The Salacak ferry to Karaköy, which used to hug the point to pick up passengers from the yalı and other houses here, was discontinued in 1978, when all the flimsy vine-clad houses clustering around the jetty disappeared beneath the foundations of the new coastal highway.

Fortunately, the ferry was immortalised not just in old postcards but also in the film of Agatha Christie's *Murder on the Orient Express*. The boat station now looks like a beached whale stranded in a wasteland of tarmac. The yalı's own dusty path is still cobbled and overhung with fig trees, but it now leads up from a pull-in off the busy dual carriageway.

Whether or not it is still technically a yalı – it is no longer possible to spit from it into the Bosphorus – the house retains its chief natural glory: an unsurpassable view of the setting sun. It is at its best in early autumn, when the sun sinks directly behind the Thracian hills, transforming the stagnant waters of the Haliç into a pool of burnished gold, whose reflection sets the yalı's panes on fire. From its balcony the ripples in the Bosphorus dance and the Golden Horn lives up to its English name. It is at this moment that Süleyman the Magnificent's Süleymaniye Mosque gives the illusion of advancing towards the Galata Bridge from its perch on the Third Hill, to remain beside the pyramid of the Yeni Cami and beneath the dome of the Great Church of Haghia Sophia, glowering and squatting amid a confusion of buttresses, until all three monuments disappear in the gathering dusk.

The yalı dates from the time when Ottoman society began to leave the stifling city for a healthier life on the shores of the Bosphorus. The headland was empty then but for Sinan Pasha's mosque, built after his conquest of Yemen, vestiges of the fourteenth-century palaces of Bryas and Domastris and the sixteenth-century ruins of the wooden palaces of two of Turkey's most illustrious grand viziers, Sokollu Mehmed Pasha and Rüstem Pasha.

It is not known why, or to whom, Selim III granted a parcel of royal lands at Salacak. But by the 1790s, with a Europeanised and Francophile sultan on the throne, and the Bosphorus known as the Canal of Constantinople and said to surpass the Grand Canal of Venice in beauty, they would have been much coveted. During this decade a complex of four yalıs was built among the foundations of the earlier buildings. The masons and carpenters reused any serviceable beam, tile or brick that they found.

In 1968, when Nuri Birgi and his architect, Turgut Cansever, began resurrecting the yalı, they discovered numerous traces of a much older construction. *Horasan* – an old-fashioned mortar of brick-dust and lime – had been used to cement its basement floor and supporting wall. The southerly garden wall had traces of sixteenth-century masonry. The bricks among the stone rubble of its foundations were late Byzantine or early Ottoman. Pieces of seventeenth-century woodwork were found in its roof; alas, these crumbled to powder when touched.

More importantly, supporting one corner of the balcony was a column, gilded and painted in pomegranate flowers similar in style to those in the ceiling of the Sokollu Mehmed Pasha Mosque. This suggested that the yalı was either on or very near the site of the grand vizier's country house.

The first renovation must have taken place around 1810, perhaps following a fire or minor earthquake. The outer left-hand wall of the present front hall conceals part of a wooden structure thickly painted in the distinctive pastel shade of empire blue – a fashion that lasted until the passing of the French Emperor. Although virtually all principal areas of the city were then owned by charitable endowments, an 1853 survey reveals the most northerly pair of the four yalıs built during the 1790s by then belonged to a well-to-do dealer in hoof and horn named Tırnakçızade. The basements were perhaps being used as a warehouse for these valuable commodities, which were exported to Europe to be made into soap and polished articles such as shoehorns, combs and knife handles. Nuri Birgi claimed that a cache of hoof parings, nails and polished bits had been found swept up beneath a blocked-up staircase.

The yalıs remained in the hands of the Tırnakçızade family until 1890, when acrimonious disputes over inheritance drove the heirs to cut the property in two by building a wall between them. The southern yalı was put up for sale. In 1890 it was bought by a Georgian pasha in the service of the Sultan and became known as the Çürüksulu Mehmet Pasha Yalı. He transformed it, inside and out, from an eighteenth-century symmetrical Ottoman box into the quintessential nineteenth-century Bosphorus mansion.

Part of the northern end of the house appears to have been pulled down when the dividing wall was built, providentially allowing room for the addition of a west-facing terrace that was to become the yalı's glory. What survived of the north wall was rebuilt, using sound early-nineteenth-century beams and clapboard wherever possible. Much of this material remains to this day, distinguishable by its *aşıboya* pigment, having presumably been protected from the rain-bearing Lodos winds by the eaves. As part of the rebuilding, the front door was moved along the east face, and a wooden balcony overhanging the garden was added to the landing of the charming south staircase. At one point an outside staircase was added to the east side of the house, reassigning the front entrance to the first floor.

Once the fine German brick-and-tile fireplace had been installed in the upstairs drawing room, the elephant-eye partition had been erected to screen the downstairs reception room from the hall, fashionable door handles had been fixed, decorative corners had been affixed to new outer window frames, a Blüthner piano had been placed upon a full-length carpet of pink stripes, and new sofas from Paris had been installed, the yalı had a curiously European air about it best described as *alafranga* (*alla franca*).

Sherlock Holmes would at once have deduced that the yalı's garden was the creation of Çürüksulu Mehmet Pasha and not of Nuri Birgi. Not only are the trees a hundred years old, but almost every variety of plant is a native of the pasha's homeland, the Caucasus. Like all traditional Bosphorus gardens, it is surrounded by walls; the entrances are on its eastern and southern boundaries.

A venerable black pine is the focal point around which all the earth paths lead, past fishponds, tazzas and a medley of beds. The walls are a riot of ivies, honeysuckles and jasmines. A platoon of cypresses marches round two of its boundary walls. A sweet chestnut, a wild cherry, a paulownia and an Oriental spruce tower above plantings of yew, bay, box and laurel. Oleander and euphorbia choose the sun, myrtle and hydrangea the shade. The raised rose bed is bordered by a clipped box hedge, and the topiary of privet is protected by a wall of trained roses beneath which lavender, sage, rosemary and thyme jostle with snowdrops, lily of the valley and cyclamen. But the chief glory of the garden is the gargantuan wisteria that was planted along the southern end of the house to adorn the wooden balcony giving off from the half-landing.

The last Georgian to live in the yalı was Belkıs Hanım, proverbially beautiful daughter of Çürüksulu Mehmet Pasha. She was as charming as she was intelligent, as reckless as she was extravagant, as tall as she was slim; her long black hair and fascinating eyes are said to have enslaved virtually every man who met her. Her first husband was Atatürk's diplomatic lawyer, Ethem Menemencioğlu. When he was away too long on an assignment to Afghanistan, she divorced him to marry Ratip Bey, a hugely rich Egyptian. When it became too expensive to winter in his Parisian *hôtel particulier*, she then left him and married a second diplomat. But when her third husband was ruined in the mid-1950s, she retired to the Bosphorus.

During her marriages Belkıs Hanım had come and gone from the yalı but, at the end of the Second World War, with the German consular buildings closed, she leased it as a temporary consulate, and until its reopening in 1951 it was used by German nationals requiring permits or assistance. When the Germans returned to Ayazpaşa, she leased it to diplomats down from Ankara for the summer. She returned complete with her daybed, on which she would recline like Madame Récamier in a cloud of lilac silk gauze. Her presence and the faded charm of the yalı, untouched since 1914, were what chiefly enchanted the visitor. Her Paris circle and that of Count Ostrorog at Kandilli overlapped. Arbiters of taste, leaders of fashion and *soi-disant* intellectuals poured through the yalı, as they did through that of the Ostrorogs further up the Bosphorus. Marthe, Princess Bibesco and the Comtesse de Noailles discussed their own poetry and their contemporaries' writing beneath the tresses of the wisteria.

When the winter rain first infiltrated the upstairs drawing room, Belkıs Hanım's *lys rouge* – a renowned diamond and ruby brooch – disappeared. When the ceiling fell, it was rumoured that the house was mortgaged, and developers called with pre-written contracts in their pockets; Belkıs Hanım was looking for someone to resurrect the house and preserve the garden.

In 1968 her old friend the ambassador Muharrem Nuri Birgi bought the Çürüksulu Mehmet Pasha Yalı from her. He had to pay the price of a speculator. As much again was needed for its renovation, which took two-and-a-half years, and Nuri Bey always claimed that he sold three properties to pay for it. Supervising from Brussels, he left it in the capable hands of the architect Turgut Cansever. Once the roof was watertight, the kitchens modernised, the central heating and two sit-up-and-beg baths installed, the wall dividing the pasha's small and large dining rooms – originally the central axis of the house – was removed, providing a room stretching the width of the building in which Nuri Bey intended to display his *pièce de résistance*, the remarkable collection of Chinese blue and white porcelain, most of which he had bought in London salerooms during the 1950s.

On Turgut Cansever's advice, Nuri Bey ruthlessly removed those of the pasha's improvements considered out of keeping with the character of the house. Out went the elephant-eye partition screening the hall, the German brick-and-tile fireplace, the door handles and the decorative corners to the windows. Regrettably, the wooden balcony leading off the southern staircase landing also had to be removed in the name of architectural purity, but it was replaced by a long window through which the sun streams all day. For the centre of the dining-room ceiling, Nuri Bey produced a remarkable carved cabbage from the collection of wooden pieces that he had amassed over the years and kept in sacks.

Before painting started in the yalı – exquisite in translucent pinks, greys, blues, yellows and whites, chosen to reflect each piece of an eclectic collection – recesses and shelving had to be built, woven matting ordered from Hong Kong and glass door handles sent from Murano. By 1972 the yalı was ready. Then the precious consignment of goods and chattels arrived from Brussels off the Üsküdar ferry and was brought up the hill, package by package, on the backs of the bearers. With the meticulous care of a true collector, Nuri Birgi arranged the brilliant Anatolian kilims on the floors and turned them into stair runners, placed the rare books in the library and the Beykoz glass on one wall. At last all the Turkish daggers, imperial Ottoman decrees, prints, paintings and watercolours, sculptures and images found their appointed places, and until his death on 30 September 1986, remained the decor for his stage.

For friends and visitors alike, the Beyazıts' yalı feels as if Muharrem Nuri Birgi has simply left for his weekly visit to the hamam in Galatasaray, which will be followed by 'a nice little lunch at the Park Hotel' before he comes back on the evening ferry.

Cornucopia Issue 7, 1994

The Çürüksulu
Mehmet Pasha Yali, Üsküdar

Clifftop elegance

Today the yalı is exactly as Muharrem Nuri Birgi resurrected it in the late 1960s and early 1970s. Beautifully preserved, its restrained exterior and spacious interior reflect the classical age of Ottoman style, and its clifftop location commands timeless views of the Bosphorus and the Golden Horn

Above One of the upstairs guest bedrooms. If the Bosphorus side of the house was a stage set, these rooms were its tiny private dressing rooms, flooded with sunlight and overlooking a richly scented garden
Left The house seen from the water
Opposite Nuri Bey's old study, hung with prints of sultans, gives onto a terrace above the Bosphorus. The design of the fabric on the chairs echoes the sash windows and the tangle of vines outside

Above A pretty staircase balustrade, possibly added by Çürüksulu Mehmet Pasha in the 1890s
Right This alcove, set with low divans, was known as 'Beykoz' in Nuri Bey's day. Then, the 'vişne' (cherry) vodka was as legendary as the view, the Persian calligraphy and the Turkish Beykoz opaline vases that gave the room its name

Above A long Spanish table stands in the dining room. The walls were painted three times before Nuri Bey found the blue-grey he wanted to set off his blue and white china. Time, and the strong light off the Bosphorus, completed the effect

Left A carved cabbage on the ceiling was an Ottoman conceit Opposite Shutters are flung back to let the sun into another east-facing bedroom; the watercolours are by Nuri Bey himself

5

THE VIZIER'S RETREAT

THE KIBRISLI YALI IS ONE OF THE LARGEST SUMMERHOUSES
TO SURVIVE ON THE BOSPHORUS. ITS RAMBLING ARCHITECTURE
MIRRORS THE FLUCTUATING FORTUNES OF KIBRISLI MEHMET EMİN
PASHA, THE NINETEENTH-CENTURY STATESMAN WHO GAVE THE
HOUSE ITS NAME, AND OF HIS COLOURFUL HEIRS

*Selim Dirvana, the
family patriarch, sits
beneath a youthful
portrait of his great-
grandfather Kıbrıslı
Mehmet Emin
Pasha, painted in
1850–51 when he was
governor of Aleppo,
which appears in the
background*

I f a yalı can be seen as resembling a bird, the Kıbrıslı Yalı is like a huge
white bird of prey drying its wings on the shore below the fortress of
Anadolu Hisarı. This long, low building is the largest eighteenth-
century yalı to survive on the Bosphorus. Its frontage stretches for more
than sixty metres along the Asian shore. From its vantage point halfway
up the Bosphorus, it looks out on every turn of the twisting northern course of
the channel, almost up to the point where a sharp bar of indigo on the horizon
marks the entrance to the Black Sea. Rumeli Hisarı and Anadolu Hisarı, the
rival fortresses of Europe and Asia, frame its spectacular view. The straits are
at their narrowest here, no more than half a mile wide, a crossing point that
has been used since Darius threw down his bridge of boats. Only on the land
side, along the ancient coastal road from Üsküdar, is the house hidden by walls
and trees, a greenness accentuated by wooded hills which until recently were
part of the house's parkland.

   The rambling gardens of the yalı still touch the meadows around the
mouths of the Küçüksu and the Göksu, 'the Sweet Waters of Asia'. But modern
urbanising mess has taken a heavy toll. A hundred and fifty years ago, as Miss
Pardoe wrote in her *Beauties of the Bosphorus*, it needed 'little aid from the
imagination to remember them as one of the brightest gems in the diadem of
nature'. Now the streams are sadly polluted. Bathers swim at their peril. No
longer are there flowers enough to conduct a romance in the language of their

names. The meadows where the Sultan's horses once grazed are fenced off in plots, with warnings to trespassers to keep away. But in the men's quarters, or *selamlık*, behind the yalı's high walls, the magnificence of the shady trees and flowering shrubs remains. The harem's fabled peonies continue to flower their best in June.

From the sea the house looks so much of a piece that one might imagine a single person built it within the space of a few years. In fact it grew over a period of a hundred, from the mid-eighteenth to the mid-nineteenth century.

Being 'noble so long as the person who elevated him exists', Kara Vezir Silahtar Mehmed Pasha, the Black Vizier, who built the original yalı, is now long forgotten. Briefly grand vizier in 1770, he must have been a rich and cultured Ottoman living during an unexpectedly quiet interlude in which the empire enjoyed twenty years of peace. These were the happy years before Catherine the Great's Russia became a pressing threat, when pashas built wooden summerhouses along the shores of the Bosphorus. It was the golden age of the 'true' Ottoman yalı.

No expense was spared with the building. Foundations were set on three platforms of quarried stone – mussel beds now – which still reach out into the bay to hold the yalı safe during earth tremors and winter storms. Alder, pine and spruce from the Black Sea were used for the outside timbers, Lycian cedar for the floors, Pamphylian silver fir for the window frames and Anatolian oak for the doors, cupboards, niches, pillars and balustrades. In the *selamlık*, ranges of tall sash windows with large panes of imported Venetian glass were let into all four sides of both storeys. The downstairs corner rooms, identical in size and shape, led into the central hall, which in turn led into the southerly garden. Where the two arms of the ascending staircase meet, a wall of windows stretches half the length of the house to overlook the red tiles of the harem's roof, and in those days allowed the eye a sweep of the lower Bosphorus before one carried on up to the landing off which all the upper rooms lead. As a summer retreat, the building was designed to allow maximum ventilation and to be filled with the strange aqueous light reflected off the waters, as well as to catch the sunlight over the gardens when the wind from the sea was inclement.

Eighty years after Kara Vezir built the yalı, his name had been erased from the history books. The house had passed through several hands and was in need of restoration. It was then that the man who gave his name to the yalı acquired it. Kıbrıslı Mehmet Emin Pasha was one of Turkey's most able nineteenth-century statesmen. Three times grand vizier, twice first lord of the admiralty, governor of Edirne and Aleppo, ambassador to London and St Petersburg, once proclaimed 'the voice of Law from one end of the Empire to the other', he was nevertheless frequently plagued by debt. At his death in 1871 he left a daughter by each of two marriages, an admiring public, few friends and just eighty-one Turkish liras. He owed the beginnings of his tumultuous and illustrious career to the most skilled of all talent spotters, Mustafa Reşid Pasha, instigator of the reforming Gülhane Decree, promoter of the Westernising Tanzimat movement, and six times grand vizier. Kıbrıslı Mehmet Emin Pasha's first wife was a protégée of Reşid Pasha's family; his second was picked out for him by Reşid Pasha himself. The lives of both women were intertwined with the history of the yalı, and each left her indelible mark on it.

Kıbrıslı Mehmet Emin Pasha's forebears were from Anatolia, and resettled in Cyprus shortly after Selim II's conquest of the island in 1571 – Kıbrıslı means Cypriot. Somehow they acquired farming land on its western shore, farmed for the production of sugar cane and sweet wines. For the next three centuries the profit from these farms was the source of their income; it only ceased when the farms were requisitioned by the British governor in 1948.

Born on the family estates near Paphos in 1810, Kıbrıslı Mehmet Emin Pasha arrived in the Ottoman capital at the age of seven to enter the Palace school. Fluent in English, French, Arabic, Persian and Greek, he was an attaché in the Paris embassy by the age of twenty-five, betrothed to a wild and beautiful but well-connected twenty-two-year-old Roman Catholic who had separated from the English doctor she had married when he was practising in the Levant. In 1840, when he was thirty and married to the lady in question, who had become Muslim and changed her name to Melek, Kıbrıslı Mehmet Emin Pasha and his wife bought the yalı, reportedly with the money raised from the sale of their furniture, at a time when he had temporarily fallen from grace and was searching for a house 'in a somewhat remote quarter where creditors generally come mounted on asses'.

Ten years later, the marriage to Melek Hanım was over and Kıbrıslı Mehmet Emin Pasha was recalled from the London embassy, where he was now *en poste*, not on affairs of state but to deal with the scandal attributed to the wife he had left behind in the yalı. His chief eunuch had been found strangled in the hamam of the harem and Melek Hanım was suspected. Kıbrıslı Mehmet Emin Pasha ordered the hamam to be torn down before his return from London; a lily pond was built into its foundations, as if to absolve the guilt of those implicated in the murder.

Melek Hanım's memoirs tell her side of the story. But what really happened in the hamam during the afternoon of their daughter's first reading of the Koran will never be known. Some say that the crime was committed by a female member of the household, jealous of a favourite eunuch's power over his mistress. But it was whispered that the eunuch had discovered that Melek Hanım was feigning a pregnancy in order to introduce into her household a child who was not her own, to replace the only son who had died on the morrow of Kıbrıslı Mehmet Emin Pasha's departure for London. If her husband was to save his career, he had no choice but to repudiate his wife. She was tried and exiled to Konya. Reşid Pasha arranged forthwith the contract of Kıbrıslı Mehmet Emin Pasha's second marriage, as he had the first.

Two portraits of Kıbrıslı Mehmet Emin Pasha hang in the yalı today. In the first he is depicted as the precocious young governor of Aleppo. The other portrait was painted by an English artist only weeks before he left London. He is dressed in his black stambouline frock coat, black trousers and fez. It is a penetrating study of a man who enjoys high office but is inwardly ill at ease.

The second wife, Feride Hanım, was the last of Ayaz Pasha's line. If history and fable go hand in hand, this illustrious Albanian forebear was Süleyman the Magnificent's swashbuckling grand vizier, who, before he died in 1539, helped his master to double the size of the Ottoman Empire, and had 140 children and estates stretching miles across Istanbul, from Ayazpaşa to Ayazağa. With the aid of Feride Hanım, the yalı was renovated, enlarged and modernised, with a new east wing balancing the identical west wing. A balcony overlooking the Bosphorus was added to the original façade. Every room was 'gaily painted'. Banisters carved to imitate *fer forgé* were as fine as the additional classical cornices were grand.

These extensive building works were apparently undertaken over the course of winter months between 1850 and 1870. An entirely new *sofa*, or grand hall, was built out into the garden, stretching the depth of the house from the Bosphorus to the land entrance. Its floor of cedar planks cut along the grain and riveted with iron nails has only recently been replaced by marble. The atrium, possibly inspired by the seventeenth-century wooden dome in the nearby Köprülü Yalı, must have had scaffolding up for months as artists worked on the frescoes of peonies. Beneath these, master plasterers would have worked on the delicate task of moulding the Neoclassical columns and friezes. It still has the highest, grandest hall of all the yalıs on the Bosphorus.

Kıbrıslı Mehmet Emin Pasha completed his house with a third large hall fronting onto the sea, its doors and windows opening onto the terrace, where the boats still moor. This acted, and still does, as a sea entrance. Behind it on the southern side is the winter dining room, still lined with cupboards for storing bedrolls for guests who spend the night. Perhaps the loveliest contrivance of all in the rebuilding was the winter garden, or orangery. Its walls of huge windows face south and east, and its divans are ranged along the walls; but the most strikingly original feature is the fountain in its centre, surrounded by a pavement of finely worked *krokalia*. This intricate technique, much used by the Byzantines, producing a carpet of geometric and floral designs from a mosaic of black and white Maltese marble pebbles, was carried on into the garden leading up to the *selamlık*'s front door. Sadly, time and winter rains hid these exterior mosaics with layers of silt. In places they have been covered with a tidier and more modern form of pavement.

On the pasha's death, in 1871, the yalı passed to the only child of his second marriage, Atiye Hanım, who is the forebear of those who still live in the main section of the house. Deeply traditional, she maintained a strict division between harem and *selamlık* until her death in 1922. While her salon was said to be almost like a mosque, the *selamlık* of her husband, the son of a pasha from the Peloponnese, who conveniently adopted the name of Kıbrıslı Mustafa Pasha, was far from traditional. As Atiye Hanım conducted prayers on the other side of the wall, he gave garden and cocktail parties to which the French writer Pierre Loti, with his powdered cheeks and platform-soled shoes, never refused an invitation and which the more emancipated ladies of the harem were free to attend.

Whatever the divisions in the household, the first Liberal Democratic party was founded at the yalı by the husband of Atiye Hanım's eldest daughter, together with her own three sons, Tevfik, the eldest, Nazım and Şevket. Five years later, on the eve of the First World War, Tevfik was assassinated during the coup d'état mounted by Enver Pasha's Committee of Union and Progress.

When Atiye Hanım died, the house was, on the advice of the courts, divided up into five equal parts, for which the surviving children drew lots. The west wing went to Şevket, Atiye Hanım's youngest son, who was married twice, first to a granddaughter of Sultan Abdülmecid's sister, Cemile Sultan, whom he divorced, and later to Princess Atiye, daughter of Abbas Hilmi II of Egypt. He had no children, and his heir was his second wife's son by a former marriage, who committed the unforgivable sin of selling his stepfather's inheritance over the heads of the rest of the family. An unsightly wall now cuts the old harem garden in half. From the sea, the west wing still looks as if it is part of the yalı, and so it is architecturally, but it is now a separate property. When it was sold, Mehmet Emin Pasha's great-grandson Selim Dirvana took a train to Ankara to ensure that an order for its protection was issued.

Atiye Hanım's eldest daughter, Azize, inherited the two storeys of the old *selamlık*. Her descendants still spend their summers there. Though they have introduced modern bathrooms and brought the kitchens indoors, they have left the hundred-year-old paint undisturbed. It has aged to resemble the translucent waters outside. What is left of the old harem garden, with its lily pond where the hamam once stood, runs up to the road, crudely hemmed in by the west wing's boundary wall. Although the *selamlık* gate still serves as its entrance, the *selamlık*'s turnstile food hatch is but a fading memory; it was considered a dangerous plaything for Azize Hanım's sister's four boys and was bricked in.

The rest of the central part and the east wing of the house, together with the dependencies in the gardens, were shared between the remaining Kıbrıslı

Jutting out into the Bosphorus, the unusually long Kıbrıslı Yalı looks all of a piece, but took a century to build. It was more than a summerhouse in the 1950s: the family would stay on until December, when the men rowed out to catch 'lüfer', the Bosphorus bluefish

children: Müzeyyen, youngest of the three sisters, who married an Egyptian pasha and lived with her only son in Paris; Nazım, a cavalry officer who married a White Russian but never had children; and Refika, who married the handsome grandson of Edhem Dirvana, a *sipahi*, an officer of the old landed cavalry corps, and had the four boys who played with the food hatch. Müzeyyen sold her part to Refika.

Anecdotes are still told of the fun and generosity, the true Ottoman hospitality, enjoyed by visitors in the years between the foundation of the Republic and the late 1950s. The Dirvanas and Kıbrıslıs kept open house. Edhem Bey was overheard to remark to his wife over lunch one day, 'I do not recognise that young man at the end of the table,' to which she replied, 'Neither do I, but he has been with us for a fortnight.' Şevket filled the yalı with a gilded circle of writers, philosophers and artists. Yahya Kemal, Rıza Tevfik and Fazıl Ahmet were among those who unrolled mattresses taken from the cupboards in the winter dining room to sleep under the windows fronting the Bosphorus, guarded only by the moon and the waters.

Nazım, the cavalry officer, has a particular claim to family fame. He crossed the Bosphorus through the fierce current from Rumelihisarı to the yalı steps on his horse in full dress uniform, not for a wager but to prove to his commanding officer that horses were better and more reliable than rowing boats. The four Dirvana sons, Mahid, Emin, Süleyman and Selim, grew up in the ferment of the new Republic's early years. Mahid, the eldest, and his wife, Nesterin Hanım, returned each summer to the yalı. It was they who restored the orangery and had the main hall paved with marble. It was she who discovered the original ceiling in her salon overlooking the Bosphorus (the ceiling was probably lowered for warmth during the First World War). A widow now, she still occupies her apartment here in summer.

Emin was a soldier, bluff and upright, whose toothbrush moustache, no-nonsense manner and faultless Oxford English astonished London when he was Turkish military attaché in the 1950s. He went on to be Turkey's first ambassador to the new Republic of Cyprus in 1960. Süleyman is a doctor who has remained in Istanbul to practise.

Selim, the archaeologist of the family, married Mihrimah Hanım and became father of Refika Hanım's only grandchild, a daughter. Born on the eve of the Second World War, Mihda was brought up in the yalı during the lean wartime years, huddling over stoves in winter, boating and swimming in summer, and always surrounded by horses and dogs.

Refika Hanım died in 1961. Money had been tight for some years. Then, apparently quite unexpectedly, Selim Bey's wife inherited her American mother's fortune. The yalı survives in the fine condition we see today largely thanks to this timely injection of resources.

The dining room, painted a vibrant pink instead of the earlier pastel yellow. The original fireplace, considered too risky in a wooden house, has been replaced by a delicate fountain topped with a fanciful cornucopia

Selim Dirvana, now a widower, looks back down the years to his great-grandfather, Kıbrıslı Mehmet Emin Pasha, and forward to the future of the great-grandchildren among whom he lives, in a modern house built over the foundations of a garden kiosk. His daughter, Mihda, married the influential businessman İlkay Bilgişin, and their children and grandchildren, Komilis, Kaslowskys and Bilgişins, now spread through Kıbrıslı Mehmet Emin Pasha's east wing and the garden buildings.

The yalı lives on, a unique monument to the declining years of the Ottoman Empire and full of vitality for the twenty-first century. Its story will continue to be the story of one family: living history which storybooks could not better.

Cornucopia Issue 8, 1995

6

AHMET VEFİK PASHA'S LIBRARY

A ROOM FOR THE BOOKS

SECLUDED ON A CLIFF BESIDE THE FORTRESS OF RUMELİ HİSARI,
ON THE EUROPEAN SHORE OF THE BOSPHORUS, IS A 'KÖŞK' –
A TYPICALLY OTTOMAN GARDEN PAVILION – THAT WAS ONCE
THE RETREAT OF A BIBLIOPHILE AND BON VIVANT

Ahmed Vefik Pasha's library today. Tiles, murals and panels of verse had replaced his 15,000 volumes when the fashionable architect Vallaury completed his transformation of the room in 1902. The Ottoman Baroque fireplace has had its ornate pediment reinstated

The building which for a quarter of a century housed Ahmed Vefik Pasha's famous library was begun in 1861. Today it is almost completely hidden by trees, standing isolated on an outcrop of rock above the village of Rumelihisarı. To one side it looks out upon a steep fall of ground, to the other upon the curtain walls of the castle which Mehmed the Conqueror built on the European shore. Below, through a fringe of trees, the hills and villages on the Asian shore are reflected in the waters of the Bosphorus as it snakes towards the narrowest point in its eighteen-mile course. Only from the second Bosphorus bridge, named the Fatih Bridge after the Conqueror, and from the footpath climbing up from the village, can the library be seen, a dark red box at the apex of a granite terrace sheltered by a gatehouse and high walls.

The library underwent two transformations to meet its twentieth-century requirements, but the essentials of the original structure remain. A photograph in the library of Leiden University [following pages] shows the interior during Ahmed Vefik Pasha's lifetime, when bookshelves two books deep covered every available inch of wall space, even precariously overhanging the fireplace. A cornice below the vaulted ceiling supported a shelf crowded with vases, and an elegant library table, piled with books and crowned with a globe, stood on a polished floor covered with rush matting. The windows which once opened onto the garden (but now lead onto a veranda) still have their original iron shutters and red-brown marble surrounds, chosen to set off the books.

The photograph was taken from the only door leading inwards from the central hall, which was both a writing room and extra shelf space for the books. The hall runs the width of the library and is lit by three windows overlooking the ravine and village path. Its marble floor mirrors the marquetry of the ceiling. Unseen is the cellar, cut into the granite rock beneath the building and entered by steps from the garden. Connected to the curious crescent-shaped pond which still stands close to the front door, the cellar was part of the system devised by Ahmed Vefik Pasha to ensure the house remains dry: winter rain and floodwater drain instantly.

Ahmed Vefik Pasha was born in Istanbul in 1823. His family had owned land in Rumelihisarı since the days when it was called Asamaton and their yalı stood on the shore, its land running up the gulleys beside the towers of the Conqueror's fort. At eleven he moved to Paris, when his father was appointed ambassador. He returned three years later, already a dedicated bibliophile who pestered his father to buy him books in French as well as Turkish.

In 1839, employed in the Chamber of Translators at the Porte (part of the new foreign ministry), he was as well versed in the English and French classics as in Oriental literature, speaking Arabic and Persian as well as French, Greek and English. He befriended Henry Austin Layard, then a young diplomat in Istanbul. Layard, destined to find fame as the excavator of Nineveh, was to return to the city as British ambassador when Ahmed Vefik Pasha was briefly grand vizier during the tumultuous first year of Abdülhamid II's reign.

Book-collecting in all the seventeen languages with which he was familiar remained a passion throughout his life of service to the Ottoman Empire. Postings as ambassador to Tehran and Paris afforded particular opportunities. Ahmed Vefik Pasha is said to have purchased more than twenty complete library collections so as to secure particularly rare volumes he coveted.

On his return from his diplomatic postings, his main concern was to construct a building which would preserve his unique collection of the best of Eastern and Western literature, science, philosophy and poetry from the twin scourges of Istanbul libraries: fire and damp. His original intention was to construct a belvedere on the highest part of his lands above the fortress of Rumeli Hisarı. The Ottoman authorities' refusal to meet the enormous expense of his final spell in Paris meant a change of plan. Land was sold to the American educationalist Dr Cyrus Hamlin, who had previously been curtly refused, and a new site was selected in the garden a few dozen metres above his house. As a result of official meanness, or ambassadorial extravagance by the portly, high-living pasha, we now have both the pasha's library and the imposing mass of Robert College (now Bosphorus University), erected by Hamlin on the land he had purchased.

This photograph of the library in Ahmed Vefik Pasha's day appeared in the 1893 catalogue of the sale of the pasha's books after his death in 1891. It is in Leiden University Library, along with most of the books, which encompassed the best of East and West

Ahmed Vefik Pasha spent his last nine years out of favour with an increasingly autocratic Sultan, exiled in his library. It was then that he completed his translations of Molière's plays into Anatolian dialects. These were regularly performed in the library. Whether he spent his wealth on adding to the library or dissipated it in other ways is a mystery, but, following his death in 1891, the property had to be sold to pay his debts. Both the 15,000 volumes and the buildings went up for sale in July 1893. Münir Bey, secretary general of the foreign ministry, was responsible for the catalogue. The bulk of the books were purchased by Leiden University, where they still constitute an important part of the library. Some were knocked down to Rıza Pasha, a noted bibliophile and the man who bought the library building.

Rıza Pasha employed the fashionable Levantine architect Alexandre Vallaury to enlarge and modernise Ahmed Vefik Pasha's stone box. The transformation was completed in 1902. By extending both ends of the marble hall it was possible to run verandas around its three exposed sides. Steel girders were mounted into the rock to support the balcony which hung over the cliff's edge. Windows were mounted into the clapboard veranda walls,

*It was common for yalı
owners to build viewing
pavilions high above
the Bosphorus, but
Ahmed Vefik Pasha's
library was unique*

Right The library
perched on its outcrop
of granite rock. The
pasha was determined
to keep his books
safe both from fire and

set on stone balustrades and embellished by latticework beneath the eaves. The outside was now as conventional as that of any late-nineteenth-century Bosphorus mansion and was painted in oxblood red. Even its glass-paned front door, flanked by a pair of marble stalactite columns, conformed. But the interior was an innovation.

Although the ceilings of the verandas matched that of the hall, the wide corridors gave an intense feeling of light and space. There is an abiding charm to the stylised star-patterned floor tiles and the cornices in *kalem işi*, a fashionable form of paint on plaster used from the mid-nineteenth century by Italian artists refurbishing the empire's mosques. Within the library itself, the books above the fireplace were replaced by an ornate pediment and a panel of indigo-blue and green glazed tiles. French windows were cut into the wall letting onto the balcony overlooking the Bosphorus. Similar chocolate-red marble was found to match the surrounds of the other two windows. Niches replaced the shelving. But the glory of the room was the magnificent *kalem işi* workmanship, deep red arabesques on the vaulting and along the cornice where once the vases stood, glowing from a blue background.

When in 1929 the building came up for sale a second time, it was in need of renovation. Once again the outcome was romantic. A fifteen-year-old girl, born in Istanbul but brought up by her parents in Paris, returned to the city of her birth and was taken by her father to view the building as a possible summer

from winter rain and floodwater. The glazed veranda was added later by Vallaury

Left The marble entrance hall. The iron shutters are painted to look like wood
Right On the vaulted ceiling, the pale Neoclassical background is overlaid with Islamic motifs outlined in deep red

retreat. It was clearly unsuitable but she fell in love with the library. Her father eventually agreed to buy it for her on one condition: that she would never sell it in her lifetime. Now in her eighties, retired from active practice as a lawyer, Sevim Hanım, wife of Dr Osman Saka, has faithfully fulfilled the promise.

A year after the purchase in 1929, a local builder repaired the roof and added two rooms above the hall. In 1950 a kitchen and a pantry were added. In 1969 Turgut Cansever – who at the time was working on another clifftop yalı along the Bosphorus, for Muharrem Nuri Birgi [Chapter 4] – began the reconstruction of the two most exposed sides of the veranda, which were becoming detached from the cliff. He undertook the modernisation that transformed it into a house of late-twentieth-century comfort without losing the essentials of the pasha's achievement.

The library is cherished by the Saka family. They know that its walls still breathe the spirit of its creator, Ahmed Vefik Pasha, the scholar-statesman, who held Haroun al-Rashid as his hero and who could discuss theology as if in a Protestant seminary, read the Koranic writings with as much pleasure as the poetry of the Psalms, and quote whole pages of Shakespeare.

Cornucopia Issue 9, 1995

7

WATER'S EDGE

HEKİMBAŞI SALİH EFENDİ WAS THE LAST PHYSICIAN TO THE
OTTOMAN COURT. HE WAS ALSO A SCHOLAR AND REFORMER.
BUT PLANTS WERE HIS PASSION, AND THE GROUNDS
OF HIS YALI WERE FILLED WITH THE SCENT OF CARNATIONS.
THE GARDENS HAVE GONE, BUT THE HOUSE LIVES ON

*Above Freya Stark
admired the yalı, now
in the shadow of the
Fatih Bridge, for its
'noble proportions'
Opposite The first-floor
reception room leads
onto a covered veranda*

Until recently most yalıs on the Bosphorus were closed for the winter. Once the October winds began to whip the leaves off the trees, owners returned to the city, leaving guardians to close the shutters, let loose the guard dogs and await the spring. The descendants of Hekimbaşı Salih Efendi still follow this tradition. When I visited their yalı in January, the family had driven up from the Asian shore of the Sea of Marmara. They had expected me to arrive by car from the European side of the Bosphorus. In fact I surprised them by appearing from the sea, as most visitors would have done in the heyday of the house.

As we set out from Yeniköy in a motor launch, hugging the European shore, the only other craft moving south were a mob of small fishing boats, each with its accompanying cloud of gulls. As we turned to cross to the Asian shore, the shearwaters skimmed the surface across our bows. I was landed on the yalı's deserted terrace.

With the exhilaration of a trespasser, I skirted the gnarled trees, crossed a paved courtyard and eventually found an open door. Sensing, rather than hearing, movement above me, I climbed the stairs curving to the drawing-room floor. And there at last I found the family, awaiting my arrival in their winter room – the landward entrance hall at which they had expected me to arrive. The hall itself, warm and welcoming, was flooded with sunshine and heated by a hissing stove.

The twentieth century took a severe toll on the yalı of Hekimbaşı Salih Efendi, but it is still possible to imagine it as it was a hundred years ago, substantially larger and surrounded by the principal botanic garden of Istanbul. Most of that garden and all the *selamlık* are gone. But the harem, a boathouse and some of the grounds remain. Midway between the Black Sea and the Sea of Marmara, the yalı's rust-red frame faces south and west, its roofs descending in steps along the water's edge. Wooded hills rising sharply behind the house form the first of its natural boundaries, protecting it from the treacherous northeasterly winds. A southern headland guards it from the worst of the summer storms, when waves lash its fragile frame and ramparts of foam drench windows and terraces with salt spray. In summer the sun sets directly behind Mehmed the Conqueror's fortress on the European shore, Rumeli Hisarı, its crenellations silhouetted on the water in gold.

In the 1840s, Salih Efendi acquired a modest late-eighteenth-century dwelling on a sheltered stretch of shore halfway between the villages of Anadoluhisarı and Kanlıca. Its single storey, built along the extreme edge of the water, contained only three rooms, with a row of arched windows overhanging the Bosphorus. Its main assets may have been its hundred or so *dönüm* (hectares) of land and the spring water which was tapped on the hillside and collected in a cistern where the hill met the road. Miss Pardoe's much-quoted description of yalıs in *The Beauties of the Bosphorus*, dating from 1836, fits the house exactly: 'Nothing is more irregular and consequently more picturesque than the style of building on the Bosphorus. Because the Turk builds for himself, they have the appearance of being put together by fragments.' Such was indeed the method of Hekimbaşı Salih Efendi. Having acquired the yalı, Salih Efendi, the last chief physician – or *hekimbaşı* – to the court of the sultan, was over the next forty years to enlarge the building and to establish in its grounds a botanic garden of international repute.

Born in the district of Tophane in 1816, Salih Efendi was the son of a *hadji*, a pilgrim to Mecca, whose forebears came from the Black Sea. This was a time of reforms, when fluency in French was becoming essential to those seeking advancement in Ottoman service, and the stambouline coat, striped trousers and fez were replacing flowing robes and turbans. Salih Efendi was among the first and most brilliant of students at the Ottoman Imperial College of Medicine, newly established at Galatasaray. He in turn taught there, and laid out the college's physic garden, compiling accurate and reliable reports on each plant that formed the basis of the Istanbul Botanic Archives. His botany lectures were meticulous, his gift for teaching renowned. He is said to have held forth on the propagation of the wild carnation, producing specimens from the folds of his handkerchiefs, not just in the lecture hall but on board Bosphorus steamers, competing with coffee-sellers and boot-cleaners shouting out their wares. His passion for botany was initially inspired by Dr Karl Ambros Bernard. Born in what later became Czechoslovakia, Bernard had come to Istanbul in 1839 and died tragically from a tooth infection five years later. Salih Efendi adopted his teaching methods, which were based on the teachings of Dioscorides, and translated into Turkish Bernard's classic textbook, used by students until quite recently. His greatest achievement was to have the language of medicine in the Ottoman Empire changed from French to Turkish.

A myth arose that the Sultan's chief physician was a six-day-a-week horticulturalist and a one-day-a-week doctor. Doubtless it originated at the college, where he ran a Sunday clinic dispensing herbal remedies. For fever and ague it was camomile, mallow heads, eucalyptus leaves, linden flowers and quince pips; for toothache, linseed packs; for earache, roasted onion centres; and for colds, coughs and chills the feet were to be wrapped in bags of hot onions.

From his appointment as chief court physician in 1849 until his resignation in 1876, Salih Efendi was in and out of government. As the Ottoman equivalent of minister of health, he was involved in introducing quarantine laws to combat the spread of plague and setting up hospitals to treat its victims. Following the 1864 cholera epidemic, as head of the Imperial College of Medicine, he chaired the 1866 international conference on hygiene at Galatasaray.

Salih Efendi was in attendance when Sultan Abdülmecid died of tuberculosis in 1861, aged thirty-eight. He seems to have accepted the verdict of suicide when Abdülaziz died four days after being dethroned in the summer of 1876. But he was unwilling that same year to endorse the imported Austrian neurologist's verdict of 'emotional instability' as justification for Murad V being deposed after only three months and Abdülhamid II ascending the throne. Murad was imprisoned by his younger brother in the Çırağan Palace, where he lingered on for twenty-eight years. Salih Efendi's resignation, the reason for which must have been widely known, aroused imperial displeasure. The new sultan wanted to exile him to Van. With the Tsar mobilising his troops on the frontier, Salih Efendi succeeded instead in retiring to his yalı.

Though Salih Efendi was quintessentially a nineteenth-century Ottoman, there was nothing traditionally Ottoman about his yalı. It never had the characteristic central hall with rooms leading off it. Beneath its tiled roofs, pitched at different angles and levels, its plain façade conceals a labyrinth of rooms. The west-facing rooms, imperceptibly zigzagging to allow an extra glimpse of the sea, run along the water's edge, their high windows protected from the waves and salt spray by shutters which, when closed, give the house the appearance of an uninterrupted wall of red. Kitchens at one end adjoin the only surviving eighteenth-century room. It is, as it has always been, the dining room, and still has its original wooden ceiling.

Some enlargements of the yalı had evidently been completed by 1866, as a photograph of thirty-three visiting doctors attending the Galatasaray conference shows them in the main reception room of the *selamlık*. Once there was a staircase at either end of the house, giving access to the reception rooms on the first and second floors. Only the harem staircase now survives. It now leads to the first-floor hallway, off which the upstairs reception rooms lead, and to the main room, with its central balcony and view across to the handsome towers of Rumeli Hisarı. The top floor is a warren of bedrooms, with cupboards of all sizes fitted beneath any projecting eave, all with well-seasoned floors and simple nineteenth-century ceilings. A rectangular gap in a dividing bedroom wall allows candles and night lights to be shared, one between two rooms.

The main halls, one above the other on the ground and first floors, stand at the back of the house. The sea-level entrance, on the south side of the house, has a marble floor. Its doors, which once led north into the *selamlık* garden and south into the courtyard of the harem, suggest Salih Efendi's house was not strictly divided. In the harem's paved courtyard is the only extravagance of the house, a Baroque cascade fountain, or *selsebil*, on the wall beside the hamam. The hamam itself, with its domed roof pierced with 'elephant-eye' skylights, and its antiquated system for bringing rainwater from a specially built cistern, is remarkably preserved (though the furnace next door that heated the water and circulated hot air through its floor and walls was superseded in 1900 by a simpler wood-burning stove). A tunnel at the back of the house once connected the two gardens.

The first-floor hall is the land entrance as well as the winter room of the house. From the road, some thirty metres above sea level, it is reached by steps which zigzag down through terraces. Inside, its sash windows on three sides overlook the gardens and the foundations of the greenhouses. Low sofas still run round the walls. Its inner doors lead to the sea rooms and the stairs. They also once led to the *selamlık*.

The house grew according to Salih Efendi's means and the needs of his family. The botanic gardens he enlarged at every opportunity. Enveloped in felt cloak, hood and galoshes, discoursing on the finer points of grafting, layering and pruning, he conducted tours of his greenhouses that were proverbial. In the summer the gardens were perfumed by carnations, lilies and peonies. In a sheltered corner of the garden there was an orangery. The terraced walls were covered in roses; one bearing his name, the *Hekimbaşı gülü*, flourishes up and down the Bosphorus.

When Salih Efendi retired to the yalı it was complete. But his need for a substantial house was gone. At sixty-three he had buried two wives and his four sons. But a new lease of life came in 1879. Cemile Sultan, autocratic sister of Sultan Abdülmecid, wanted a sixteen-year-old Circassian girl, new to her household in Kandilli, to learn French. Her aged, respectable neighbour and friend was summoned. He found Payidar's pale skin, lustrous black hair and green eyes irresistible. The former chief physician obtained the Sultan's permission for the girl to leave the royal household.

A devoted wife for sixteen years, Payidar bore Salih Efendi three daughters, each of whom inherited her mother's strong character and gift for music, as well as her beauty. On Payidar's death in 1923, the yalı and its grounds were divided between them. The eldest, Übeyde, inherited the northern end of the property: the main boathouse, the botanic garden and her father's first-floor library, elevated on timber columns and tacked onto the end of the *selamlık*. By 1966 it had fallen into ruin and her heirs sold it off with the vestiges of the botanic garden. Meliha, the middle daughter, inherited the *selamlık* at the centre of the property. Having no children and wishing to pursue a musical career in the new Republican era, she sold her share at once. In the 1970s a bungalow was built on the site.

By 1947 the hillside terraces above the road had reverted to a wilderness of secondary forest and were requisitioned by the Treasury. In 1990 the carriageway of the second Bosphorus bridge – the Fatih Bridge – was driven through the top of the orchard. But the harem, with its portion of waterfront garden – the inheritance of the youngest daughter, Sakibe – has survived. She presided over it until her death in 1982, letting out the ground floor to her friends Memduh and Sevim Moran after she lost her husband in 1962.

The facilities were limited; the kitchen, hamam and other conveniences were shared. This did not inhibit the yalı's cultural life. Guests included the soprano Leyla Gencer, who sang with Sakibe's daughter, Mehlika, in the city's new conservatoire chorus. Freya Stark stayed with the Morans, dedicating to them her *Sketch of Turkish History* prepared in the yalı.

By 1977, when the position of the second Bosphorus bridge was being decided, the yalı's timbers were bleached a silvery white and the whole building had started to slip perilously into the sea. TAÇ, the historic buildings foundation, agreed to help, and Grade I listing would save the yalı from destruction by the bridge. But a condition was extensive renovation to TAÇ specifications. The last eleven *dönüm* of land were sold to pay for the work, which took three years. The family lived in the house throughout, moving from room to room while the building was refloated on concrete piers and raised several inches to escape the seawater. Except for the upstairs rooms and the original eighteenth-century ceiling in the little dining room, which survived complete, every outside timber, every window frame, shutter and joist, was replaced. Finally the yalı was repainted with *aşıboya*, the traditional red iron-oxide and linseed-oil paint, to preserve its wood from beetle and rot.

Today the yalı lies in the shadow of the Fatih Bridge, largely insulated from the traffic noise, but subject upstairs to a barely perceptible shake. Salih Efendi's granddaughter is now in her eightieth year; she and her daughters, Süveyda and Zerhan, devote much of their energies to the yalı's preservation. The doctor, scientist, administrator and plantsman looks down from sepia photographs on the walls: a smiling face, framed by a snowy white beard.

Cornucopia Issue 10, 1996

The yalı in the 1950s. In the days of the Sultan's chief physician a botanic garden covered the terraced hillside behind the house

Left The chief physician (with beard and fez) at the international cholera conference he chaired in 1866

Opposite Scrubbed floorboards, a faded carpet and well-worn varnish on the handsome doors

An airy first-floor bedroom, with wrought-iron stove and Empire-style bed, remains unchanged since the early 1900s

Right and opposite Evening light pours into the reception room. Freya Stark described 'five high windows arched to the ceiling'

THE TALK OF THE BOSPHORUS

BUILT IN 1895 AS A GLITTERING PRIZE, THEN CLOSED BY WAR AND
EXILE, THIS HUGE, FLAMBOYANT MANSION SET TONGUES WAGGING.
SIZE APART, IT WAS SEEN AS SCANDALOUS FOR A TURKISH PASHA
NOT TO BUILD HIS BOSPHORUS YALI IN WOOD. TODAY THE SUMMER
RETREAT OF THE BRILLIANT LINGUIST, SOLDIER AND REFORMER
ZEKİ PASHA STANDS FORLORN, OVERSHADOWED BY A MASSIVE
BRIDGE, CLOAKED IN CREEPER AND MYSTERY

*The panel of an Italian
commode in the grand
salon of the Zeki Pasha
Yalı, inlaid with pietra
dura and framed
in gleaming ormulu*

No one who has sailed the upper reaches of the Bosphorus
can miss the bulk of Zeki Pasha's great mansion rising in
the shadow of the Fatih Bridge. Large, ornate and curiously
urban, its oatmeal-coloured walls are festooned with fronds
of virginia creeper. When I first crossed the Bosphorus to
see the yalı from the water, the winter sun had just risen above the Bithynian
hills, outlining each fold in a charcoal line. While the Asian shore was still
in shadow, the yalı was standing within its square of walls, seemingly sewn
into a ribbon of twentieth-century development, its reflection slanted across
the water, dancing on pale ripples of sunlight. Strangely, the noise of traffic
from the bridge was no more than a murmur above the screams of the
mobbing gulls.

The house stands to the north of Rumelihisarı, the village which sprawls
around Mehmed II's fortress on the European shore. Here, at the point where
Darius is said to have walked his armies into Thrace, the Bosphorus narrows
to no more than half a kilometre in width. Boatmen have always taken
advantage of this headland, where the channel's zigzagging current changes
course for Asia beneath the yalı's walls. Despite having to dodge multistorey
supertankers carrying Russian oil to the outside world, the easiest way to
cross between Rumelihisarı, on the European shore, and Anadoluhisarı, on
the Asian side, is still by boat.

When the house was built in 1895 it was denounced as unorthodox and astonishing. Other than the imperial summer palaces, which by the middle of the nineteenth century were all built dressed in stone, plaisances on the Bosphorus were still traditionally constructed of wood. Zeki Pasha's yalı is uniquely built of reinforced carbon-dust brick blocks, sealed together with conventional cement mortar to resemble four towering walls of crazy paving. These earthquake-resistant façades are symmetrically decorated with a profusion of Renaissance plaster mouldings, fixed around a medley of balconies and windows on all five storeys. An observatory is hidden behind a Neoclassical balustrade on the roof. The late-nineteenth-century Europeanness of this surprising building is, however, contradicted by a pair of enchanting Ottoman porches with overhanging eaves, seemingly pinned onto the corners of the western, landward-facing façade. Double staircases run up to them from the garden. The paradox is contrived, even eccentric.

The man responsible for the flamboyant ensemble which was the envy of late-nineteenth-century Istanbul was Zeki Pasha, one of Abdülhamid II's most trusted and able soldier-statesmen. It is said that during the last decade of the nineteenth century, the size and situation of a property reflected status and success more surely than at any other time in the four-and-a-half centuries of Ottoman rule. Zeki Pasha's summer mansion was the finest on the Bosphorus.

Zeki Pasha was the son of Ali Remzi Efendi, himself the orphaned son of Mahmud II's Greek *kürkçübaşı* (head furrier). Ali Remzi had been adopted by the minister of war Hüsrev Pasha and later entered the service of Osman Pasha, governor of the province of Aydın, where Zeki was born in 1849. Intelligent, blue-eyed and ambitious, he joined the elite First Artillery Regiment at Tophane, taking with him to the cadet school an extraordinary gift for music and languages, and an ability to teach as well as to learn.

While serving in the Turco-Russian War of 1877–78, he was appointed aide-de-camp, first to the commander-in-chief, Süleyman Pasha, then, after the war, to Sultan Abdülhamid himself. Assigned to the Palace as tutor to the Sultan's sons, he later had a seat in the Sultan's cabinet and was appointed inspector-general of military schools and commander-in-chief of artillery (*tophane müşiri*). His collaboration with the cultured and witty German Colonel von der Goltz in modernising the armed forces and reorganising the military command structure was so successful that even the suspicious British, who reported 'faction rivalry within the High Command', considered him to be 'one of the best men the Turks have got'.

By 1895 he was at the high point of his career, newly married for the third time and father to a brood of successful children. In all probability the Sultan's gift of five *dönüm* of land (5,000 square metres) at Rumelihisarı – four on the hillside and one on the waterfront – for the construction of a yalı was made because the earthquake that in 1894 had severely shaken the capital had badly damaged Zeki Pasha's house on Büyükada, the largest of the Princes Islands, in the Sea of Marmara.

Bills of lading and an account book for the construction of the yalı have survived. The work was scrupulously supervised by Zeki Pasha's aide-de-camp, who has a wider fame as the father of Vasfi Rıza Zobu, the first Turk of good family to become a celebrated actor, bringing respectability to a profession that hitherto had been the preserve of the minorities.

Although it is not proven, almost certainly the architect of the exterior of the yalı was Alexandre Vallaury, son of a Levantine French confectioner whose patisseries, sold in the family establishment on the Grand' Rue de Pera, were legendary. Vallaury was ultra-fashionable, the architect responsible for the surge of public buildings peppering Beyoğlu, styled 'Banker's Renaissance'. His *chef d'oeuvre* was the remodelling of the old Ottoman Bank in Karaköy (jointly owned with the Régie des Tabacs, the tobacco monopoly), which he had enlarged into the bank's splendid three-storey headquarters, a building still standing on Bankalar Caddesi today.

The design of the interior of the yalı may have been left to one of Vallaury's pupils, who would have trained at the École des Beaux Arts in Paris. The internal organisation has roots in Ottoman architecture – all the main rooms lead off each storey's central hall – yet it also resembles a late-nineteenth-century bourgeois apartment in the fashionable sixteenth *arrondissement* in Paris. The awkward entrance hall is squashed against the stairwell. Its poorly proportioned staircase, lit by a skylight, links each floor in steep flights to the topmost landing. Yet four splendidly well-proportioned *appartements*, identically arranged in a succession of six rooms per floor, lead off the long central halls. The sea-facing rooms are still gorgeously decorated and gilded in the style of late-nineteenth-century Paris, all with inlaid parquet floors, recessed mahogany doors, fine marble fireplaces and windows with espagnolette bolts. The hall floors are laid in oak; the stairs (apart from later repairs to the first flight in stonework) in elm; and the main entrance hall in marble.

Parents, children and a retinue of servants moved from the family's winter mansion in Nişantaşı – house and garden now the site of the American Hospital – to the new stone yalı on the Bosphorus. They did so in time to escape the capital's political unrest and an outbreak of typhoid in the city. Adviye Hanım, Zeki Pasha's young wife, had just given birth to Sabiha, a third daughter. In 1913 Sabiha, who died in 1993 aged ninety-eight, was to marry Ali Kemal. A victim of one of the more unsavoury incidents in the independence struggle, Ali Kemal was lynched by a mob in Izmit in 1922. Widowed and in virtual exile between the two world wars,

Sabiha brought up her only son, Zeki, in Switzerland. In his turn, Zeki Kuneralp was to become one of Turkey's most distinguished and admired diplomats after the Second World War.

For thirteen successive summers from 1895, the house was in full use. Sabiha remembered in old age how cold and damp it could be. But her most vivid recollections were of voices echoing up and down the elm stairs, trips in the launch, fishing off the jetty and hearing her father singing Neapolitan love songs at the piano. The passengers at Rumelihisarı's ferry station are said to have waited to glimpse Zeki Pasha, resplendent in uniform, being saluted onto the *mouche* (gunboat) bound for his headquarters at Tophane. And village tales still tell of the Imperial Artillery Band playing in the yalı's garden when the Sultan's anniversary was to be celebrated.

In June 1908 the life of the yalı came abruptly to an end. Abdülhamid, shaken by an insurrection in Rumelia – Ottoman Europe – and the mutinous mob of his troops, promised to restore the suspended Constitution of 1876 and to dismiss some of his closest advisers. Zeki Pasha and his family were ordered to Rhodes, where they stayed for four years in comfortable exile, with interludes in France, Austria and Switzerland. In 1913 Zeki Pasha returned to Istanbul, to the old family yalı on Büyükada, rather than the newer house on the Bosphorus. He died in 1914, a few months before the birth of his grandson, the future diplomat Zeki Kuneralp.

From 1908 to 1918 the yalı was closed. During the troubled years before the Great War, neither Mehmed V nor the Committee of Union and Progress had need of it or wished to make claim to it. During the terrible years of the war itself, many yalıs, if not turned into hospitals or barracks, were shut.

At the end of the war in 1918, Prince Vahdettin succeeded his half-brother as Mehmed VI. The empire had shrunk to no more than Anatolia and a tiny foothold in Europe. Under Allied occupation the capital was a frenetic whirl of soirées and balls for the privileged few, while the majority suffered serious shortages of food and fuel. The worse conditions became for the common people, the faster and more frivolous grew the social scene.

During the early months of Mehmed VI's short and troubled reign, another Sabiha, the most beautiful of the Sultan's daughters, took over the empty yalı. Princess Sabiha was newly married to her cousin, Ömer Faruk Efendi, and for four years they made it their summerhouse in a world that was seemingly falling to pieces around them.

In March 1924, a month after their eldest daughter, Princess Neslişah, had celebrated her third birthday – and scarcely six months after the birth in the yalı of the second daughter, Princess Hanzade – the Ottoman Empire ended. All the members of the former ruling dynasty were expelled from the new Republic. Neslişah Sultan still remembers events before their departure for Europe [the

Princess died in 2012, aged ninety-one]. Her memories are vignettes divided between Dolmabahçe Palace, where she was born, and the yalı, their horses, and how they directed the work in the gardens. She remembers noticing, presumably from an upstairs window, how porpoises made use of the race below the yalı's walls in rounding the point. The winter of 1923 was glacial. Icebergs floated down the Bosphorus and branches of cedars broke under the weight of the snow; snowmen lingered on in the garden for weeks. Inside it was scarcely warmer than out.

In the hectic and unhappy time before their departure from the capital, the imperial families had to make what arrangements they could to leave their estates in capable hands while waiting for the politics of the new Turkey to stabilise. So it was that Bedriye Hanım was given charge of the yalı. She was the wife to one of Mehmed VI's favourites, Refik Bey, who until March 1924 had been director of the Imperial Treasury and for this service was probably the obvious choice for the task. Through her husband she had close ties with Zeki Pasha's family. Through her father, Gazi Edhem Pasha, one of the richest of the last Ottoman field marshals, she inherited valuable building land in Osmanbey and the necessary financial resources when she moved in with her daughter Meliha in the summer of 1924. She could not have foreseen that she was to reign over all domestic matters until her death forty-two years later. After surnames became compulsory, she adopted the name Milona in memory of her father's famous victory against the Greeks in 1897.

In 1928 Meliha became engaged to Saffet Baştımar. He was a landowning businessman from the Black Sea, with newly opened tobacco factories in Izmir and Samsun and a flourishing trade with the United States. Moreover he had aspirations to represent Trabzon in the Grand National Assembly in Ankara. The political situation in Ankara had stabilised and it was now clear that there would be no restoration of the sultanate. A financial arrangement between Princess Sabiha in Europe and Bedriye Hanım in Istanbul for ownership of the yalı to pass into the name of the future son-in-law on marriage to her daughter Meliha in 1928 must have seemed an obvious expedient.

During the Second World War the tobacco trade across the Atlantic was disrupted and Zeki Pasha's great house, together with the beautiful Esma Sultan Yalı in Ortaköy, was used as a depot for Saffet Baştımar's consignments of tobacco awaiting shipment once trade resumed. From 1947 the building was transformed again from a wartime warehouse into a yalı for Bedriye Hanım and her family. For Saffet and Meliha Baştımar's two children, Refika and Can, who were both at school at the time – Refika at Notre Dame de Sion and Can at the English High School for Boys – and whose home the yalı is today, it was the heyday of the house. It was a time when their friends poured through, either to play tennis on the newly laid tennis court in the garden, or to swim off the jetty with the boxer dogs once the morning rubbish had swept past on the tide. Structurally, only the first flight of the elm staircase had to be replaced in stone.

The late-nineteenth-century Venetian glass chandeliers, with their flowery sprays which had so remarkably survived the war, were rehung; the cornices and high mirrors were regilded; some of the French furnishings were replaced. It was then left only for the longest dining table on the Bosphorus, bought from an Egyptian family fallen on hard times during the 1930s, to be reinstalled in the main dining room on the first floor. This Scottish-made table was later sold to an industrialist, who built a room specially to house it in his yalı across the water in Anadoluhisarı.

In 1961, Saffet Baştımar died in London, aged only sixty-nine. In 1967 his widow, Meliha, to finance the development of Istanbul's first shopping complex – on land at Osmanbey and Şişli, complete with cinemas *à l'américaine* – sold the tobacco factories in Izmir and Samsun. Three years later, with the family spending increasing lengths of time in the yalı, they sold the hillside above it in Rumelihisarı to install its first coal-fired central-heating system.

Bedriye Hanım, who had taken such care of the yalı for four decades until her death in 1966, was spared the knowledge of the decision, taken in 1978, to place the footings of the Fatih Bridge on the hill immediately behind the yalı. During the autumn of 1987, a section of the bridge was swung directly over the yalı on a moving trolley. This winching and swinging operation was the signal for the owners of all houses beneath the bridge compulsorily to change all heating systems to oil. Security of the new multi-million-dollar structure necessitated the change, but the individual property owners had to pay for it. By the following year the second Bosphorus bridge, the Fatih Bridge, was completed. At 1,090 metres, it just exceeds the First Bosphorus Bridge in length and at the time of building was the fifth longest bridge in the world.

The coast road from Rumelihisarı to Baltalimanı, the neighbouring village to the north, is wider than it was a hundred years ago. Steps lead down from its uneven pavement to the yalı's creeper-clad entrance gates. The gate nearest the village has a notice warning of dogs. Within the walled garden there is an overwhelming feeling of peace. The trees are showing their age. The decorative marble fountains on the walls are all but obscured by curtains of ivy. Notwithstanding the huge bridge that passes directly over the old tennis court, the visitor is curiously isolated from its noise and feels caught in a time warp. Not even the kennel for the rottweilers breaks the spell.

As the evening shadows lengthen across the garden, it needs no great imagination to discern the ghosts of those who have lived in and loved Zeki Pasha's great yalı.

Cornucopia Issue 17, 1999

The Zeki Pasha Yalı's crystal bonbonnière and glasses, a gift from the Greek royal family

At either end of the western façade is a decorative Ottoman Revival wooden porch with overhanging eaves. Each is linked by a double staircase to a garden where military bands once played. In the hundred years since it was built by Zeki Pasha, three separate families have occupied the house, their fates curiously entwined by marriage, revolution and war

Below Refika Menemenci, whose grandmother, Bedriye Hanım, ruled over the yalı from 1924 until her death in 1966. Refika now shares it with her brother, Can; as children their friends poured through the house to play tennis and swim from the jetty

9

The Ratip Efendi Yalı

SOME ENCHANTED EVENINGS

In the 1950s, this palely beautiful summerhouse on the Bosphorus made the perfect playground for the cream of café society. Now its spacious, luminous rooms, emptied of fuss and colour, reveal their natural beauty

Princess Fazileh, great-granddaughter of the last Ottoman sultan, in 1957, the year she became engaged to King Faisal II of Iraq at the yalı. During that magical summer, the King enjoyed himself so much that it was hard to persuade him to leave for a few hours to let others sleep

Nigel Nicolson says that some houses, like some people, are immediately likeable, while others take time to know. The mid-nineteenth-century summerhouse on the upper shores of the Bosphorus owned for three generations by the Ratip family – and now by the Mardin family – belongs firmly in the former category. It stands on a sheltered curve of the channel between the villages of İstinye and Yeniköy on the European shore. Enclosed by high walls, hidden from passers-by, its charms are as fresh to those who have known it a lifetime as to those whose first visit was yesterday.

The wooden yalı was originally built as one of a pair. They were probably the first substantial constructions ever, or at least for many centuries, to have stood on the site, for this had once been a monastery. Sadly, its twin has gone, torn down in the 1930s to make way for a fashionable new Republic summerhouse in a style best described as Bosphorus Third Empire.

The deceptively simple exterior of the Ratip Efendi Yalı conceals a wonderful and richly decorated interior, set off by a breathtakingly elegant flight of stairs. It is generally supposed that the twin houses were commissioned by some well-connected pasha as dowry pieces for his daughters, though no records survive of when, or how, they were built, or of any architect. They were almost certainly the creation of local master craftsmen, their prodigious talents passed down from generation to generation.

Viewed from the water the yalı lies palely beautiful amid its own mature trees. Huge magnolias, a dozen palms, together with pines, cedars, Judas trees and overgrown laurels, run riot up the hill by which the yalı is cushioned; they do battle with armies of giant hydrangeas, rambling roses and cords of entwined wisteria. The perimeter walls and fine entrance gates enclose a full acre of ground, cut into terraces on three levels.

The hillside itself is dotted with springs. These waters have been channelled through finely decorated fountains to cascade into a series of oval fishponds dug into the terraces. Close to the shore, between the boathouse and the yalı, a freshwater spring bubbles up through clear sand. As a shrine dedicated to St George, its walls are covered in frescoes of uncertain date. The therapeutic properties of these waters may well have been known from as early as the time Jason sailed by with his Argonauts, and villagers still come with their jugs when there is sickness in the home.

Rushing around as we do today, hostages to mobile phones and laptops, it is hard to conceive of those long, leisurely sojourns on the Bosphorus enjoyed by a throng of Turco-Egyptian textile magnates known as the *Mısırlılar* (the Egyptians). Each summer from the 1850s to the 1960s they migrated here from their palaces in Cairo and their *hôtels particuliers* in Europe. Reckless spenders, they came to enjoy the fruits of the nineteenth-century cotton boom. Following a vogue set by the Egyptian khedives themselves, who had built a series of summer palaces on both sides of the water, they arrived by car, by train or by boat as the wisteria came into bloom. Like homing pigeons returning to an old-fashioned loft, they settled, with their entourages of servants, into the yalıs they had bought or built beside the Bosphorus.

The Ratip fortune had been made in one generation by an exile of the Ottoman Empire who had fled to Kavalalı Mehmed Ali Pasha's Egypt after his father had fallen foul of Sultan Mahmud II in the early nineteenth century. It is thought that Ratip Efendi acquired the yalı in Yeniköy – ideal for generous entertainment and useful for accelerating acceptance in the capital – sometime during the 1860s.

By the turn of the century, Ülfet Hanım, his half-Egyptian daughter, was spending her summers happily ensconced in the yalı, conducting her fashionable life in many tongues. She is remembered particularly for her love and knowledge of Turkish classical music and for the evening concerts she gave in the house. But it was to be during the lifetime of her son, Ebubekir, that the yalı took on its role as the cultural crossroads between Europe and the Middle East for which it is most vividly remembered.

During the four-month, summer-long stay in the yalı, one day merged into another. It was open house. Swimming parties led to lunch; fishing, sailing and rowing parties led to five-o'clock tea and idle gossip around a samovar in the shade of a spreading umbrella tree. Gone is the sight of 'Papa and Mama Ratip' passing through the yalı's handsome gates in their Rolls-Royce, their huge Egyptian chauffeur in full uniform and fez at the wheel. Ebubekir Bey was a handsome figure with a monocle and moustache, Ceyda Hanım a beautiful woman in Dior's New Look. Gone, too, are the Fifties sports Mercedes, the seven live-in servants – an international household led by Beshir, the striking Sudanese whose shiny black shoes, well-ironed trousers, white jacket and fez made him the mascot as well as the majordomo of the house.

Ebubekir Ratip died at the age of eighty-five, in 1977, his substantial inheritance all but eaten up. His wife outlived him by three years. They were the last truly colourful *Mısırlı* family to summer on the Bosphorus. Both were bound, either by friendship or by blood, not only to almost every member of the international café society who took their motorboats and waterskis to the French Riviera, but to nearly every member of the then ruling families of the Middle East.

It is difficult, half a century later, to unravel the complex relationships between members of the Ratip circle. Ebubekir Bey's connections were mainly Turco-Egyptian – he was related to the Khedive – but a Ratip nephew was married to Fevziye, the former Empress of Iran. His wife, Ceyda, provided further cosmopolitan links. She was the eldest of the newspaper proprietor Ahmet Cevdet İkdam's three daughters. Her half-Russian mother, a concert pianist, was the daughter of a St Petersburg court jeweller. Ceyda's first husband, killed in a car crash in the South of France, had been Prince André Obolensky. As a young widow, staying in Cairo with her middle sister, Reya, in the early 1920s, Ceyda met, and later married, Ebubekir. Reya's husband was the Turkish diplomat Şemsettin Arif Mardin, son of the last governor of Syria and the Lebanon, and the legendary Leyla Hanım Efendi, daughter of an Egyptian diplomat, who had been brought up in the embassies of Paris, Vienna and St Petersburg, watching her father's collection of paintings by Corot, Courbet, Boucher and Ingres being added to the walls. It was in Leyla Hanım's Cairo palace that Ceyda and Ebubekir were introduced.

During the summer of 1957 the Ratip summerhouse on the Bosphorus contributed a bright thread to the tapestry of history. The crowd of friends who came daily to swim from the terrace included foreign diplomats down from Ankara (the French, Italian, Swedish and Greek ambassadors), neighbours dropping in from up- or downstream, the Princesses Neslişah and Hanzade, grandchildren of the last sultan, still unable to own property on Turkish soil, with their own children, and the young King Faisal II of Iraq.

The King arrived every day at nine in the morning and left at three the following morning, for he was courting Princess Fazileh, the beautiful daughter of Hanzade Sultan, to whom he became engaged in the coolness of the yalı.

When she received his emerald ring, she could not have imagined that a year later her short, plain but charming fiancé would be murdered, following the Iraqi Revolution of July 1958, or that later, married to Hayri Ürgüplü, she would sell the ring to pay for her own yalı.

That summer the young King's suave, good-looking, pro-English uncle, Crown Prince Abdülilah, then acting as regent of Iraq, came regularly to tea carrying a grey cat on his shoulder, which he stroked constantly. He, too, was foully murdered following the July revolution. Less regularly, the diminutive but handsome young King Hussein of Jordan arrived, not with his Hashemite cousin Faisal, but with the Egyptian Prince Mehmet Ali, Hanzade Sultan's wealthy husband, who moored his yacht alongside the yalı's quay.

A year before King Faisal's engagement, on 14 July 1956, the roads were closed along the European shore to allow a cavalcade of cars to flow in the direction of Yeniköy for the biggest wedding in Istanbul since the war. The marriage of Reya Mardin's son Şerif was being celebrated in the yalı. His bride was Suna Aksoy, the beautiful daughter of the successful bureaucrat and honorary consul in Monte Carlo and his İzmirli wife, whose family had owned cotton fields in the Menderes delta for generations.

Those who glimpsed the bride and the throng of wedding guests passing on their way could not be blamed for imagining that the disruption was in honour of Turkey's beauty queen: if they failed to recognise the crownless King Umberto of Italy with his sister, the ex-Queen of Romania, certainly the young future prime minister Bülent Ecevit, later a regular guest, will have passed unnoticed by the watching crowds.

The fifty-year marriage of Ebubekir and Ceyda Ratip was childless. When she died in 1980 the yalı passed to Osman, the son of Şerif and Suna Mardin, grandson of Reya, Ceyda Hanım's younger sister, and so Ebubekir Ratip's great-nephew by marriage.

The Mardin Yalı, as it should now be called, has recently been lovingly and impeccably restored and is in hands as safe and as sensitive to its history as any yalı on the Bosphorus could hope to be.

Cornucopia Issue 18, 1999

History in the making

Top Fazile and King Faisal's engagement at the yalı in 1957: from left, Prince Abdülilah (the King's uncle); Hanzade Sultan (Fazile's mother); Prince Ahmet (brother), the engaged couple and Ebubekir Ratip. Kneeling is Faisal's cousin Prince Raad of Iraq (son of the painter Fahrelnissa Zeid). Faisal was murdered in the 1958 Iraqi Revolution before they could marry

Right In the fashionable village of Yeniköy, where the Bosphorus broadens out, Ratip Efendi's yalı has long been a setting for memorable gatherings

Far right His grandson Ebubekir Ratip's Rolls-Royce in the Swiss Alps

Yalı and Köçek St. Vasiliy / The rich Armenians settled here between the ... Köçek. The families of Allahverdi, Oherotom and Soymooozjan ... the rug, among them with its ... beauty and simplicity of style. ... ... to the Turkish ... ... hand on a Europeal plan. On the left arm ... ... Near Köçbet Square Vasiliki Kalli's charming yalı and next to it Ssoymoss's

... ve Köçekem . Yenlkör'ün köylval Releroset ve dolu dirıla dirdir ... ... -ler tenagloını yerleymeytrdir. Bulgarıstan Cenetelın, Rocymooozjan ve Allahverleen-... ... ... Yenlkör dovtirım serptali. Boycymooozjan tannittil ile Allahverden-... ... ... Almanla, Rocymooozjan. Turk Ampirl ile Etnokal akat altııfotctin ter pilen ile çlundıdılar. ... ... tabo Vasıllkı ... ... Germanin köpeğl ... ... almun loeynı edilln-... ... ... köybasıl meydanı tarafında Vasıliki Kallanat satıf yalısı, onun jor-... ... görgülidiir.

Above Detail of a
painted ceiling
Left Ebubekir Ratip
sporting a fez, monocle
and riding boots
Right The elegant
double staircase, an
outstanding feature
of the house

THE HOUSE THAT
CAME OUT OF THE BLUE

IT WAS ONLY TO STOP A PROPERTY DEALER PAINTING IT BLUE
THAT THE GERMEN FAMILY ACQUIRED A YALI TO LOOK AFTER.
ON A GLORIOUS STRETCH OF THE ASIAN SHORE, THIS COVETABLE
PAVILION, ONCE THE MEN'S QUARTERS OF A LARGER MANSION,
ENJOYS SOUTHERLY VIEWS ALL THE WAY TO THE TOPKAPI

*The Germen Yalı was
formerly the men's
quarters of a substantial
house in Vaniköy.
While modest in size,
it has had a succession
of distinguished
owners, including
a future sultan*

My first view of the Germens' enchanting summerhouse in Vaniköy was not from the sea but from the First Bosphorus Bridge. The single-storey pavilion was built, probably in the 1840s, as a *selamlık*, serving the main mansion next to it as a place where guests were received and to which men could retire. It stands boldly on the water, turned to catch the widest view of the lower Bosphorus, its windows commanding a panorama stretching from Bebek on the European shore via Seraglio Point to Üsküdar on the Asian side.

Though modest in size, the Germen Yalı has always had owners of exceptional distinction and refinement who are in tune with its particular combination of simplicity and elegance. For some sixty years the Germens' pavilion and the main living quarters next door, the harem, have been separately owned, yet they are both structurally unaltered and still painted the distinctive Ottoman oxblood red.

The whole of the estate is said to have been acquired by the Palace sometime in the last decade of the nineteenth century as a summer residence for the blue-eyed, fair-haired future sultan Mehmed V Reşad. As heir apparent to his suspicious half-brother, Abdülhamid II, Mehmed Reşad, a timid, delicate poet and dervish, must have been living at the time under strict supervision. Some authorities believe that the mansion was acquired for Mihrengiz, Mehmed Reşad's third wife, who married into the imperial family in 1887 at the age of eighteen. On her husband's death in 1918, it is thought that she disposed of the property to the master of the robes to the Sultan, Esvapçıbaşı Sabit Efendi. Others suggest that it was acquired for the very much younger Dilfirid, Mehmed Reşad's fifth wife, who was born in 1890. Whichever of the wives was living there, the splendidly ornate sea door is some confirmation of the tradition of a royal connection, while the modest size of the *selamlık* indicates that Mehmed Reşad was an occasional visitor rather than a resident.

Sometime during the late 1920s or early 1930s Sabit Efendi sold off the *selamlık*, now the Germen family's yalı, to the politician and eminent professor Nihat Reşat Belger. Major refurbishment was then put in hand. Although protected from both the biting northerly winter winds and the currents racing round the point, it is fully exposed to the *lodos*, the sinister tropical storms that arise without warning from the south. White-tipped waves grow into rolling seas which flay the house. Water crashing over the roof leaves salt eating into the woodwork and destabilising the pier. Professor Belger reduced this threat by extending the terrace overlooking the water.

Internally, he made a kitchen out of the Ottoman *kahvehane*, or coffee room. Water was piped in from the hillside behind the house, and he installed a plain marble fireplace on the southern wall without disturbing the delicate proportions of the rooms. The doorknobs he had fitted throughout the yalı have a 1920s feel; so, doubtless did the Japanese bridge spanning two ponds in the garden, long since filled in.

Professor Belger was a household name in the first decades of the Republic. Opposed to autocracy of any persuasion and disillusioned with Enver and the Committee of Union and Progress, he took refuge in Paris in 1906, combining political activity with advanced medical studies. During Turkey's War of Independence (1919–23) he represented the Turkish Nationalists in France, where he established an international reputation as a gastroenterologist. In the early 1930s he returned to Turkey to live in the yalı and continue his political and medical careers.

Belger was the epitome of the new Republican ideal: practical man of science, active democrat and aesthete. The last of those attributes is vividly reflected in the Germen Yalı. He was elected to the Grand National Assembly, and became director of the Yalova Spa and Atatürk's personal physician. In the 1950s he was briefly minister of health but he fell out with the increasingly autocratic regime of Menderes. By this time Professor Belger had moved to Ortaköy, on the European shore. In 1947, at the age of sixty-five, he had decided to sell the yalı. Noisy neighbours and the smell of the grain mills in Kandilli are said to have precipitated the move.

The house was bought by İhsan Tunalı, a *bon vivant* who had retired early from the diplomatic service to join his brother-in-law Cenap And in his infant Ankara wine company in Kavaklıdere. He purchased the yalı as a surprise present for his young wife, Nerime Hanım, registering her as owner on her birthday. Half a century later, she told me how her husband died in the yalı only six years afterwards and, unable to face the summers there alone, she rented it out. When the relentless upkeep and continual repainting of the southern façade became luxuries she could no longer afford, Nerime Hanım made an arrangement with Fethi Doğançay, the property-dealing husband of Atatürk's youngest adopted daughter, Ülkü, to take it off her hands in exchange for a comfortable apartment in the then fashionable district of Şişli.

Good luck had it that in the late 1950s Seniha Germen and her two daughters, Sezen and Güli, the present owners, were spending the summers in Vaniköy. Having set their hearts on the yalı, they were alarmed by the refurbishment plans of Fethi Doğançay, whose workmen had stripped off the traditional dark red *aşıboya* paint in preparation for repainting in blue. Their bid was accepted, and in late 1958 they found themselves the owners of a house of six small, well-proportioned rooms, each one with four or five tall sash windows arranged to give views in two directions: across the garden to the verdant Asian hills, and out onto the moody Bosphorus.

From a central *divanhane*, or hallway, which runs through the house from the garden to the terrace, three rooms lead off on either side, each one benefiting from the soft aqueous light and reflection from the sea. The yalı had again found owners of exceptional taste. Seniha Hanım, beautiful, witty and cultured, a member of the intellectual Allamezade family from Izmir, was the widow of Murat Germen, friend and admirer of Atatürk, who had died of septicaemia in 1938 while governor of Izmir. She never remarried, and devoted her fifty years of widowhood to her daughters.

The family first struggled with the yalı's exterior. At a time of scarcities they managed to procure some Romanian silver fir for the cladding of the southern façade and Russian pine to repair the rotting window frames. With great expense and difficulty they also managed to procure from Holland oil paint for boats similar to *aşıboya*.

The interior was also a labour of love. The exquisite plasterwork of the high ceilings, each one of a different Neoclassical design, was meticulously reworked. Soon the latticed strapwork, including single and double diagonals, became again one of the main features of the house. In 1966 new pine floors were laid, in which the ceilings are subtly reflected.

Until her death in 1989, Seniha Germen took the lead over the management of the yalı. Now it is Güli's turn to be in charge of the *ustas*, specialist craftsmen repainting and repairing the complicated details of the woodwork. Güli is married to Sinan Vlora, a successful architect living in Switzerland. On both sides Vlora is descended from Albanians: from Kavalalı Mehmed Ali Pasha, first Khedive of Egypt, and from his kinsman Prince Vlora (Avlonia Pasha), who went to Egypt with him. Linen from the khedival palace at Çubuklu, brought by Sinan Vlora's mother, Princess Atiye, daughter of the last khedive, Abbas Hilmi II, is still in use in the yalı.

The elder of the two Germen sisters, Sezen, a brilliant professor of philology, worked at the Council of Europe in Strasbourg for eighteen years until her recent retirement. For forty-two years both sisters have spent at least part of every summer in Vaniköy. They arrive as soon as the weather permits and stay until autumnal cold and damp oblige them to decamp. But the house is never deserted. Their faithful Trakyalı maid and gardener are always there to open up the house at a moment's notice.

Life has changed dramatically since the Germens moved in. Above all, the Bosphorus itself has changed. The ferries no longer call at Vaniköy, fishing boats rarely supply the riches of the sea from a few metres off the yalı's jetty, and the twice-daily bathes have had to be abandoned in the face of extensive pollution from neighbouring Çengelköy.

Seniha Hanım died before an explosion blew out most of the yalı's original Venetian glazing, an incident that occurred during renovation of a neighbouring modern house. But she had shared her daughters' outrage when, during the winter of 1971, the massive stone land wall, together with the handsome, newly restored entrance gate, complete with its original handles, was swept away without notice or compensation during the municipality's road-widening scheme. In one swoop, thirteen metres of the yalı's garden, together with its outbuildings, disappeared. Its two ancient plane trees are now shading the central reservation of the road.

The Bosphorus, mistreated, vandalised and disfigured as it has been in the past hundred years, still has not lost all its magic. Sezen and Güli no longer pull up a bucket of mussels from the pier if a visitor unexpectedly stays on for dinner, but the flowers of the Judas trees still turn the hillside magenta each May; the smell of the lime trees still overpowers the senses each June; withered magnolia petals still carpet the terraces and lawn, smothering the honeysuckles, jasmines, roses and hydrangeas on the boundary walls. And a lone boatman from Yeniköy, perhaps the last of the real Istanbul *efendi*, needs no instruction as to how to land visitors arriving from Europe.

Cornucopia, Issue 21, 2000

THE GERMEN YALI, VANİKÖY

Tiny but perfect

The house is small and luminous and has spectacular views on two sides. Past the picturesque village of Vaniköy and the First Bosphorus Bridge is the distant silhouette of the Topkapı. The dining room and drawing room have long windows facing south and west to take full advantage of the outlook

The yalı looks across the Bosphorus to the village of Bebek on the European shore. Flourishes were added to the windows when Abdülhamid II gave the yalı to the future Mehmed V Reşad. The chalet style became fashionable in the 1890s when Abdülhamid built the new Yıldız Palace

Overleaf The central 'divanhane', or hallway, runs through the house from the garden to the terrace. The author is seen at work as 'Hiawatha', the American Consulate's classic launch, sails past

The look of cool elegance was set by Seniha Germen, who acquired the yalı in the 1950s as a young widow. The handsome eighteenth-century chairs were hers, and the gleaming silver her mother's. Today her two daughters keep the house alive
Below The flamboyant front door, embellished window surrounds and ceramic stove date from c.1900

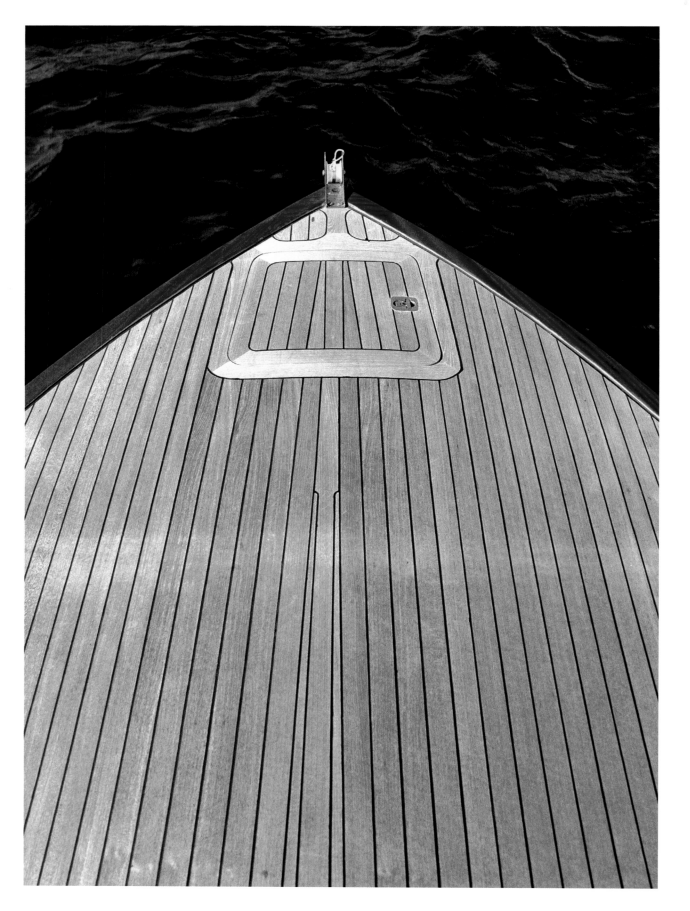

IN THE SPIRIT'S WAKE

<small>AFTER TWO DECADES OF PAINSTAKING NEGOTIATION,
TWO ARCHITECTS ACHIEVED THEIR DREAM OF BREATHING
NEW LIFE INTO AN OTTOMAN SPIRIT FACTORY</small>

The wooden deck of the sleek launch used for ferrying the Sumahan's hotel guests between the European and Asian shores

The derelict nineteenth-century Ottoman spirit distillery at Çengelköy has been miraculously transformed from an industrial wasteland on the lower Asian shore of the Bosphorus into a tip-top twenty-first-century hotel, Sumahan on the Water, uniquely standing on its own private quay at the very water's edge. The Bosphorus, a beautiful sinuous riband of deep water dividing Europe from Asia, has over the past twenty years been the victim of unprecedented urbanisation. In contrast to the developments that have sprung up around it, the Sumahan (literally spirit-house) is, like the two bridges halfway between which it stands, both aesthetically and functionally right.

The transformation of the old distillery is the realisation of a couple's dream, achieved over two decades of painstaking negotiation with planning authorities and backers. Fitting perhaps, if small comfort to Nedret and Mark Butler, the architects whose dream it was, since the history of the Sumahan has always been complicated and romantic. The original building dates from the reign of Mahmud II, when royal distilleries were well-constructed factory complexes built in local stone on prime sites. The distillery produced *suma*, or raw spirit, a clear, pungent liquid that can be made from almost any staple, from grain to grape – the Çengelköy factory used figs to distil its *suma*.

On Mahmud II's demise in 1839 the waterside factory passed to his wife, the beautiful Bezm-î Âlem Valide Sultan, mother of his two sons and successors,

Abdülmecid I and Abdülaziz. She was renowned as a benefactress to the poor and to the women of Istanbul, though her reputation owed nothing to her liberality in dispensing *suma*. She was vehemently teetotal, even destroying the Palace's precious collection of crystal drinking vessels. Following her death, ownership of the complex becomes unclear. It has been suggested that the factory was acquired by an Armenian businessman, and there may be truth in the story that an Englishman ran it during the Allied occupation of Istanbul at the end of the First World War. At all events, it continued to produce raw spirit. By 1921 it was evidently making the traditional aniseed-flavoured spirit drunk throughout the Mediterranean region: the smell of rakı issuing from the village's twenty-two taverns was so strong that respectable citizens were obliged to walk down the street to the ferry station with handkerchiefs dipped in cologne held to their noses.

In the early 1930s the distillery changed hands for the last time. The whole complex of buildings either side of the Kuleli coastal road was acquired by Tevfik Cenani, an industrialist who had come from Ottoman Bulgaria and made good. No stranger to Çengelköy, to escape the summer heat of Beyoğlu, he had bought the enchanting two-storey wooden *köşk*, or villa, on the hillside above the road that had been owned in the mid-1920s by the Ottoman ambassador to Vienna, Mahmud Nedim Pasha. Set like a jewel on a rise above the village, its interior painted with curious Russian murals, it was the ideal summerhouse for his unmarried sister, his wife and later their adopted son, the child of a close relative.

Born in 1887 in Burgaz, in modern Bulgaria, Tevfik Cenani had arrived in Turkey in 1912, probably among the hundreds of thousands of Muslims fleeing before the various Balkan armies. At the close of the Ottoman Empire he was producing aviation fuel for the infant Turkish air force, and owned an olive-processing factory and a freighter on which his various goods were shipped. The acquisition of the spirit distillery at Çengelköy was one of his few bad investments. Mustafa Kemal's determination to nationalise key sectors of the new Republic's faltering economy saw the Turkish state take over the Régie, the French-run tobacco monopoly, in 1925. Similarly, alcohol production was taken over the following year, seriously affecting the viability of private distilleries.

To stem mounting losses, Tevfik Cenani – now known as Tevfik Cenani Ercan to avoid confusion with the Kanlıca Cenani family – tried his hand at the canning business and the production of briquettes for the Coal Board. On his death in 1949 the entire loss-making complex was leased to the nationalised TMO, the Soil Products Office, which was searching for a depot on the Bosphorus. When his widow, Nadire, died in 1958, the doors of the hillside *köşk* were closed, and for a decade the family turned its back on Çengelköy.

It was not until 1971 that Tevfik Cenani's descendants decided to reopen the house. His granddaughter, the young Tayyibe Nedret, then in her sixth year as an architecture student at the University of Minnesota, visited Çengelköy hunting for a Turkish subject for her thesis. Only then did she realise that her family owned the extensive ruin of the old spirit factory straddling the shore and the coastal road. And that was the genesis of the dream that eventually resulted in Sumahan on the Water.

At that time part of the factory, with its central chimney, was still used to make coal briquettes. The TMO's sand and gravel were everywhere, and the dilapidated complex was very much in public use. Huts were spread over a makeshift sandy beach; an outdoor cinema had been set up against one wall, and village boys had colonised the recreation ground, tying their boats to it and fishing and diving from it.

But Nedret could see the beauty of the incomparable waterside location and the potential in the masonry walls, arched windows and fine chimney. Encouraged by the enthusiasm of Mark Butler, her future husband and a fellow architecture student, her thesis envisaged an ambitious complex of two distinct zones, one either side of the road, with a bridge connecting the two.

Married in 1972 after graduation, Nedret stayed in the US, working first in Minneapolis, then with Mark on a postgraduate study of urban design at the Massachusetts Institute of Technology. The Sumahan dream was on hold until they settled in Istanbul in 1976. For five years they played about with a variety of proposals for the site in ever-changing applications for Ministry of Tourism backing. But the climate wasn't right: there was no real appetite for sophisticated tourist development, and the planning process became more complex, while finance for a grandiose project remained at best problematical.

The breakthrough came in 1994 when Nedret and her brother, Tevfik Ercan, decided to divide the property and he took on the buildings across the road from the distillery, together with the earlier stone portion of the complex, which incorporated the chimney. Part of this has now been turned into a restaurant. Nedret's share, apart from the wooden house on the hillside in which she and Mark live, was the long row of distillery buildings downstream of the central chimney and the slipway to the water alongside it. With the scale of the project no longer so ambitious, or so expensive, the Butlers' architectural plans at last got the nod, as well as financial backing.

Work began. Once the debris of half a century had been cleared, standing walls were stabilised. Reconstruction required concrete foundations to be encased in steel, like a ship's hull, and sunk deep into bedrock. The whole service area of the hotel is well below sea level – during construction two pumps were kept at work to avoid the building floating away. Now it is earthquake- as well as water-proof.

The overriding aim was to keep as much as possible of the old structure and not to lose its spare but warm industrial feel. Where there is the least clue as to how the original was arranged, it has been echoed. It is fortunate that the lie of the land, as well as restrictions on redevelopment of historic buildings, dictated one floor – the third and top one – giving onto the road, with a further two giving onto the water. The resulting privacy of the lower two storeys, meticulously designed around the factory's series of arches, is a major bonus. The arches dictated a duplex format for many of the suites overlooking the water. From the quay, the unsurpassable view to Seraglio Point and old Stamboul, seen below the span of the First Bosphorus Bridge, epitomises the reborn Sumahan: old and new combined to best effect.

So the dream has been realised. Truncated perhaps, confined as it is to only part of the old distillery site, Sumahan on the Water is nonetheless an adornment, rather than another blot on the Bosphorus: a gift to Istanbul.

Cornucopia Issue 34, 2005

SUMAHAN ON
THE WATER HOTEL,
ÇENGELKÖY

Distilled style

Twentieth-century design classics and understated luxury are the hallmarks of the Sumahan, transformed from a waterside distillery into a boutique hotel. The property was inherited by the architect Nedret Butler. She and her husband, Mark, also an architect, spent two decades realising their dream

Opposite Rarely do Bosphorus properties stay in the same family, but Nedret Butler (bottom right, with her husband and daughters) has hung on to her legacy. The Sumahan was inherited from her grandparents Tevfik and Nadire Cenani (bottom left)
Top The family in the 1930s, in the garden of the wooden 'köşk' above the village

A fishing boat chugs past the industrial chic of the Sumahan on the Water hotel. On the left is the nineteenth-century distillery's brick chimney

12

THE ETHEM PERTEV YALI

THE PALACE LADY'S SUMMERHOUSE

THE DESCENDANTS OF THE KÖPRÜLÜS, A GRAND OTTOMAN FAMILY,
HAVE RESTORED LUSTRE TO ONE OF THE PEARLS OF THE BOSPHORUS,
AFTER A CENTURY AT THE MERCY OF FLUCTUATING FORTUNES

The romantic Ethem Pertev Yalı, informally known as the Palace Lady's Summerhouse, was built by the eponymous Palace Lady in the 1860s with only a harem building, seen here in its original, unrestored glory. Men's quarters were added when it was bought by its second owner, the successful pharmacist Ethem Pertev

One of the many joys of the Bosphorus is to arrange a boat to take you out at dawn, when a breathless silence lies over the great waterway. As the sun slides up over the eastern hills, the houses that line the Asian shore emerge from the habitual film of mist, first as greyish outlines, then in soft colours reflected sharply in the still-black water of the channel. It was on one such outing that, looking north from below the Fatih Bridge towards Kanlıca, I first saw and grew curious about a small blanched wooden yalı, far less spectacular than some of its more ancient Ottoman-red neighbours. It was its elegance that caught the eye.

So I was not entirely unprepared when I was invited to have a critical look at the house, the Ethem Pertev Yalı, which had recently been restored by Murat and Nina Köprülü. I was dropped off at the Kanlıca ferry station and walked to the gate of the house a couple of hundred yards downstream, along the narrow road squeezed between the water and the unspoilt wooded hillside. I found the blanched wooden exterior now renewed and painted a pure white – symbol of the meticulous restoration effected on a dazzlingly elegant example of late-nineteenth-century Ottoman architecture.

The waterside houses of the Bosphorus have captured the imagination of generations of travellers. They were victims of fluctuating family fortunes during a decaying Ottoman Empire, a new Turkish Republic, two world wars and three revolutions. The ups and downs of the late twentieth century took a particularly heavy toll. Until the 1980s, new houses were preferred to expensive restoration of these fragile structures, which fell victim to fashion, fire and neglect. But, as the 1980s gave way to the 1990s and the new millennium, fashion, and with it serious money, returned to the Bosphorus. The distinguished Köprülü family, descendants of a line of seventeenth-century grand viziers, are the latest, and among the most successful, to restore a national treasure that might otherwise have been lost.

As far as I know, the Ethem Pertev Yalı is the only house on the Bosphorus built by a woman about whom nothing is known for certain except the year of her death. The only clue to her in the house that she lived in for almost five decades lies in its naming. Although officially it bears not her name but the name of its second owner, Ethem Pertev, the building is referred to in some accounts as 'the Palace Lady's Summerhouse', 'the Veiled Lady's House' and also as 'the Decorated Building'. Surprisingly for a relatively recent building, those names and the assertion that it was a sultan's gift are about all we have to go on from written sources in speculating about its origins.

The Palace Lady's Summerhouse is said to have been built in the early 1860s. The dating seems right, both stylistically and in relation to the development of the Bosphorus shoreline. So the gift may well have been made in 1861, following the death of the extravagant, reforming Sultan Abülmecid, who loved women as much as he did presiding over the political reforms of the Tanzimat. It is probable that the recipient was not one of the Palace concubines – women who enjoyed exceptional freedom, whose veils 'were the thinnest in the city' and who were seen 'flying around the Bosphorus rowed by handsome boatmen, their thin gauze *ferace* cloaks quite transparent'. More likely, she was one of the children born and brought up in the Palace, perhaps Georgian. Ottoman law safeguarded these children. In her book, *Three Centuries: Family Chronicles of Turkey and Egypt*, the painter Emine Fuat Tugay writes that after the father's death there was no legal difference between such a child and the children by the legal wife in either status or inheritance. The mother, on the other hand, could only inherit if she was legally married. At all events, the lady in question was evidently still young, as she died only in 1908, and the gift modest: a small site, doubtless chosen to take advantage of a sweeping view of the upper and lower channel and also of a valuable Byzantine well.

The anonymous lady's house was curiously built: in two identical but quite separate units supported on three piers which stood on the bedrock of the channel, though from the outside they look of a piece. Two floors and a loft were linked internally and are now united by a decorated balcony; below was a pair of *kayıkhane* (boathouses) occupying the spaces between the three supporting piers. Doubtless the Palace Lady furnished the house appropriately:

porcelain, glass and rugs, as well as books and paintings, are displayed to good effect in the sea-facing rooms. But to a contemporary observer it was probably no more than a small, timber-clad mid-nineteenth-century yalı overhung by a red-tiled roof: a vernacular common on the Bosphorus.

The story of the Palace Lady's Summerhouse becomes less obscure in 1905, once the Palace Lady, perhaps by then too elderly to summer there, let it out for its excellent fishing to Ethem Pertev, a successful pharmacist from Tirnova in Bulgaria. Ethem Pertev was the first to sell ready-made medicines over the counter in the expiring Ottoman Empire and was already a household name for his syrups and pomades. Three years later, on its owner's death, he bought the yalı and then a vacant plot of land next to it, to build upon it the separate *selamlık* essential to any Ottoman gentleman's establishment.

By 1910 the yalı, tucked beneath the steep Bosphorus hillside, was undergoing radical building work. The harem was renovated. The timbers of all four façades were renewed to give the appearance of a building at once fashionable and cosmopolitan: in the riot of arabesque scrolling, every eave, string course, portico, door or window frame was restored.

It may have been then that the sea-facing mansard window was added to crown the wide, tiled roof. It was certainly then that the real glory of the house, the ornately carved balcony cantilevered over the water on stout brackets, was reworked to give the impression of being wrapped round the lower floor, holding the two halves of the building together. Not only is its very position over the water a delight, but the cantilevering is set to discourage the wash of passing boats from affecting the living quarters, and its screening obstructs the gaze of any curious passer-by. While protecting against wind and wave, it allows perfect privacy to a household enjoying the channel unseen through a screen of handsome bargeboards separating six irregular niches carved in seemingly inexhaustible varieties of decorative patterning.

A handsome, well-proportioned, timber-clad *selamlık*, painted white to match the harem, was duly built by Pertev on the newly acquired plot of land. A square of garden separated the two buildings. Fronted by the quay, and with the Bosphorus running fast and deep from north to south, the whole effect was perfectly balanced: cosmopolitan Art Nouveau at its best. It must have been at this point that the yalı that Ethem Pertev had bought from the Palace Lady acquired the sobriquet 'the Decorated Building'.

Ethem Pertev and his house came successfully through the 1914–18 war and the collapse of the Ottoman Empire. The manufacture and export of Pertev products for health, beauty and cleanliness – toothpaste, face creams, shampoo and brilliantines – flourished more than ever following the declaration of the new Republic in 1923. Pertev, who is remembered for his part in training a new generation of pharmacists, was the Turkish tycoon of his day.

The Pertev story was to end in tragedy, however. The youngest son was killed in one of the yalı's boathouses while tending to the boats during a storm. Ethem lost all interest in fishing off the quay. He no longer had the will to bend pins to make fish-hooks and bait them with olives and pomegranate seeds. In 1927 he died a broken man. Five years later his surviving children sold the house.

Some sources claim that Hayri Kaptan, captain of the No 74 ferryboat, bought the yalı from Ethem Pertev. The captain was a popular man who ran the cleanest, swiftest and most reliable ferry on the entire Bosphorus. His punctuality was proverbial and his schedule included the morning and evening runs. When the ferry left and arrived back at the *iskele*, or landing stage, its hoots were part of all Kanlıca's daily timekeeping. Perhaps it was village pride wanting to keep the jovial captain's memory alive that ascribed ownership of the yalı to him.

There is no doubt about the fact that in 1932 the house was bought by Mürşide Güneşin, a widow with two young sons, Adnan and İrfan. Fire had destroyed their family town house in old Stamboul. Possibly she bought in Kanlıca because she knew the village: two Cenani cousins with whom she shared a common grandfather were already living there, in one of the most beautiful Bosphorus houses, the romantically dilapidated Saffet Pasha Yalı.

Murşide Güneşin occupied the Ethem Pertev Yalı for three decades, until her death in 1963. It was a time of privations: the Second World War was followed by shortages in the İnönü and Menderes years. The only repair work that seems to have taken place was some necessary patching-up in the 1940s after a freak accident, when a ferry coming down the Bosphorus in fog slammed into the harem. The captain found himself, still in the wheelhouse, confronted by Murşide Hanım six feet away in bed. She is alleged to have calmly asked him to leave before she herself left the room, closing the door behind her: she was lucky to escape with her life.

Nor did Murşide Hanım's two sons, both married with children and using the two parts of the yalı only to summer in, undertake the restoration which was becoming ever more urgently needed. To accommodate their increasing needs, a concrete structure which came to be known as the Bunker was built in the quadrangle. By 1998 the yalı's once-white timbers were bleached to a silvery grey, rotted and splintered. Bits of old tin patched the worst of the gaps and leaks. The dilapidated iron fence that ran along the quay posed little challenge to trespassers from the sea, and the quay itself was more concrete than stone. When the Art Nouveau steps leading up to the *selamlık*'s front door, which were studded with iron rods that once supported vines and creepers, became dangerous, and a neighbouring wisteria, which for years had smothered the walls of both houses, invaded the inside of the harem, the time had come for the family to take stock: the yalı was falling down.

News reached Murat and Nina Köprülü in 1998 that Adnan and İrfan Güneşin's daughters, the grandchildren of Murşide Hanım, were thinking of selling the family's summerhouse. The Köprülüs had long been on the lookout for a yalı. Murat's association with the Bosphorus reaches back to the days when Köprülüs were second only to sultans. The legendary seventeenth-century Köprülü Yalı above Anadoluhisarı, the oldest surviving house on the Bosphorus, was built by his forebear, Amcazade Hüseyin Pasha, the last of the five Köprülü grand viziers [page 34]. Though American, Nina was no stranger to Turkey when she married Murat. As a child she had spent her summers at Aphrodisias, where her godfather, the late Kenan Erim, directed excavations, and her mother, Martha Joukowsky, worked on the Bronze Age mound behind the theatre. She herself was well versed in the fine arts and classical architecture.

The following year, 1999, Nina found time to visit the yalı on a lightning visit to Istanbul. It was a *coup de foudre*: the sale was sealed and the Köprülüs' link with the Bosphorus had come full circle. But that was the easy part. The young Köprülüs soon realised that, if they were to achieve the authentic restoration the house demanded, a bedrock-to-rooftop rebuild was needed.

Work began in 2001. As the yalı was dismantled under the stewardship of the architect Mark Butler, who was engaged with his wife on creating the Sumahan Hotel further down the Bosphorus, it became clear that neither structure nor ornament could be preserved for reuse. But simple demolition and rebuild was not an option if authenticity was to be achieved. The expertise of Hüseyin Öztürk and his firm of contract builders gave the resourceful Nina the courage to go through with the project. Painstaking dismantling was undertaken and every surviving feature and its original material was minutely recorded. A worldwide search was then on for those materials and for the craftsmen who could produce workmanship of the quality that had gone into the Palace Lady's harem and Ethem Pertev's later *selamlık*.

To keep the profile as it originally was, the first task was to rebuild the piers of the two boathouses so as to support the structure rising above them. The digger for this job was not wasted. Excavation work was carried on into the hillside, scooping out a great pit to make a fine new interior kitchen. This innovation was part of the answer to the familiar problem of the restorer: how to provide the modern conveniences that a yalı always lacks with minimum prejudice to aesthetics and authenticity. Elsewhere, the architects were more radical: air conditioning was installed, and seven bathrooms for the seven bedrooms were achieved without violence to the original structure – two fitted into the loft, three on the second floor and two in the Bunker, now transformed into an annexe for guests.

The most contentious change, which seemed to me also to be the most successful, was to replace the two sea-facing rooms on both floors of the harem with spacious, long single rooms, effectively unifying the two separate halves of the building. Each has ten windows: the six that face the sea remain irregularly spaced, and there are two on the north side and two on the south. Cunningly, the staircase of Turkish pine with its cedar banister rail has been turned, to give more room on the upstairs landing, and carried on up to the attic.

When it came to materials and workmanship, change was kept to the minimum. Finding stone for the cladding of both harem and *selamlık* happily proved easy: the original quarry forty miles from Istanbul at Gebze was still open. Extra stone was ordered to clad the Bunker. The same stone suited the masons for their work on the quay, and also the garden designers for rebuilding the steps and pathways. If it was not available in Turkey, all the necessary wood was brought from Canada, kiln-dried and ready for use: American cedar and pine for the cladding of the houses, teak for the decorative facings. The quest for harmony, if not complete authenticity, which by now was unattainable, even stretched to casting all the brass fittings in the United States. A single fine, if damaged, brass doorknob had survived on an outside door and another on a garden gate. They were duly copied to perfection.

Patrick Chasse, who teaches landscape architecture at Harvard, specialising in Japanese gardens and the Japanese principle of hide and reveal, took on the task of transforming the courtyard between harem and *selamlık*. He spent three months studying the Ottoman garden, taking note to plant nothing that had arrived on the Bosphorus later than 1910. Hydrangeas, magnolias, pencil cypresses, roses, the original wisteria, tamed and retrained, and a fountain where the Byzantine well was discovered, set off the one distinctly non-Ottoman feature: a small swimming pool in the centre of the garden.

The watchword for the interior designer, Mica Ertegün, was 'Oriental sensibility', as well as authenticity in such matters as reproduction of the original patterning on the ceilings and decorated wooden ends to the new sofas. Fabrics, hand-stencilled for the most part, were sourced from Paris, as were chandeliers in the dining room and library. All the paints replicate the pale colours used on the Bosphorus as the nineteenth century gave way to the twentieth. Pictures and furniture were acquired with similar care over period and taste.

When the Ethem Pertev Yalı was finally ready in 2004 for the Köprülüs to move in, one final authentic touch was added: a 1906-model Twelve Foot dinghy built by the restorer of wooden boats Rıfat Edin. Gilt on an elegant gingerbread.

Cornucopia Issue 36, 2006

A new chemistry

The gleaming yalı after its restoration in 2005. To the right of the harem building is the single-storey 'selamlık' added by the pharmacist Ethem Pertev around 1910. The original twin boathouses beneath the harem, visible in the photograph of the unrestored house, have been filled in

*Opposite The ornate
balcony overhangs
the Bosphorus on
Istanbul's Asian shore,
with the Fatih Bridge
and the fortress of
Rumeli Hisarı beyond*

*Above The pool of the
austere new garden
by the American
landscape architect
Patrick Chasse*

Above The dining room
is hung with twenty-four
engravings of Ottoman
figures, dated 1714
Left The 'selamlık'
building, an enfilade of
three rooms, has been
turned into a library

WINDOW ON THE BOSPHORUS 145

*The designer Mica
Ertegün has opened up
the yalı. The first-floor
master bedroom (above)
and the drawing room
(right) both run the length
of the harem. Silks were
specially woven in France
to old Ottoman designs*

Travels in Anatolia

13

THE COUNTRY HOUSES THAT RIDE THE STORM

IN THE RAINFORESTS OF THE BLACK SEA MOUNTAINS, WHERE
JACKALS HOWL AND THE RIVER FIRTINA (THE STORM) CRASHES
TOWARDS THE SEA, LIVE THE HEMŞİNLİ, WHO WERE HERE WHEN
JASON CAME IN SEARCH OF THE GOLDEN FLEECE. MORE RECENTLY
THEY PROSPERED AS BAKERS AND RESTAURATEURS IN TSARIST
RUSSIA, RETURNING EVERY YEAR TO THEIR HAUNTING HOUSES
IN THE HILLS EAST OF TRABZON

The hide of a mountain goat hangs by a door in the Yücel mansion in Çamlıhemşin. 'Every door, cupboard, niche, shelf, floorboard, platform and shutter is wooden, with the dull, rich tint and aroma of seasoned woods'

Previous pages Minutes from the Med: Lake Köyceğiz (Chapter 14)

Even before Jason led his band of heroes along the shores of the Black Sea – then known as the Euxine – to fetch the Golden Fleece from the foot of Mount Caucasus, the Hemşinli inhabited the rainforests in the surrounding valleys of the Kaçkar Mountains. The pragmatic Hemşinli are a singular race even by Black Sea standards. Isolated in remote, narrow valleys, they have preserved their own language, dress and customs.

The heartland of the Hemşinli is the valley of the River Fırtına (or Storm), one of the most beautiful places in the world. This is a wild and wet land of thundering rivers and misty landscapes, where jackals howl unceasingly and beehives are hidden high in the trees out of reach of the honey-loving bears. For fifty kilometres the waters of two streams thunder down from mountain glaciers and lakes beneath the cockscomb crags of the Kaçkar Mountains until they meet in Çamlıhemşin, the old first station on the Hemşin trade route over the mountains twenty-five kilometres from the Black Sea, and the main town in Hemşin.

Farmsteads cling to the wooded slopes behind the tea plantations and hazel groves that cover the foothills. Built on stone foundations, these wooden houses date back five hundred years and are ideally suited to the harsh climate of the Pontic Alps and to the extended families who for eight months of the year lead self-sufficient lives by tending small herds, keeping bees, growing maize and exploiting the abundant woodlands.

Among these wooden farmsteads is an unexpected collection of grand country houses, their imposing white and blue façades incongruously prominent amid the weathered timbers of their neighbours. They are quasi-palatial homes, and the finest of these astonishing edifices stand on an almost sheer hillside in the old district of Makrevis, now known as Konaklar Mahallesi, the 'District of the Mansions'. They are scattered an hour's walk above the town of Çamlıhemşin, reached from the road to İspir. Last spring a bulldozer attempted to cut a road to them. So far, it is a sandy track which zigzags up through maize fields and chestnut woods to the clay hills upon which the lower houses of the district are built. It ends abruptly in a landslip, and it is still a twenty-minute climb on foot to the grandest of these late-nineteenth-century mansions.

At first there is a steep scramble to a pasture so precipitous that a ladder of footsteps cut into the hill marks the way. Then a muddy path, swept by the branches of cherry laurel, weaves a way through a cluster of ancient wooden buildings. Eventually it arrives at a gate beneath a trellis festooned with gourds, rows of beans ramping over poles, maize drying on tripods, terraces choked with wild flowers suffocating plantations of hazel, fig, cherry, apple, pear and walnut. It is only then that the three konaks – the object of my journey last September – come suddenly into sight, towering above the path. Two are of brick and plaster, painted white and lavender, the third of weathered timber. No nineteenth-century watercolourist could have done justice to the romance of these buildings, framed against a backdrop of dark green forest and vaporous grey sky.

All three houses share a watermill and are huddled together to benefit from the ancient system of land division that created narrow strips running straight up from the valley bottom. The Ottoman cadastre, the land registry, defined these strips in sixteenth-century Makrevis as 'betwixt river and cloud'.

Two of the houses belong to a well-known Hemşinli family who took the name of Yücel in the 1920s. The third was never completed. Each has overhanging eaves below pitched tiled roofs and basements with room for some thirty cows. From the outside the animals' quarters appear to be the ground floor of the mansion itself. Their integration goes further than appearances. Trapdoors from the principal living rooms give access in bad weather, and the plumbing of the houses is adapted to ensure that the washing and kitchen waste flows through the basement quarters, helping to flush the slurry out to pits further down the hillside.

The houses were built at intervals over a period of fifty years. The earliest, the uncompleted mansion begun in 1850, combines an Ottoman baroque interior and a simple classical exterior. It is said to have been built for a prominent *kadi*, or judge, whose work must have taken him away from

Hemşin into provincial Anatolia, where the vogue for the square Ottoman konak (mansion) was enjoying its heyday. His building is certainly similar to the best of the late-eighteenth-century merchant houses in Kayseri and Karaman and was adapted to the needs of Hemşin life by incorporating cow stalls and stables into the basement. But the fabric of the house is deteriorating fast and the structure is suffering; soon there will be a serious collapse.

The konak next to it, belonging to the Yücel family, is considerably larger and the best-preserved of all the mansions in the district. It was built in 1902 by two brothers with the profits of a lucrative restaurant trade in Crimea. Abdullah, the elder, went to Sevastopol in the late 1880s and soon sent for his brother Mustafa. Within a few years their chain of *lokantas* were so successful that they were able to leave them in the hands of managers during the winter months to return to Hemşin with a wealth of Tsarist gold. 'Architects of their own fortune', in the language of the valley, they 'enlarged their gates', exchanging the family's small wooden farmhouse, with its steep pitched roof thatched with maize stalks secured by ropes of chestnut bark, for a flamboyant brick-and-plaster mansion with a watertight roof and baked red tiles. To look at, the konak they built is similar to the *kadi*'s house, but the stucco work is much more elaborate, embellished with bands of decorative brickwork patterning beneath the eaves and between the first and second storeys.

From the muddy path below the houses, wide steps lead up to a shared terraced yard where galoshes, boots and shoes of all sizes and shapes announce a large household. Inside, every door, cupboard, niche, shelf, floorboard, platform and shutter, and even many a door handle, is wooden, with the dull, rich tint and aroma of seasoned woods – spruce, chestnut, silver fir and lime. A wide passageway bisects the house, cutting across its large central hall. On one side is a massive domed hearth framed by a stone arch and lit by a window high in the chimney wall; on the other side is the main living room, or *hayat*. The hearth, large enough for a whole family to gather inside it, is still used when the mists envelop the valley. The roof above it is pierced by a huge chimney. In the *hayat* the furnishings are simple, the view sublime. A table, a stove, some divans, a couple of home-made walnut chairs for pulling up at mealtimes are all that fills the long room, and from the enclosed balcony it looks across the valley towards the clusters of houses clinging to the ridges. Only the shutters appear to be decorated, carved with star and crescent and retaining traces of paint. Otherwise the room's decoration reflects the lives of the Yücels: the skin of a local mountain goat, a couple of old Russian shotguns, a photograph of a wedding group taken in the konak. Tatar vases and a Russian samovar sit on a shelf above ancient and indestructible Hemşinli serving trays crafted from compressed hazel roots.

On each side of the *hayat* is a series of simple rooms reserved for the family's newly married couples, *gelin odaları*, or bride's rooms, with turn-of-the-century iron bedsteads from Crimea. Family weddings in the konak take place in winter and involve the whole valley in three days of feasting.

If the large room occupying the northeastern corner of the house is traditional, with raised platforms where guests can sleep and ranges of cupboards where their bedrolls can be stored away, the warm, sunny southeastern corner of the house is innovative. It was converted into a kitchen after the Second World War. Here a remarkable home-made brick-and-iron Aga-like range, complete with lids to contain the heat of the hotplates, is used for cooking and to heat the household water. Ingeniously devised hot-air channels draw enough heat from a couple of smouldering sticks to dry out sodden clothes, a great boon in a place where it seldom stops raining.

A vast upstairs hall runs the length of the house, laid out with spruce floorboards up to fifteen metres long. The ceiling is supported by a line of decorated chestnut columns impervious to worm. The hall is lit by long windows north and south and by light streaming in from the upper balcony. The warren of bedrooms either side of the hall have small glass panes set into their walls to allow lantern light from the hallway to filter through on long winter nights. The floor gives access to covered terraces behind the house, enabling dry hay to be brought in and stored among the rafters in the attic granary before being dropped down to the basement stalls.

The head of the family, Muzaffer Yücel, is a direct descendant of Mustafa, the younger of the two brothers who built the konak in 1902. He was born in the family's summer quarters further up the valley at Pokut in August 1916. In 1932 he left Hemşin to seek his fortune, and spent eleven years as a pastry cook in Tehran, assisting a paternal uncle who had opened the Persian capital's first Turkish *pastahane* (pastry shop). On his return in February 1943 he married his thirteen-year-old cousin Rukiye. She arrived at the konak on the back of a white donkey for the three-day feast and for more than half a century presided over the konak, meticulously maintaining the house, its gardens and animals, and bringing up two daughters. In the meantime Muzaffer Bey built up a successful *pastahane* business in Izmir, returning each summer in the Hemşinli way.

Rukiye Hanım and her family used the third konak of the group as the storehouse, tool shed and annexe. Smaller than the others, it is no less enchanting. The arrangement of the cow stalls, living quarters and bedrooms is similar. The panelling in the guest bedrooms is, however, the best work of all. An invocation to Allah and the date 1306H/AD1880 are inscribed below the eaves, where a balcony runs the entire length of the sunny southern and western sides. Until quite recently the larder would have been piled high with cheeses, pumpkins, gourds, walnuts, dried mushrooms and preserves of raspberry and cherry laurel. Heavy barrel-like beehives made from hollowed-out lime trunks are now stacked one above the other, awaiting an agile youngster to get them out into the treetops again.

Rukiye Hanım's death last April has ended an era in the konak. Her cows made one last journey to the high summer pastures, the *yayla*. Then they were given to neighbours. Muzaffer Bey is now eighty years old, and wintering alone in the konak is an impossibility. Both daughters, Gönül and Sürreya, together with Gönül's three children, live and work in Izmir. Gönül, herself married to a Hemşinli, keeps to tradition. Like her parents, she celebrated her marriage in the konak, as did her elder daughter a quarter of a century later.

Last summer Gönül took on the role which had been Rukiye Hanım's: when the snow began to melt on the high ground, it was Gönül, supported by her younger daughter, Nurgün, who took the cows up to the *yayla* for the last time. By the middle of September the konak had been closed for the winter and for the first time there were no cows in the basement to warm, as well as to supply it. Like the other brick-and-plaster mansions of the valley, it will now only be opened in the summer.

Meeting the dignified, hospitable people of the valley today, it seems unjust that the first written description of the Hemşinli, nearly six centuries ago, should have been so unflattering. The travel-weary Spanish diplomat González de Clavijo, returning to his native Castile after two years at the court of Tamerlane, described a four-day journey in September 1405 which took him through a country called Arhakel, 'so rocky and steep that burdened horses cannot travel'. His party had to build bridges of beams from rock to rock in order to cross the crests. As today, there were 'no sumpter beasts in use here, but men who are porters have to carry all burdens on their shoulders'. He found himself 'in some danger' among a people 'of a barbarous race... for though they are Armenians and profess to be Christians, all are robbers and brigands'. It seems likely that they had forced Clavijo to pay a high toll for the right of passage. He also describes the recent overthrow of the Christian overlord, the Lord of Arhakel, by the neighbouring Muslim *atabey*, the Lord of İspir. It may have been at about this time that the Hemşinli converted to Islam.

Many of the houses Clavijo saw in 1405 are still standing, and the seasonal pattern of life for the Hemşinli has remained largely unchanged since that time. It is dictated by the weather in the valleys. In early summer, once the snow has receded and the rhododendrons are ablaze on the lower slopes, they move up to the *yayla*, first just above the treeline, at around 2,000 metres, and then still higher. There they remain, making cheese and cutting hay, until early September, when the crocus springs up overnight, pale purple on one ridge, white on another, with the deeper, larger colchicum around the middens. Their appearance signals the end of summer and the moment to return to the valleys.

The Yücels were not alone in earning their fleece of Russian gold. The valley is scattered with displays of late-nineteenth-century wealth. One of two konaks belonging to the Tarakçı family, perched at a much higher altitude than the Yücels', is famous for possessing the first lightning conductor in the district. It also has thirty-six bedrooms, arranged on three floors. Below the Yücels, the Melik family konak, standing on a hill beside the new sandy road, is unique in concealing a two-storey cowshed. As these houses were built within a few years of the Yücel house, it seems likely that the disused lime pit and brick kilns which stand beside the river were set up specifically for their construction.

Until the last century, household incomes had been supplemented by the wages of the young men who travelled south across the passes to become tanners and artisans in the towns on the eastern Anatolian plateau, such as Erzurum, where the Yücel forebears worked. But from the 1880s until the First World War hundreds of men from the Hemşin valleys went north across the Black Sea to exploit the new prosperity of Crimea. Turkey's defeat in the Turco-Russian War of 1877–78 had reopened the Bosphorus to Russian trade, and the cosmopolitan towns and resorts of the Russian Black Sea coast prospered as never before. On the eve of war in 1914 there was hardly a town in greater Russia without its Turkish bakery. Moscow alone had 120. Most belonged to men from the valleys of the Kaçkar Mountains, and it was Russian gold that allowed them to build their prestigious brick-and-plaster mansions, imitating the new merchant houses then being constructed on the littoral of the Black Sea, even copying the paintwork on the stucco façades.

This prosperity lasted less than forty years. Most of the Hemşinli made their way back to the valleys, fluent in Russian and some with Russian wives, after the outbreak of the First World War. Some disappeared in the turmoil of Bolshevik Russia. The good times were not to return until the influx of new money and tourism again started to transform the valleys in the mid-1980s. The first to be affected by this new wealth was the town of Çamlıhemşin itself. It is now more concrete than wood and is an administrative sub-district of the province of Rize – a traditional centre, with shops, teahouses and a splendid modern post office.

For the traveller, the treasure awaiting discovery is the Fırtına Valley. Its river passes under a series of high-backed stone bridges, uniquely picturesque and resistant to the fierce spates of melting snow, their dates obscured by festoons of creepers. Above the riverbed, those without access to the bridges have rigged up a system of wire pulleys, or travelling boxes, in order to reach the road on the opposite bank.

The river arrives at the coast in a confusion of boulders. In the frequent storms on which the tea plantations of the lower slopes seem to flourish, whole footbridges, haycocks and parcels of hazelnut husks bound up with tea bushes are swept down to the shore, where the debris stains the sea red-brown to the horizon.

The road that runs up from the coast to Çamlıhemşin divides just below the town to follow the two summer trade routes to the interior and the passes some thirty kilometres away and more than 3,500 metres above sea level. Out of sight of the Yücel konak, the left-hand route, towards Georgia, heads for the highest pass of the Kaçkar, through the fingers of the Altıparmak range. Its first twelve kilometres have been broadened and improved. But the tarmac stops abruptly at the gates of the new national park below the village of Ayder. The 'District of Hot Waters', old Hamameşen, is now a popular health resort with a splendid Turkish bath built over the hot springs.

To reach the pass, four-wheel-drive vehicles filled with cows and the chattels of the *yayla* bump along the remnants of the old paved road to Kavron. Thereafter the journey is only possible on foot. Above Kavron the rare visitor is unlikely to meet anyone but the *yayla* dwellers. They will, however, be surprised to see herds of unattended native black bulls. Once the snows have melted, these are penned into the highest valleys, where they fight it out among themselves in preparation for Artvin's ancient bullfighting festival – which is strictly bull against bull.

A forest of native Caucasian trees clothes the mountain between Ayder and Kavron. It is a unique collection of beech, plane, oak, chestnut, lime, spruce and silver fir, cared for by the Forestry Department in the recently declared national park. Trees should no longer be vulnerable to felling but a new scourge has caught up with them, in the shape of the processionary caterpillar. Spruce and even some beech are recent victims. Glistening sacks of the sticky grubs appear, hanging from the branches in spring. By late summer the trees are draped in the telltale tresses of the dispersed sacks, and the trees themselves show signs of distress. Unless a treatment can be discovered soon, the damage could prove to be irreparable. Less insidious are the occasional avalanches, which sweep stretches of mountainside clear of trees, leaving a form of tundra, to be colonised by jungles of rhododendron.

Where beech predominates, curiously fashioned spruce poles will be seen forming stilt-type ladders into the higher branches of those trees that catch the morning sun. On closer inspection, these turn out to give the valley's beekeepers access to the hollowed-out barrel-like lime trunks which serve as hives. Attached to upper branches, they protect the bees from valley mists and, so the story goes, the honey store from marauding brown bears.

If the right-hand road above Çamlıhemşin is followed, rather than the one to Ayder, the track leads over the pass to İspir. This is the main route across the mountains to Erzurum and follows the Fırtına, passing beneath the Yücel konak. Once the last tea plantations, oleander bushes and hop-hornbeam, along with the lines of cherry laurel, are left behind at around 650 metres, the road climbs steeply over thickly afforested spurs, bordered by banks of cotoneaster, viburnum, wild rose, honeysuckle, violet and cyclamen.

The route then plunges down into the gloom of the Zilkale gorge, where waterfalls are lost in a wilderness of giant ferns that are tall enough to conceal an army of men. All sound is drowned out by the thunder of the water. Amidst this semi-jungle, a rare forest of unharvested boxwood survives, interspersed with ancient yews, privet, alder and holly.

The valley itself was guarded by two fortresses, both now ruined and both of uncertain date. The remains of the lower, Zilkale, possibly built by the oppressive Lord of Arhakal described by the fifteenth-century Spanish ambassador, stand on a spur commanding the gorge, towers and turrets emerging from an overgrowth of creepers, shrubs and trees. Out from the darkness of the gorge, the water meadows, ablaze with wild flowers and alive with butterflies by June, give way gradually to gardens of azalea underplanted with white peonies, blue aquilegia and the remnants of giant snowdrops. Myrtle thrives above the treeline, together with raspberry. Finally, above the valley mists, among the granite bosses, the spread of the miniature white rhododendron emerges from beneath the melting snow.

Today hordes of people are streaming westward to buy and sell since the opening of the old Iron Curtain frontier between Turkey and Georgia. The modern Hemşinli, secure still in the valleys, watch as their coastal trading post at Pazar is transformed into yet another of the overgrown, malodorous towns sprawling around the mouths of rivers between Batum and Trabzon.

The Hemşinli still, above all, excel as pastry cooks. After their return from Russia they moved to Atatürk's new capital to hold sway in the Republic's flourishing new restaurant and hotel business. For more than three decades the Bulvar Palas in Ankara was the most agreeable hotel in which to stay, the Milka the bar for lunch, and the Washington the restaurant to dine in. But whether employed in Ankara, Istanbul or Izmir, the Hemşinli will be home each summer.

Cornucopia Issue 12, 1997

Houses of the Storm Valley

The River Fırtına (the Storm) passes under a series of high bridges built to resist fierce spates of melting snow. This was once the main route from the Black Sea to Erzurum on the high Anatolian plateau. The great mansions of the Hemşinli people, built with Tsarist gold earned in Crimean resorts, stood high above the river valley

Above The densely forested Fırtına Valley echoes to the howl of jackals

Right The Yücel konak (on the left), painted in white and lavender blue, was built in 1902. It is still a twenty-minute climb on foot from the nearest road. The basement conceals the stables. The hayloft in the attic is reached from the hillside behind. The house on the right was never finished

Opposite A single room can be boudoir, bedroom and bathroom. The humidity and the long climb from the valley floor make baths essential. Here a pail of steaming water brought in from the kitchen sits beside a concealed tub

Overleaf On the first floor a projecting glazed balcony makes a comfortable alcove with dreamy views. A trapdoor conceals a long stairway to the stables

*Above Muzaffer Yücel,
the patriarch of the
family, sits back in the
giant arched fireplace,
which has room for six
people to sit inside, lit by
a window in the chimney
wall. These fireplaces
are the focal point of
every country house here*

*Left The older wooden
house next door is
used for storing food.
Here beans and garlic
are left to dry on the
covered balcony*

*Opposite Everyday
objects of satisfying
beauty: a perfectly
carved bowl, a
handsome green bottle,
and wooden lockers to
keep maize flour safe
from rodents*

14

LAKE KÖYCEĞİZ

THE LAKE THAT TIME FORGOT

SPEEDING EAST ALONG THE MEDITERRANEAN COAST ROAD TO
ANTALYA, IT IS EASY TO MISS THE GREAT LAKE OF KÖYCEĞİZ
HIDDEN AMONG THE ORANGE GROVES. INSULATED FROM BOTH THE
HIGHWAY AND THE TOURIST THRONG, THIS IS AN AREA THAT IS
ECOLOGICALLY FRAGILE. ON THE LAKE'S SHORE IS A REMARKABLE
MANSION LIVED IN BY THE GREAT-GRANDDAUGHTER OF THE PASHA
WHO FOUNDED THE MODERN TOWN OF KÖYCEĞİZ

Famed for their old-fashioned courtesy, Lake Köyceğiz's black villagers descend from slaves and freemen who worked the cotton plantations around Dalaman that prospered in the cotton boom of the 1860s. Those men who did not return to Africa married local women and settled around the lake

It was chance that took me to the lake at Köyceğiz forty years ago, shortly after the devastating earthquake which flattened Fethiye. I was pressing towards Muğla on the route taken by Sir Charles Fellows, described in the diaries of his travels in the late 1830s. But I had no time to look for the 'Derebey castle at Koogez', or the 'fine country house with outlying gables, rather Georgian... half hidden by trees' glimpsed there by Freya Stark and recorded in 1956 in *The Lycian Shore*.

For all that, fate in the form of a puncture detained me under the burning August sun on a dusty bend of the track between old Dalyan and modern Köyceğiz, a stone's throw from the lake. Under the westernmost crags of the Taurus, which were thrusting out to sea on each side of the lake like giant pincers, with pines clinging to both ridge and flank, I was stranded in a world of white feathery reed heads, bowing to their reflections in gold-brown water. Attempts to fit a spare wheel which also turned out to be punctured were disrupted by a cloud of dust as lines of swaying camels, led by donkeys, made their way past me with the day's harvest of cotton roped to them in brown bales.

Help came when a roguish-looking black man with a Cherry Blossom polish to his skin and a mouthful of dazzling teeth arrived to tend his nets and eel traps. With no further ado, he picked up the tyres and walked with me to the village of Eskiköy. In the coffee shop, while repairs were in progress,

'Arap Ali', aka Ali Çetin, told me his story. His ancestors had come from the Congo via the Algiers slave market. Having earned their freedom, they and the local women they had married settled near Eskiköy to farm and fish eels. According to him, that was the norm. In some generations some of the children were black and others were not. There was never any prejudice, and there was evidently none that afternoon.

Hurrying away, I determined to return to explore Köyceğiz, not least to explore the question always asked by visitors to the region – why so many villagers, like Arap Ali, are black.

Last year I returned to that dusty verge at the margin of the lake, this time with leisure to explore. The road, now bypassed by a new highway, was deserted but for a pile of eel traps stacked beside the jetty, collapsing among the reeds. Apart from the modern town of Köyceğiz, with its exposed southerly aspect and broad esplanade against which the lake water laps, all was seemingly untouched by late-twentieth-century development. Jungles of willow, alder and the occasional pine ring the shore amid walls of unstable reeds. The few villages seem to be set back from the water.

The old village of Köyceğiz, a stronghold of the Menteşe – Turkic lords who had settled in Anatolia at the end of the thirteenth century – is only some four kilometres as the crow flies from the modern town, tucked away on the northeastern corner. A substantial islet shelters it from the southwest wind and any prying eyes. Even from the highest point of the islet, Gâvur Adası, or Infidel Island, only a broken minaret can be seen. The ruins of the fortified village are lost amid thick vegetation.

Though correctly told in Köyceğiz that the old village was 'just across the lake', I took several wrong turns off the main road. Among the rills of this patchwork land I followed red muddy tracks beneath soaring Lombardy poplars and sloshed between lurching *Liquidambar orientalis* and giant Australian eucalyptus, recently introduced to drain the fields.

Eventually I stumbled upon an elderly black lady, with a curious turban above a thick plait of hair, sitting at her porch beside the track. She waved me towards a ruined nineteenth-century mansion, and another, the condition of which could not be discerned. I walked up the path between the two houses until I found a bank from which I could look over the walls. I was observed. A gate flew open and, full of smiles, the great-granddaughter of the pasha who founded modern Köyceğiz ushered me into the garden of the konak he had built in 1878. Sema Menteşeoğlu told me the story of her family while her chickens scratched about under our chairs.

Centuries before the Mongols appeared in Asia Minor, waves of nomadic horsemen had been moving westwards. Among the hordes who poured almost unresisted through the splintering chaos of Anatolia during the breakup of the Seljuk state, a branch of the Akkoyunlu tribe, led by Menteşe Bey, reached the Mediterranean seaboard in the late thirteenth century. Based in Antalya, they won the old kingdoms of Caria and Lycia by attacks from the sea, dominating the coast from Ephesus to Finike.

The Menteşe beys of the fourteenth century traded with the Crusader knights in Rhodes and were known to Chaucer when he was controller of customs at the Port of London. Even after 1424, when their lands were incorporated into the Ottoman Empire, they kept their independence as hereditary petty princes.

Sir Charles Fellows halted at 'Koogez' on 25 April 1839. He found that the 'palace or establishment formed the whole village... in fact there was no other house in the place... Half of the quadrangle, which would have accommodated many hundred dependents, was in ruins... and adjoining it was the ruin of a large barrack'. It seemed that a generation before, 'ten ships of war floated upon the lake and all the country around was dependent on him [the Menteşe bey] and served him through fear'. But the power of the family was 'now extinguished'.

'I am lodged in one of the half-ruined apartments of the palace,' Fellows continued. 'A few years ago my lodging would have been a prison or the hold of a lawless brigand or pirate.' The Menteşe powers had finally been broken by the Ottoman sultan Selim III's land reforms.

The fortunes of the Köyceğiz Menteşe continued to fluctuate until the last quarter of the nineteenth century, when Ali Rıza Pasha opened the lucrative chromium mines above Fethiye and caught the cotton boom. Hugely rich and a great local benefactor, Ali Rıza founded the modern town of Köyceğiz. Despairing of an heir by his wife İkbal, he adopted one, paying his weight in gold for the child. As so often happens, İkbal thereupon produced an heir. The trouble was that not only was the adopted son unsatisfactory; the couple's blood son, Cemil, did not turn out too well either.

When Ali Rıza died in 1914, the lands were divided between the two sons. Menteşe fortunes waned after the First World War as Cemil flitted between Istanbul, Paris, the gaming tables of Monte Carlo and his estates in Rhodes. He shipped his belongings, including his horses, his grooms and their trappings, to and from Köyceğiz as necessary.

On Cemil's death in 1934, the land was once again divided. His middle son, Niyazi Menteşe, having studied agricultural science in Germany, returned in 1951 to run the farms at Köyceğiz. His young wife, Hürrem, who had been raised in Istanbul, was astonished to find that there was no electricity or telephone, village houses were made of basket reeds, and the inhabitants were for the most part black.

Sema, their only child, was born here in 1952. From an early age she accompanied her father on the rounds of his estate, riding behind him on his favourite grey mare. At boarding school in Izmir, she started to paint. Later, painting took her to Perugia, where she trained; exhibitions in Italy and in Turkey followed. So did marriage.

By 1992, when Sema returned to live there, the estates had become run-down and a good deal of the land had been sold off to villagers. The household was much reduced and the house itself perilously in need of repair. The trusted black steward and the head cook, Periş Anna, the black woman whose speciality was glutinous Turkish pastries, had both died.

While shuttling to and from Izmir, bringing up her two daughters, Yonca and Çağlar, Sema set about putting the house and estates in order. It is still a struggle for Sema and her mother, who lives on the top floor, but the restoration of the konak is well advanced.

On my recent visit, there was only time for a quick tour of the house, considerably altered in the past hundred years. The loss of its distinguished Venetian 'crow's nests', more usually seen crowning palaces on the Lombardy plain, and of the tiled hamam in the garden is compensated for by a sound roof and indoor bathrooms; the outside kitchen complex is now Sema's studio. Leaving Sema's walled garden, we walked towards the lake, soon passing the remnant of an imposing wall, with chimney flue, chimney breast and place for a *coffre-fort* still set into the masonry. Sema explained that this building had been Ali Rıza's *selamlık* and the place where he stored his gold; it must have also been on the site of the 'Derebey castle'.

As we pushed on, the shell of the Derebey's compound became more obvious. Crumbling grey walls almost completely obscured by overgrowth revealed themselves as the remains of a sesame factory in what may formerly have been the market square. One upended early Ottoman gravestone had become a tethering post for a villager's cow. Through a huge wall of ivy we reached the building known locally as the Seljuk Mosque.

Its flat timber roof, carried on transverse joists, had been temporarily saved from collapse by the addition of some reinforced concrete pillars. Forming a canopy which affords shelter from the elements, a single broad vault opens onto the square in which the medrese, the theological college, doubtless stood. Adjoining the mosque, above its finely carved balcony, is the village's most distinguished landmark, now broken and overwhelmed by creepers. Possibly fourteenth-century, the Köyceğiz minaret is said to have been built in 'the early Cretan vernacular with a strong Venetian influence'.

Only a stone's throw further on, we reached the barrier of reeds running along the shore. There was just enough time before sunset to visit the small island known as Gâvur Adası. Sir Charles Fellows found 'five or six cottages of Greeks and a ruin of an early Christian church'. Today, all are choked by reeds; nature has won the struggle to destroy virtually all trace of the 'infidels' – the Christians – who gave the island its name of Infidel Island.

While we know something of the story of the Menteşe enclave, the history of the lake itself is largely unknown. The ancient writers Thucydides, Stratonicus, and later Strabo, wrote extensively on the flourishing city port of Caunus – situated no more than half a dozen kilometres downstream from the lake, where its waters meet the Mediterranean – but they are silent about what went on upstream.

Today, as in antiquity, fish swarm into the delta below Caunus and up the Dalyan river to spawn in the lake and its tributaries. Grey mullet are the most numerous and most highly prized. In Strabo's day, and doubtless earlier, they were caught in *dalyan*, long netting traps set across the river. The traps probably lay near the lake: a fragmentary Caunian inscription sets out regulations concerning catches of fish. Nowadays over-exploitation is a real threat. Caunian salt, famous for its purity and recommended in antiquity as an addition to eye salves and antiseptic pastes, provided the means to preserve the harvest each spring as the fish rushed upstream, and in late summer as survivors and their progeny returned to the sea. Köyceğiz roe is highly prized, as it was in antiquity, and is still preserved in the same way – sealed with a layer of beeswax. It is sold throughout Turkey.

The abundance of fish still sustains a teeming population of birds. Dippers, divers, warblers and kingfishers share their fishing grounds with eagle owls, cormorants and pelicans. White egrets roost up to fifty in one tree, festooning the branches so thickly that they seem to be covered in snow. All winter these gregarious herons, their chalk-white plumage relieved only by their black legs and feet, fish aloof from the hundreds of ducks and geese that occupy the middle of the lake.

At certain seasons, often preceding an earth tremor and coinciding with a decided sniff of sulphur in the air, there is a distinctive change in the colour of the lake waters. The eastern half turns emerald green, while the western half takes on an opaque, slaty, blue-grey hue. The change is most extreme in the southwestern corner, where the lake is at its deepest, scarred by troughs up to seventy metres in depth. Hot springs bubble up offshore and in the *kaplıca* – the thermal bathhouse – at Sultaniye. I was told by an astute local observer, a professional man not easily given to flights of fancy, that within an hour of the Adana earthquake a few years ago, a pall of steam smelling strongly of sulphur was followed by the sight of the lake changing colour as if a giant was whisking soda crystals in the waters. It took four months before the eastern half of the lake began to return to its normal golden brown.

The only village on the western fringe of the lake is Hamitköy. In its coffee shop near the mosque I learnt that it was founded by an Egyptian from the Lower Nile in the eighteenth century. A search for work had led his family to the shore of the lake to grow onions in the rich alluvial soil. It was a time when two onions were worth a sheep and two sheep were worth a slave. I was told that the village's copious supplies of water run miraculously warm in winter and cool in summer. Two volunteers from the American Peace Corps came to live in the village in the 1970s. Their reading matter, it seems, included illustrated fashion magazines with advertisements of ladies in underwear. Furtive glances at these modern wonders changed the quality – nylon for silk – as well as the content of the village dowry chests for ever.

As in Eskiköy, Köyceğiz and Dalyan, the villagers include a handful of black people. Their forebears seem to have come from different parts of Africa at different times. The 'Arap Ali' I had chanced upon in 1960 talked of ancestors from Zaire (Congo). A cousin in Hamitköy told me that he was descended from labourers brought in the mid-nineteenth century to work on the vast cotton plantations established by the khedives of Egypt.

There is little doubt that armies of African workers, mainly Sudanese, came as slaves or indentured workers to Dalaman from the late 1860s onwards. Cotton was introduced when Europe's supply was cut off by the American Civil War, and the price of cotton surged as a result. The labourers do not seem to have brought women with them, acquiring wives locally. After working the cotton fields for a number of years, they returned to Africa or settled as free men in the Dalaman area.

It was the Khedive of Egypt, Abbas Hilmi II, who at the end of the nineteenth century built the Bavarian-style building which is now the headquarters of the Dalaman State Farm. Cloaked in bougainvillea and jasmine, approached by avenues of palms, it was one of the many buildings which this spendthrift monarch commissioned. 'The trouble was,' Arap Ali's cousin grinned, 'that his architect mixed up the plans for the farm with those for the railway station in Alexandria. The waiting rooms and booking halls had to be adapted first to domestic and subsequently to official use.' The building is still clearly identifiable as a railway station – only track and trains are missing.

Back to the bustle of Köyceğiz, where market day was in full swing. I stood beside the Caunian lion guarding the main square, holding Köyceğiz fish roes in one hand, honey in the other, and stared wistfully down the lake towards Dalyan, Caunus and the sea. The lake is too precious, too fragile for its own good, I thought. Please let no one wake it from its sleep.

Cornucopia Issue 20, 2000

Designed to be raised above the marshy ground on long poles of alder, one of the last basket houses of Lake Köyceğiz. The chimney, typical of Muğla buildings, is constructed so as to fall away from the house in an earthquake

BASKET HOUSES OF THE LAKE

Capacious Moses baskets, mini Noah's arks, giant sedan chairs, or even unusual mobile homes, these singular constructions perfectly resist the vagaries of the lake's environment and are virtually impervious to earthquakes. Their oblong frames, with hearth and chimney accommodated in an apse, are woven in a fashion similar to traditional Sussex sheep hurdles. The pliant local form of wattle, used by gypsies to make crude baskets, is plaited through stakes of the sweet-smelling, insect-repellent *Liquidambar orientalis*, the source of church incense. Walnut, lime or pine floors and doors, unpaned windows, shutters and outside verandas are then incorporated before the whole building is roofed with either lake reeds or local tiles. Traditionally they were crowned with the distinctive Muğla chimney, and their walls coated inside and out with a lime-and-mud plaster.

In Hamitköy, where the ground is marshy and liable to flooding, they are raised on long poles of alder, which become as hard as iron when constantly wetted and dried. During earth tremors, nothing more serious occurs than that the chimney falls outwards, the plaster shakes off the house and the frame sways to and fro on its rockers.

The houses are dry, cool, comfortable – modern architects, take note. A fine example now stands in the garden of Ali Rıza Pasha's konak, bought on a whim by Fritz von der Schulenburg when he was taking photographs for this article and brought to the konak on the back of a local lorry. Protected from the elements by modern roofing, it seems destined to survive its neighbours in Hamitköy and become something of a museum piece.

KÖYCEĞIZ

A visit to the lady of the lake

Minutes from the Mediterranean, Lake Köyceğiz is a beautiful backwater lost in time. The distant peak of Ölmez Dağı, outlined against the early evening sky, is where the gods of ancient Caunus were held to live. Sema Menteşeoğlu (overleaf) returned in 1992, after thirty years, to find her family home in perilous disrepair. The black steward, linchpin of the estate, had died, and much of the land had been sold. Just a handful of people remained in the ancestral village

Above The artist Sema Menteşeoğlu wears a medal presented by Abdülhamid II to her grandfather Ali Rıza Pasha, who built the small but handsome house in Köyceğiz in 1878. It is very much an artist's home, constantly evolving and embellished with her own creations. Sema trained in Perugia under the sculptor Bruno Orfei and brought her painterly eye to the house's restoration. Here she stands by one of her signature painted door panels

Left The pet cockerel rules the roost outside Sema's studio, once the kitchen building. The shady veranda is where olives are pressed for oil and jams are made. The old-fashioned café chairs are still made locally

Sema Menteşeoğlu's artist's studio, which still looks very much like the kitchen it used to be. A Palio pattern painted by Sema and her daughters livens up a cupboard (opposite).

Black and white checks are repeated round the work surface (above). Sieves for sesame and wicker-covered demijohns for wine or oil speak of the room's utilitarian past. The

green olives on the top shelf (opposite) were picked on Gâvur Adası, an islet in the lake. Sema made the three-legged mulberry table herself

Top *The lake teems
with sulphur-tolerant
turtles, crabs, eels and
rare birds*
Left *A dappled corner
in the walled garden of
Ali Rıza Pasha's konak*

Above *The Dalaman
State Farm, built by the
Khedive of Egypt for
his huge cotton estate,
mistakenly used plans
intended for a railway
station. He would stay
here on his way to
and from summers on
the Bosphorus*

15

THE GREAT MOSQUE AND HOSPITAL OF DİVRİĞİ

SUBLIME PORTALS

THE IMPERILLED GREAT MOSQUE AND HOSPITAL OF DİVRİĞİ,
A MEDIEVAL MASTERPIECE OF ISLAMIC ART IN THE
REGION OF THE UPPER EUPHRATES, IS SO REMOTE THAT EVEN
THE INTREPID RARELY MAKE THE PILGRIMAGE TO SEE ITS
MAD, EXTRAVAGANTLY CARVED ENTRANCES

*The doorway of the
Hospital of Divriği,
endowed by Melike
Turan, 'the just queen',
in 1228. The portal's
soaring, freestanding
arch, unfettered by
a rectangular frame,
creates a drama new
to Islamic architecture,
heightened by the
exquisite carving of
roundels, pentagons
and five-pointed stars*

Articles, I read once, work best if facts are kept on short rations. Rationed they seem to have been on the early-thirteenth-century Great Mosque at Divriği and its Hospital, which together are one of the great masterpieces of Islamic architecture. Few of the traveller-scholars crossing Asia Minor to record architectural wonders visited the remote Ulu Cami (Great Mosque) and Şifahane (Hospital), set on a hill above the town. Recognised in 1987 as a World Heritage site – the only designated individual building among Turkey's nine sites – its flamboyant and sophisticated originality more than justifies this belated accolade.

Within the triangle of Sivas, Malatya and Erzincan, modern maps show Divriği easily accessible by road and rail. Do not be misled. It takes time to reach this small mining town, centre of Turkey's principal source of iron ore. Though it is set in the midst of a congregation of prosperous central Anatolian towns, even during the heyday of the great Seljuk Empire, when trade was flowing in all directions, Divriği was remote, and withdrawn from the sultan's court at Konya.

Overlooked by the forbidding Demirdağ (Iron Mountain), hidden among the troughs and gorges of the Çaltı Çayı – unregulated tributary of the young Euphrates, carrying white waters to the Keban Dam – Divriği stands on the valley floor, skirted by willows and poplars and flanked by steep hills rising in a stark confusion of copper-green, sand-yellow and blue-grey. In a bare and unpopulated land where outcrops of limestone are snow-white, and springs as clear as crystal taste of iron, it is not unusual for the severe continental winters to cut Divriği off from the outside world for weeks at a time.

Little is known of Divriği's ancient past. It first attracted attention in medieval times as Tephrike, a formidable stronghold. There an Arab emir of Malatya settled a community of heretical Paulician Christians within the citadel, with an eye to their controlling defence and trade along the border with Byzantium. In AD 969 they duly suffered notorious persecution at the hands of the Byzantines.

Within fifty years of the Byzantine defeat by the Seljuk Turks at Manzikert in 1071, an incoming Turkic tribe, the Mengujek (Menguçlu), were established on the Çaltı Çayı at Divriği and on the Euphrates, at Kemah and Erzincan. Though allied by either blood or marriage to the Sultans of Rum, the three petty fiefdoms were nonetheless their rivals.

For almost two hundred years, which ended when the Mongols overran the Mengujek lands in 1251, the emirs at Divriği prospered. It was a time of reconciliation and synthesis of earlier cultures when political alliances, taking little account of religion, were quickly forged to hold back the Mongol threat. Within the citadel, the massive bastions and curtain walls of the castle were rebuilt to present a formidable deterrent to invaders, and a three-aisled castle mosque of 'unshaped field stones' was completed in 1180. The twelfth-century town spilled out beyond the walls, and new markets opened to merchants and artisans of every race and creed; conical *kümbets*, memorials to the Mengujekid dead, were erected among the settlements of newly arrived Türkmen migrants.

In the second decade of the thirteenth century, when Seljuk Anatolian architecture was at its peak, the poet and mystic Mevlâna Celaleddin Rumi, teaching at Konya, was journeying to and from Damascus and may have passed through Divriği. It was then that the ruler of the provincial but cosmopolitan little town, Ahmet Shah, and very possibly his wife, Melike Turan, commissioned a dual foundation of Friday mosque and hospital.

That the Seljuk state attached great importance to medicine and that hospitals were free to all is well known, but what was unusual was to have a mosque and a hospital beneath one roof. It has been suggested that this was a safeguard against theft. More probably it was for convenience rather than security, for the site that was chosen was on a steep, barren and empty hillside, a twenty-minute walk from both the citadel and the new settlements above the river.

Of the construction of the mosque-hospital complex and its use over the centuries few records remain. The resources lavished on it by Ahmet Shah and Melike Turan doubtless derived from trade as well as the rich iron-ore deposits in the region. Details of the quarrying, the levelling of the platform on which the building was to stand, its construction and the decoration on its three portals, and the more restrained ornamentation of the side walls, the windows and the interior of the building, are unrecorded, but they must have involved hundreds of workers over several years.

From inscriptions we learn that the foundation date was 1228. We also learn that the architect and master mason was one Khurram Shah of Ahlat and that in 1241 the *mimber* (pulpit) was completed by the woodcarver Ahmet of Tiflis. It is assumed that the nearby quarries producing the ashlar blocks of red and yellow sandstone, ideal for stone carvers, were owned by affluent Christian denizens. But the transportation of the stone and the levelling of the platform cut into the hill may well have required a migrant workforce. Stylistic evidence points to separate teams of craftsmen.

The Seljuks exploited the rich artistic heritage of the towns they took from the Byzantines. By the thirteenth century itinerant master craftsmen from Persia, Caucasia and Syria were working within their empire. The craftsmen working on the mosque-hospital complex were almost certainly cosmopolitan travelling masters employed for a season or two to carve freely, perhaps even according to whim. The result was the near-miraculous transformation of three entrance doors into monumental virtuoso portals.

The redoubtable Evliya Çelebi, serving as a customs clerk in Erzurum in the seventeenth century, was captivated by Divriği. Describing the 'invincible' castle, he tells of its marvellous cannons, which were fired with great noise at every festival. We learn how in summer, when the citadel's cisterns ran dry, water was pumped up from the river through a deep shaft, and he tells of the fine houses of an 'embellished city'. Ever fond of cats, he describes the luxurious fur of the brick-red Divriği cat, used by merchants, pashas and beys to line their topcoats against the cutting winds of the Anatolian winter, and taken to Persia as coveted presents or to be auctioned in cages in the bazaars of Erdebil.

Importantly, he finds 'the delicate works of art' on all the walls of the Ulu Cami in 'perfect condition'. 'The carving is so skilled that even the Yıldırım Mosque in Bursa… the carved *mimber* in Sinop and the Ebulfeth Mosque in Athens in the land of Rum cannot compete with the skill and inventiveness of Divriği's Mosque.'

In the late autumn of 1876, Captain Fred Burnaby, an English cavalry officer on regimental leave, struggled into Divriği from the west in dense mist and deep snow, having waded several miles through slush 'nearly breast high'. As a soldier on regimental leave from the British army, crossing Anatolia by horse with his soldier-servant, his interest lay more in the old ruined citadel 'perched on a seemingly inaccessible rock' than in the 'numerous minarets and domes lying as it were in miniature below'. Locals assumed that he had ridden in on 'business connected with the mines', which he was told had been worked 'several hundred years ago when people knew how to get at the treasures which lie hid beneath the ground'. Having been told that 'for the present there was no active trade in Divriği', he walked to the citadel, which he found inhabited only by dogs and lizards.

How long the hospital remained in use and when the mosque's prayer hall closed we cannot be certain. By 1900 the hospital was being used as a hay barn. During the Second World War, treasures from the Topkapı Palace were housed in the mosque for safekeeping.

I first glimpsed Divriği during the high summer of 1961. I arrived by train from Ankara, taking the *ekspres* to Kayseri, the slow mail train, or *posta*, to Sivas, and finally the Simeryol to Erzurum, which reached Divriği as the sun came up. The Simeryol (Sivas-Malatya-Erzurum) line was the dream of the new Republic, and Divriği was doubtless covered in order to shift its valuable iron ore economically. Designed to connect the chief towns of Anatolia and eventually to join up with the railway to Kars and the Russian frontier, it was begun in 1933 at both ends, which explains why not all the tunnels met in the middle. It took six years to build, and at times 10,000 men were working to make bridges, cut tunnels and finally shovel earth over hardcore to build the single-track railroad.

The journey can still be done by train, though most visitors now come by car. They may rub shoulders with the engineers and executives of the mining and smelting enterprises that are still the source of Divriği's wealth, but they will not encounter a Divriği cat. The old trades are no longer practised: brick-red carpets are no longer woven from local wool coloured with dyes derived from local minerals; the long-toed leather slipper which resists mud and slush is no longer made. But the Divriği people are still as 'generous and charitable' as Evliya Çelebi reported, and I can vouch that the black, purple and white mulberries, from which the Divriği compôtes (*hoşab*), molasses (*pekmez*) and sherbets are made, remain unrivalled.

Cornucopia Issue 43, 2010

The entrance to the Hospital, with a staircase leading up to the first floor, and an octagonal pool mirroring the octagonal skylight

Below In this bird's-eye view, summer sun washes over the North Portal of the Great Mosque. The entrance to the Hospital is in shadow on the right of the picture. The roof, now lead, would originally have been packed earth. The taller conical structure conceals a dome. To its left is the lower tower of the mortuary chapel

Overleaf The sixteen columns supporting a vaulted ceiling give the mosque the air of a monastic cloister

Following pages: Left A double-headed falcon with bells attached to its beaks, symbol of Seljuk authority Right The magnificent North Portal

Secret Ankara

PHILIPS RADIO

16

THE EMBASSIES' BIG MOVE TO ANKARA

A BRAVE NEW WORLD

A NEW CAPITAL CALLED FOR NEW ARCHITECTURE.
ANKARA IN THE 1920S AND 1930S PRODUCED A FASCINATING
DIVERSITY OF STYLES AS THE FOREIGN POWERS DRAGGED
THEMSELVES AWAY FROM THE BOSPHORUS AND SETTLED
RELUCTANTLY ON THE ANATOLIAN PLATEAU

*Ankara in the 1940s.
A mounted Atatürk
surveys his new
capital in Heinrich
Krippel's Victory
Monument of 1927*

*Previous pages
Ankara Station,
photographed by
Othmar Pferschy. The
Art Deco building,
opened on 30 October
1937, was by the
Turkish architect
Şekip Akalın. Before
designing it, the
untested young man
was sent on a tour of
Europe's stations*

Atatürk showed himself to be an iconoclast and an innovator in switching his capital from Istanbul to Ankara. In this, as in much else, Mustafa Kemal's bold action was eventually emulated, by Australia, Brazil and Pakistan, among others. A spate of new public buildings resulted – the Grand National Assembly, the ministries, the presidential palace itself – which remain as monuments to late-1920s and 1930s taste. So too, in their more individualistic ways, do the principal embassy buildings of the period.

In 1919 Mustafa Kemal's Nationalists moved their headquarters to the old farm school in Keçiören, on the outskirts of Ankara – or Angora as it had been known since classical times – from Sivas, a day's journey to the east. Ankara, an important trading post in Hittite times, was then just a small town in Anatolia, 300 miles from Istanbul. Although the Baghdad railway had reached there as early as 1893, it had only intermittent contact with the outside world. Its sense of isolation had been exacerbated by a fire during the First World War which had destroyed swathes of the old lath-and-plaster houses that lined the steep cobbled streets huddled about the citadel.

The arrival of the Nationalists did little to change the physical aspect of Ankara while Anatolia remained in the grip of civil war and invasion that followed the First World War. But on 18 March 1920 the last Ottoman sultan, Mehmed VI Vahdettin, definitively adjourned parliament in Istanbul.

SECRET ANKARA 195

The way was open for a legitimate provisional Turkish national assembly to open a month later in Ankara. Mustafa Kemal was elected its president. While operational headquarters remained in the old farm school on Ankara's outskirts, he and his inner circle appropriated the stationmaster's house, below Ulus, Ankara's market area, built up among the extensive ruins of the Roman provincial capital of Galatia.

Few, if any, recall rural Ankara as it was in 1920 – snowbound in winter, sun-baked in summer and in other seasons a muddy morass. During the summer of 1921 the strains of war against the Greeks, compounded by malarial fever, drove Mustafa Kemal and his entourage into the hilly district some six kilometres southeast of Ulus, already known as Çankaya. There he took over the best of the agreeable timber-framed merchants' summerhouses standing among vineyards and orchards, and directed the final stages of the war which cleared the Greek invaders from Anatolia and decisively weakened the hold of the Allies in Istanbul and elsewhere.

The Sultan had already fled his dead empire aboard a British warship when the victory of Turkish resistance received international recognition at Lausanne two years later. On 24 July 1923 the Treaty of Lausanne, with

The view of Ankara from the Citadel today. Of all the Anatolian cities, Ankara is the most intriguing, but even to the initiated it reveals its secrets slowly

annexes detailed almost to absurdity, was ratified by the Allies 'in a brightly caparisoned Swiss University hall'. 'None of us can pretend that it is a glorious instrument,' the British high commissioner wrote of the treaty to his deputy in Istanbul. He likened Mustafa Kemal to 'a boxer who, after being counted out, had risen from the ring, stunned his opponent and knocked the referee through the ropes before making off with the prize money'.

The triumphant Turks proclaimed Ankara their capital on 23 October 1923. A circular to diplomatic missions was then issued: 'The Angora Government would like to see the Diplomatic Missions there too. They should choose sites on which to build and the Government would be happy to make these sites available to their Governments.' The new regime envisaged a diplomatic quarter, offering small sites off a track which was to become Atatürk Bulvarı (Atatürk Boulevard), cutting through orchards and agricultural land from the new government area, soon known as Bakanlıklar (the Ministries), to Çankaya.

This should not have been the shock it was to the representatives of the Great Powers in their palaces at Beyoğlu and on the Bosphorus. A capital away from indefensible Istanbul had been advocated as long ago as 1898 by Sultan Abdülhamid's German adviser, Goltz Pasha. Sooner or later the embassies were to be weaned away from the fleshpots of Istanbul to Ankara – 'a place where diplomats were not alone in being disconcerted by its primitive character' – by the need to transact business with the new government. That government stubbornly refused to transact it anywhere but in Ankara, where it offered the inducement of land to build on for those who would come.

Come they eventually did: first the Soviets and the Afghans, in the aftermath of their support for the Nationalists in the War of Independence; then the Americans, aloof from the occupying powers of 1918; then the French, who soon saw the way the wind was blowing after 1923; and, in due course, the British, obliged to negotiate the future of northern Iraq. And so they acquired sites, and then they built – some accepting plots in the 'diplomatic quarter' and buying additional land to accommodate housing and offices; others buying sites elsewhere which they thought better suited to their needs. And most built prestigiously and well – monuments to the status and taste of their individual nations – during the late 1920s and 1930s.

Cornucopia Issue 39, 2008

Monumental Modernism

When a new French ambassador to Turkey was appointed in 1928, the Quai d'Orsay instructed him in no uncertain terms to 'steer clear of the fleshpots on the Bosphorus'. As Ankara was where dealing with those who governed Turkey was now done, he was to 'live there by choice', he was told. 'It is not the end of the world.' A small mission had been established in Ankara since 1923, administered by a succession of chargés d'affaires who complained bitterly of the 'abominable' dust and water shortages. But the ambassadors themselves resided in the Palais de France in Istanbul, taking the fifteen-hour train journey to Ankara only to present their credentials and attend the annual Republic Day ball.

France's principal concern in 1928 was the governance of the Sanjak of Alexandretta on the Syrian border – today's province of Hatay – which was a League of Nations mandate that Mustafa Kemal was keen to acquire. There was a need for a resident ambassador in Ankara: Charles de Chambrun was appointed that year. ▷204

Left Albert Laprade's palais, conceived as a Modernist take on Versailles' Petit Trianon Below left The marble-clad eastern façade as it was in the 1930s

Right The Gobelin tapestry that brings a splash of colour to the light-flooded marble atrium celebrates France's cycling prowess. The Frenchman Louison Bobet was winner of the Tour de France in 1953, 1954 and 1955

The Salon des Fêtes,
used for winter
receptions. It was
originally intended to
have Art Deco furniture
to complement the
architecture, but budget
cuts in the approach to
war in 1938 meant
that the embassy
had to make do with
the old Louis XV
and Louis XVI
furniture and early-
nineteenth-century
chandeliers. The
Le Brun tapestry over
the piano depicts
Louis XIV's meeting
with Philip IV of Spain

As custom demands,
guests are still received
in the traditionally
furnished Petit Salon,
whose doors open onto
the garden terrace

Top row The desk
and chairs in the
ambassador's study
were contemporary
creations by Jules
Leleu. The room
is dominated by a
Gobelin tapestry of
Louis XIV's capture
of Lille, after Le Brun,
woven in 1737–41
Left Guests in the Salon
des Fêtes in 1938

Left In the dining
room, the Art Deco
designer Jean Dunand's
ten-metre-long lacquer
mural of a herd of
hinds, made up of
thirty-nine panels,
is dated 1938

The Turkish government duly honoured the 1923 promise of a site: a parcel of uncultivated land behind the Italians and Germans, away from the mud, dust and ruts of Atatürk Boulevard. But it was too small. Fortunately, the following year, contiguous terrain, more rock than earth, belonging to the celebrated author Yakup Kadri came on the market. Its purchase enabled building plans to be made. While the two responsible departments in Paris – the Beaux Arts and the foreign ministry – quarrelled for the next eight years over the designing and funding of the new building, a temporary chancery was opened in a French religious order's old house in Ulus, and a villa was rented for the ambassador in the new residential quarter of Yenişehir.

Four years elapsed before France's chief government architect, Albert Laprade, visited Ankara to assess the possibilities of the site. In September 1934 his plans were approved. Fresh from the success of his widely acclaimed Modernist Musée des Colonies in Paris, Laprade was France's best choice to design an embassy that would reflect 'Greater France' in the new capital, bristling with classical Modernist architecture. For the next three years, when not coercing the engineers, technicians and interior designers responsible for the details of the project, he was dealing with the petty jealousies and intrigues of the bureaucrats and the demands of four successive ambassadors.

For all that, the main work on the building, a rigorously symmetrical rectangle, its austerity somewhat offset by the quality of the building materials, was complete enough for embassy staff to move in by the autumn of 1937. The fitting-out of the interior took longer, but new funds were allocated in 1939 – there was a need for additional buildings for counsellors, attachés and garages – and more funds arrived for the garden and a reservoir before France fell in 1940.

If this grand, spare *hôtel*, which embraces under one roof offices, public rooms and the ambassador's private apartment, is a celebration of French Modernism, its fine wrought-iron gates, flanked by a pair of pavilions in the forecourt, the red and white marble facings of the façades and the levelling of the land below the western terrace evoke the Petit Trianon at Versailles.

Some see a striking resemblance to Laprade's Musée des Colonies, others to the governor's residence in Rabat and the Villa Tyng in Marrakesh. For Ankara denizens, the landscaping of the land from bedrock to formal park in the style of Louis XIV's gardener Le Nôtre is probably Laprade's crowning achievement. Connoisseurs of French Modernist furniture see Jean Dunand's black-lacquer mural for the dining room and Jules Leleu's set of desk and chairs for the ambassador's study as major works of their genre.

The Second World War put paid to the final touches of Laprade's grand design. The last of the pre-war funds received from Paris in 1940 was for a reservoir to tap water from a spring deep in the rock (this is still the ambassador's swimming pool and never warms up). Nevertheless it exhibits the unique style of 1930s French architecture. All the post-war ambassadors have left their stamp on the house, including the present envoy, who rightly sees the peerless beauty of the tapestries adorning the embassy walls as the link that blends and holds together this rare assembly of furniture and furnishings in an important house retaining much that the 1930s stood for.

THE BRITISH EMBASSY

A delightfully English house

The site chose itself, wrote Alexander Knox-Helm, the young embassy secretary who found the future British Embassy on 13 January 1926. It was then 'an old wooden house standing alone within a few acres of bare hillside'. He could not have foreseen that he would himself be British ambassador at Ankara twenty-five years later and in the intervening years would be responsible for the purchase of the land alongside, on which the present chancery and residence are sited.

In the aftermath of the First World War there was little love lost between Britain and the Turkish Nationalists, and the British had no intention of being inveigled away from Istanbul. The first post-war ambassador allowed thirteen months to elapse before arrangements were made to present his credentials in Ankara. Two railway carriages were hired for the week away. When the British party arrived in a siding below Ulus on 1 March 1925, they were surprised to find the French envoy alongside in a sleeper-coach hired for the same purpose.

With negotiations over northern Iraq – a leftover from the Lausanne Peace Conference – due to resume in Ankara in May 1926, Knox-Helm was despatched to the capital in mid-January – with a local representative from the Office of Works – to find a suitable site. The pair stayed 'in a so-called room in an outhouse of a so-called hotel' near what is now Ulus Square. Knox-Helm's instructions were explicit: an existing house, accessible by road, with its own water supply. His ambassador warned him to bear in mind 'the awful possibility that the British Embassy might one day be obliged to move there'.

Knox-Helm made a far-sighted choice: a site in Çankaya, near the President's villa, since it would be the first area to get reliable services in the developing city and the last to be cut off. A small eight-roomed house with its own spring was available – 'a shack with a cool cellar underneath a fair-sized room, a smallish dining room and two ice chambers as well as a kitchen and four small bedrooms up top'. Its owner, Salih Bozok, a childhood friend and once ADC to

Overleaf The British Embassy stands in an informal English garden, with a weeping willow planted by the Queen in 1971

the Gazi, wished to make it a gift from the Turkish government. Knox-Helm's diary records that day: 'Three things to do: first lease the house, second, fix a price for its purchase and, third, complete the formalities for its transfer.'

The site was duly granted by the Turkish government, and Salih Bozok was persuaded to rent out the house. By May 1926 it was fit for Sir Ronald Lindsay, leading the negotiations which produced the treaty resolving the Mosul dispute. Despite a three-day break while 'the British house' was closed for fumigation, the treaty was signed within three weeks.

Once the owner's scruples over accepting payment of £2,500 had been overcome, the house was enlarged and the embassy secretaries wintered there happily, spending their spare time terracing, gardening and planting trees. The lines of Lombardy poplars are their legacy, despite the Office of Works reprimanding them for planting the wrong sort of poplar.

In 1951 the old wooden 'shack' was pulled down. Knox-Helm's affection for it was evident: 'It had character but how it swayed in the winter wind. Life in it had been hard but it had been great fun… It was there that Anglo-Turkish friendship was revived and the foundations of the Anglo-Turkish alliance laid.'

When the adjoining property belonging to Mustafa Kemal's henchman Kılıç Ali came on the market in 1929, London was finally reconciled to Ankara and agreed both to the purchase and to building. At a cost of £32,284, a red-roofed, white-stuccoed chancery-residence, complete with lodge and driveway, was built within a year to Office of Works plans. Though scheduled to be the eventual chancery, it became the ambassador's residence until 1945.

On the eve of the Second World War, as the Modernist French Embassy was nearing completion and the Italian *fascista* compound was well under way, a British construction company brought in from India made a start on the long-awaited residence. They built to the highest standard and had it completed, bar decoration and electric fittings, two years later. It was appropriated for much-needed office space throughout the war: neutral Ankara was a diplomatic beehive. In the lovely, peaceful house today, it is difficult to imagine the main dining room transformed into chancery offices, the Green Drawing Room divided in two for the registries, and the three sections along the windows of the hall partitioned off to provide offices for the head of chancery and the typists. The same sort of thing happened on the bedroom floor, and the surrounding lawns were covered in Nissen huts.

The changeover from office to residence took place over the summer of 1945. Anticipating the German surrender on 9 May, partitions were removed and victory celebrations planned in an empty house, from eleven in the morning until midnight. The house saw over a thousand people streaming through, but once the dancing was over, the staff packed up and the house was turned over to workmen. The first post-war ambassador moved in that October.

The north-facing Green
Drawing Room was,
until 1990, a brown
room made gloomier
by Knox-Helm's screen
of Lombardy poplars.
The panelling is from
1939; the green walls,
silk curtains and low
stripy sofas are from
the author's days as
the ambassador's wife
in the 1990s

Above The dining room. In the 1990s the embassy's Paul Storr silver and Worcester porcelain were taken to Istanbul for summer dinner parties

Left Characterful but prone to swaying in the wind, the 'Shack' served as the British Embassy for five years

A portrait of George V,
in whose reign the
British Embassy was
built, hangs above a
George III silver tureen

The first-floor hall is large enough to be used for recitals on the Broadwood grand piano and even as a ballroom. In the Second World War, neutral Ankara was a diplomatic beehive, and the hall was partitioned to make offices for the head of chancery and his typists

Since 1945 much has been done in the British Embassy compound: the garden landscaped, the chancery remodelled, more surrounding land acquired. Above all, the residence, with its high-quality panelling, inlaid doors and Otis lifts, has been made into the comfortable, functional, well-appointed 1930s building it was designed to be. Though the structure of the house was turned from back to front at the insistence of Sir Percy Loraine, the pre-war ambassador who was never to live in it, even the strangeness of the resulting front hall and the turned-around staircase rising to the main hall is not too out of place. On the climb one passes a rare set of eighteenth-century paintings of a grand vizier's reception of an envoy – with time to note that the envoy was probably the Dutch ambassador, rather than the British. A portrait of Hobart Pasha, the romantic English seadog who commanded the Ottoman navy, benignly surveys all who reach the first-floor hall. If asked from where and when all this mix of furniture and furnishings came, the answer is: in dribs and drabs from Istanbul and London. Like an English garden, it is a happy hotchpotch of tastes – which is, after all, a typically English genre.

Until the 1970s no civilised denizen of Ankara went anywhere but to Istanbul for the summer break: the unpolluted shores of the Bosphorus and the Princes Islands were much preferred to the inaccessible and primitive coasts of the Black Sea or Aegean. Right through from the 1920s to the late 1960s, ambassadors stole a march on their Turkish hosts, packing up by mid-June and not returning to the new capital until well into September.

The British Embassy went under dust sheets as soon as the Queen's birthday party was over. Paul Storr silverware and Worcester porcelain, needed to embellish the old Istanbul winter embassy, Pera House, and the gardens of the old summer embassy at Tarabya, were packed into trunks embossed with the royal arms; and off they went, together with cook, butler, under-butler and several other domestic staff, on the overnight train to Haydarpaşa Station and on by launch to Beyoğlu. The ambassador, his wife and her secretary were ensconced in the Rolls at the head of a modest motorcade, which swept to the head of the ferry queue when it reached Üsküdar nine hours later. The British would find the French, Italians, Spanish and Germans already installed. Even the Americans and Russians, less attached to the old ways, came to Istanbul for at least a month. And the British were far from unique in maintaining a motor launch, complete with Italian crew of four, for the ambassador's use.

The only trace of the old summer routines, apart from fleeting visits to Istanbul by air, is the occasional arrival of flowers from the surviving gardens of the old summer embassy at Tarabya. Until recently the British still received a weekly hamper containing the produce of the mild microclimate enjoyed in the extensive gardens of the great summer embassy on the Bosphorus, which burned down over seventy years ago.

Easy grandeur behind a formal façade

It was not until 1941 that the Italian ambassador was officially prised away from the old Venetian palace in Beyoğlu. An embassy compound in Ankara – chancery, church and stables – was at last ready, constructed at speed to designs by the fashionable Milanese architect Caccia Dominioni.

Discussions about the move to Ankara had begun in 1926, when a site in Çankaya was refused on the grounds that it was too small. Hopes were dashed for prime land in Kavaklıdere when the Poles got in first. The plot offered by the Turkish government – beside the Germans, fronting the Boulevard in the diplomatic quarter – was too small. But, like the Germans, the Italians had good fortune in tracing the owner of the ground behind it. When, in September 1929, he was found willing to sell, a 30,000-square-metre site, part gifted, part purchased, sandwiched between the Germans and the Bulgarians, was entered into Ankara's official land registry as property of the Italian government. The falling-out between Mussolini and Mustafa Kemal may have been the reason why it took another nine years before building began. It was not until 1938 that the foundation stone of the chapel of the future embassy was laid by the apostolic delegate, Monsignor Roncalli, later to become revered as Pope John XXIII.

Those familiar with 1930s architecture will know that severe, arguably fascist, exteriors can hide both practical and elegant interiors. From the Boulevard, the red-ochre residence, its chancery discreetly attached, appears stark and forbidding. Trees, shrubs and formal garden, ravaged by the pollution of the 1970s, have recovered to give the terraced elevation both presence and shade; the steep sweep of the U-shaped double drive from a pair of lodge gates softens the arrival.

The chancery wing, comprising one central corridor, runs to a green baize door, through which the ambassador comes and goes. No one could fail to recognise the convenience of this arrangement, or the easy grandeur of the residence itself, with its western garden climbing up the hill behind. The great hall, overhung by balconies, leads into a fine withdrawing room, with a ceiling exquisitely plastered in squares filled with signs of the zodiac picked out in gold leaf. For size, for prestige, for functionality, it is a house that is a success. Its only drawback, apart from draughts (about which there are complaints), is the loss of a view to the eastern mountains, obscured by one of Ankara's more unfortunate high-rise buildings that shot up in the 1990s.

Top left The severe
red-ochre façade
of Mussolini's 1938
Italian Embassy
Above left The graphic
commemoration date

Top right The drawing
room has signs
of the zodiac on the
coffered ceiling
Above right Queen
Elena of Italy still
dominates the entrance

hall. Her husband,
Victor Emmanuel III,
was on the throne
when the embassy
was constructed. The
flag is out for Italian
Republic Day, 2 June,

established after he
abdicated. The short
double staircase leads
to the great hall on the
'piano nobile'

*Both grand and
functional, the great
hall, with its pillars
and gilded chairs,
occupies the whole
length of the palace*

A schloss among the skyscrapers

It comes as no surprise that the beautiful Austrian Embassy in the district of Bakanlıklar was planned, planted and built by Clemens Holzmeister, Austria's greatest pre-war architect. His controlling hand in the design and execution of this small Austrian gem in a vineyard donated by Mustafa Kemal was possible because from 1928 he had been visiting Ankara to oversee the construction of the capital's most prestigious ministries, banks and monuments. When he took on the Austrian Embassy in 1933, he had just completed the President's new villa in Çankaya and was soon to embark on the great parliament building.

Although the impoverished Austrian Republic had taken back the old Habsburg palace on the Bosphorus in 1924, it was another nine years before recovery from the loss of dynasty, army and empire made a move to Ankara possible. Between 1933 and 1935 an embassy to Holzmeister's design, an eighteenth-century Austrian schloss, rose behind fine gates set back from the Boulevard.

The conception of the embassy was brilliant. In order to give presence to the house and its two wings, which were to form the shape of a U around a sloping, paved forecourt, finished off by a pair of arched gatehouses, the Ankara construction company, Haydar Emre & Cie, had to dig to provide an elevated terrace on which to set the house. If the sloping elevation at its front gave height to the offices and stables in the wings, the back elevation gave form to the garden. From a wide easterly terrace giving off the central hall, a double stone stairway led down to the garden, once full of vines, later replanted with roses. It is still very pretty but, alas, now overlooked by apartment blocks.

Seeing the house today, warmly and richly painted pale Schönbrunn yellow, it is difficult to envisage how it looked in 1945, having been shut for the duration of the Second World War once the German ambassador Franz von Papen had moved on to the Czech Embassy: it had, after all, had only three years of use. Sixty years on, one wonders whether the elegant staircase in the corner of the hall always had a carpet to enhance the iron balustrades and curling ironwork banister; whether the Murano glass chandeliers, the Meissen porcelain and the nineteenth-century tapestry of the *Death of Uria*, not to mention the seventeenth-century painting of Süleyman Efendi and a remarkable collection of Persian carpets, were all inherited from the

Holzmeister's Austrian Embassy, painted in a pale Schönbrunn yellow. A long garden, once an orchard, leads to a striking circular niche and a double flight of steps up to a wide terrace

Habsburg palaces in Istanbul. Certainly the set of painted and decorated 1930s dining-room chairs, table and sideboards were specially ordered for the house.

It is a residence in which successive envoys have taken pride, not least the incumbent on a recent visit, Heidemaria Gürer. As founder of the Central Asian Summer Academy of Fine Arts, she has opened it to visiting artists devoted to Central Asia and the Caucasus. There is little doubt that Clemens Holzmeister, former director of Vienna's Academy of Fine Arts, would have been as delighted by her success as he would have sympathised with her distress at the overwhelming presence of the İş Bank, which now towers above the house, blocking out its light.

Tsarist treasures in a Soviet block

The new Russian Embassy of the 1980s dominates one of Çankaya's western spurs, a Postmodernist block which displays all the grim might of the Soviet era. Fortunately for its occupants, the great palaces of the tsars in Istanbul survived the convulsions of Lenin's revolution and, amazingly, some of the treasures of Catherine the Great's famous winter embassy in Beyoğlu found their way to Ankara to embellish the new Russian mission.

With no ties to Istanbul, the Soviets had nothing to lose by being the first to accept a plot in the putative diplomatic quarter near the district reserved for ministry buildings by the new capital's urban planners. Their new building was not even the Soviets' first mission in Ankara.

The sixty-roomed old Soviet Embassy on the Boulevard stood, large and well furnished, from 1924 until it was demolished during the 1970s, a Constructivist experiment, inspired by the Cubists, a homage to Modernism and to the aspirations of the New Order. Its admirers, who enjoyed Ambassador Comrade Surich's wild parties, likened it to a dreadnought, some even to a surging ship. The wide balconies overlooking the Boulevard did indeed resemble the decks of a sea vessel, but it was thought the architect's perilous, stormbound passage across the Black Sea had been the reason for them.

The building was immortalised in 1933 when it was used by the Soviet cineast Sergei Yutkevich for the documentary *Ankara: Heart of Turkey*, which was shot to mark the tenth anniversary of the Turkish Republic. Since then two structures have replaced it. Whether the present building, today undergoing extensive restoration, will one day be regarded as an architectural treasure of the late twentieth century remains to be seen.

The drawing room of the Russian Embassy today, full of heirlooms from Tsarist times

The old Russian Embassy in the 1930s, a monument to Constructivism

Last of the Boulevard villas

Belgian industrialists were well established in Turkey before the First World War. Once the Armistice was signed, business resumed – for instance, the *wagons-lits* service on the Orient Express and the sale of steel. Despite such substantial commercial involvement with the new Republic, the Belgian government took time to respond to the summons to Ankara.

In 1929, during the coldest February on record, when snow held up the Orient Express outside Istanbul for over three weeks, Ankara's escalating land prices forced Brussels' hand. Two plots of land fronting the Atatürk Boulevard below the Soviets were purchased at a cost of £1,468.

On 1 June 1929, Jack Nesim Aggiman's flourishing firm of Ankara architects and builders quoted £16,000 to complete the job. Meticulous accounts still held in the embassy inform us that the lime, gravel and sand were brought in from Yozgat; the marble from the island of Marmara; the ceramic and roof tiles, as well as glass, from Belgium; Portland cement and oil paints from England; and wood for doors and window frames from Romania.

A comfortable, well-proportioned, up-to-date stuccoed villa – its defining feature an off-centre open entrance reached by a semicircular stairway – was completed in six months. Its interior betrays the trademarks of an Ottoman architect: Ottoman conceits in the patterning on the ceilings and the swirls on the radiators' iron grilles but, above all, the traditional Ottoman upstairs hall, off which all rooms lead. Aggiman was paid in sterling, the most stable currency following the Wall Street crash.

A fence, more for keeping out neighbouring cows than delimiting land not yet at risk of either development or encroaching roads, was built during the 1930s. Today the embassy is one of only two villas on the Boulevard that has not been replaced by high-rise apartment blocks and shopping malls. Once one enters the gates, a whiff of Mustafa Kemal's Ankara is still sensed.

The residence has recently had new life breathed into it by an envoy sympathetic with this architectural period. The terrace above the front door has been glazed to make a much-needed winter garden. Could it be that the beautiful handwoven curtains adorning several rooms, including the library, are replicas of those once hanging in the German Embassy famously admired by the Gazi? The ambassador chanced upon them in old Ulus. The elderly lady who kept the store told him that they were her last, the weaver having died of old age. Authentic Ankara weaving, by tradition women's work, is, alas, a dying art.

The King of the Belgians presides over the dining room; the view of Brussels is by Jean-Baptiste van Moer, dated 1880

Bottom row The Belgian Embassy – one of the last of the villas that once lined the Atatürk Boulevard – as it is today and in the 1930s

A temple portico for a country house

The Polish Embassy's portico was inspired by Warsaw's Belvedere Palace. The embassy incorporates the ambassador's quarters, office space and a chapel under one roof. It was the ideal 1930s functional embassy

Few people had suffered so grievously during the First World War as the Poles. Following the Armistice of 11 November 1918, Poland celebrated her newly refound independence by opening a mission in Istanbul. With Josef Pilsudski's new Republican government keen to be among the first to answer the call to Ankara, it was unfortunate that the gift of land offered to them by the Turkish government in 1924 was the vacant plot sandwiched between the Soviets and Germans on the Boulevard. To make up for this tactlessness, an alternative site in the district of Kavaklıdere, at the limit of the diplomatic quarter, was found, which the Poles accepted on 15 May of the same year.

In Warsaw the Polish ambassador-designate to Ankara, Wladyslaw Gunther, pushed for the new embassy to be in the mould of a Polish country house estate similar in style to the Belvedere, at the time the flagship building in the capital. On 15 May 1924 the ministry of foreign affairs signed a contract with the ministry's Neoclassical architect, Karol Iwanicki, but his plans exceeded the budget. Funds were no longer available to pay for so expensive a house, and the counsellor heading the legation settled in three small buildings in Keçiören, outside the city.

During 1926 budgetary difficulties were compounded by the Turkish government's demands for payment for the Kavaklıdere plot, since the Poles had not begun to develop it and the Italians were now keen to purchase it. With the threat of losing the whole site and the need to have a suitable house in the right area in time for the arrival of Poland's first ambassador, Warsaw granted credits for the following year. By 1928 the land was fenced, construction started and, tradition has it, the foundation stone was laid by the Gazi himself.

The Polish craftsmen followed Iwanicki's drawings for a grand yet unpretentious two-storey, cream-stuccoed country house, windows and walls classically plain, crowned by a red-tiled roof. Exceptional was the central portico in the form of an antique temple front, built in the Ionic order below a flat-faced pediment decorated with the arms of Poland.

An ill wind blew during the afternoon of 25 June 1935. A fire broke out in the attic, causing major damage to the roof and the ambassador's wing: a kitchen flue too near a wooden door frame. There was no option but to call in Jack Aggiman's firm to repair the damage and ensure that the

Top left The great sweep of the staircase
Top right The dining room's Art Deco ceiling, floor and furniture were made by joiners in Gdansk. Few such complete ensembles survive

Above left The pretty Neoclassical music room with its Blüthner grand piano
Above right The embassy has a fine collection of Persian carpets

The embassy is a rare surviving celebration of the country's happy interwar years. Almost everything of the period in Poland itself was destroyed

building remained one of Ankara's most prestigious – as it certainly is today.

Once inside the Polish Embassy's large garden in Kavaklıdere, where flowering shrubs and gnarled fruit trees are watered by a stream overhung by poplars and Oriental planes, the beautiful Neoclassical Polish manor house, harking back to the golden years of the eighteenth century, appears oblivious to the swirl of life outside it. But the development of modern Kavaklıdere has inevitably impinged on the estate since it was acquired in 1926.

Nibbling away at its grounds began in 1955, when 811 square metres of garden were required for the widening of Atatürk Boulevard. Then the northern part of the garden, with some venerable trees, was taken for the Kuğulu Park, with an extra slice through the drive to make Polonya Caddesi. In compensation the Poles were given a piece of land on the far side of the stream. During the 1990s a huge building arose on its southern perimeter, taking light as well as land. Now the Kavaklıdere underpass necessitates new arrangements for access.

Despite all its travails, this remarkable embassy remains a place where Poland celebrated the happy interwar years, most examples of which were destroyed in Poland itself during the Second World War. It is a charming house, where Persian rugs look their best on marquetry floors in the well-proportioned, airy rooms, and Rococo furniture and 1930s paintings look good alongside eighteenth-century paintings and 1930s furniture. A pretty music room contrasts admirably with the Baroque panelling, plastered ceilings, marble chimney breasts, metal-worked central-heating covers and, not least, the great sweep of marble stairs from the hall to the *piano nobile*.

THE GERMAN EMBASSY

A hunting lodge in the heart of the city

Until they built the Prussian hunting lodges which have graced their compound near the Russians on Atatürk Boulevard since 1928, the Germans had a temporary building, so successful that it ended up in the Atatürk Orman Çiftliği, a model farm on the outskirts of the city, where it can be seen to this day. Even temporary arrangements were not easy in the aftermath of defeat in the First World War, and the decision to move to Turkey's new capital at the end of 1923 was complicated by the existence of two large embassy buildings in Istanbul – in Beyoğlu and Tarabya – both closed since the Armistice in 1918.

However, the establishment of good relations with Mustafa Kemal was the paramount consideration, and Berlin did not hesitate for long. Whether purchased or gifted, 28,000 square metres of sloping ground, rising from the Boulevard short of Kavaklıdere, was entered into Ankara's official land registry book as German Embassy terrain on 26 February 1924. Thereafter it was known locally as Almanköy (the German village).

The urgent need for a suitable temporary building was solved by the Hamburg firm of Christoph & Unmack, whose catalogue advertised wooden prefabricated 'facilities'. The selected house left the port of Hamburg aboard the MV *Stralsund* on 24 July 1924 and, nineteen days later, was shipped across the Bosphorus for onward transmission to Ankara by rail. The German firm of Philipp Holzmann, responsible for its assemblage, had the ingenious wooden building erected on stone foundations a month after the arrival of the Weimar Republic's first envoy, Rudolf Nadolny.

Six months later Mustafa Kemal paid the building an unscheduled visit on his way to Ulus. For an hour he inspected every detail, from the glazed Dutch-tiled stoves, sanitary fittings and dining room that could 'sit sixteen' to the clever use of local fabrics, most particularly as 'little curtains for the French windows'. Even the view from the balcony and the newly planted saplings in the park received praise. He left declaring the house had made so dazzling an impression upon him that he desired one for himself. 'As far as I know,' reported the gratified ambassador on 9 February 1925, 'the German Embassy is the only one that has been singled out by a personal visit from the Gazi.' The despatch of a Christoph & Unmack catalogue from Hamburg was given the highest priority.

A further 37,000 square metres of land having been purchased in December 1927, Berlin approved a major development of the whole site. Traditional Prussian country-style architecture was considered admirably suited to Ankara's semi-rural landscape, and the moving spirit, when it came to design, was Ambassador Nadolny himself. He greatly admired President Hindenberg's sand-yellow and garden-green hunting lodge and insisted on a near-replica. By the end of 1930 the temporary building so extolled by the Gazi had been superseded by the present chancery building, flanked by two substantial staff residences, recessed behind twin-porticoed gatehouses either side of the entrance on the Boulevard.

Ambassador Nadolny was no longer in Ankara when, in 1937, Berlin's directorate of historic buildings ran a limited competition for a prestigious avant-garde residence for the ambassador to Ankara. It was won by Konstanty Gutschow, but the plans were still awaiting Hitler's approval when he launched the Second World War with his invasion of Poland. When Ambassador Franz von Papen arrived in 1939 there was still no residence.

The first German Embassy was a stylish 1924 prefab building by the Hamburg firm of Christoph & Unmak

Left The chancery, dressed up as a Prussian hunting lodge, was built in 1930 Opposite The compound, complete with stables and riding school, is known as Almanköy

He moved into the Austrian Embassy, Austria having been part of the Reich since 1938, and later took over the Czech Embassy.

Of all the tales of wartime espionage, perhaps the most spectacular incident played out on neutral soil was the 'Cicero affair'. The position of the side gate at the back of the compound, through which the British ambassador's Albanian valet, code-named Cicero, slipped nightly on his way to the German attaché's house, is now unclear. But his onward passage through the compound's upper garden, past the stables, greenhouses and reservoir, can easily be charted. Berlin suspected Cicero's films of crucial Allied secrets, filched from the over-trusting ambassador's safe, were a 'plant'. He was paid in counterfeit sterling.

Post-war German ambassadors have enjoyed the greenest oasis in the concrete wastes of Kavaklıdere, complete with stables and the best recreational facilities. But they still await a purpose-built residence; their house is one of the staff houses designed by their Weimar predecessor, Ambassador Nadolny.

The Hungarian Embassy

National celebration in Art Deco Baronial

A forgotten jewel in the crown of Ankara's embassies is the residence of the Hungarian ambassador, built in 1929 to the designs of the successful Istanbul-born Italian architect Giulio Mongeri (1873–1951). It is a celebration of the eclecticism of the period.

Realising that the original embassy, a small villa next to the Afghans in Maltepe, was too small (it is now a kebab shop), the Budapest government traded it in for new land in Çankaya and commissioned Mongeri, who was at the vanguard of Turkish national architectural style, to draw up plans for a separate chancery and residence worthy of Hungary's miraculous recovery from the First World War.

The residence boasts a double drive leading up to a brick-and-stucco building roofed in red tiles. The porch, set beneath pointed arches, is crowned by a fine coat of arms. The hall has grand columns with decorated capitals. And its great fireplace is an Art Deco curiosity with a Central European difference. The fine hood, with its gilded arabesques, is supported by a pair of pillars: a grand surround for a plain 1930s marble fireplace to greet guests arriving on a cold winter's night.

Top The pointed arches of the Hungarian Embassy's portico are part of its eclectic appeal

Bottom A simple marble fireplace in the entrance hall is surmounted by a massive hood

A Modernist nod
to Turkish vernacular

The Ottoman Empire had been represented at Berne from 1901 to 1915, its envoy's main task having been to 'watch over' troublesome Young Turks living in self-imposed exile, removed from the scrutiny of Sultan Abdülhamid's army of spies. But Swiss interest in Turkey was not of sufficient importance to justify a permanent diplomatic mission until well after the establishment of the Republic. During the Lausanne Peace Conference of 1922–23, the Nationalists reopened the Berne legation. But it took the diplomatic skills of Ambassador Mehmet Münir Ertegün, Turkey's envoy to Berne, to set Turco-Swiss relations on a reciprocal basis. Henri Martin, first minister to Turkey, presented his credentials on 28 October 1928, to fine words of goodwill.

It was not until 1936 that the Swiss took the decision to build, the architect Ernst Egli being invited to draw up plans for a functional embassy suitable for the Swiss government's first ambassador in Ankara. The building was commissioned in good time for the Swiss to play in Ankara the same important neutral role they carried out in so many capitals during the Second World War.

Painted red, overhung by eaves, the residence, with its severe south-facing façade more window than wall, stands on a precipitous slope below the Israeli legation and above ground allotted to the Czechs, on what in 1960 became Şehit Ersan Caddesi, leading up to Çankaya.

The interior design was a foray into the modern, counterbalanced by an exterior harking back to a conservative Ottoman vernacular. For more than half a century the house was surrounded by a garden of roses which tumbled down to the Kavaklıdere stream, but recently some of this ground has been sacrificed for a state-of-the-art office block. As with most other embassies, aesthetics have been subordinated to practicality.

Ernst Egli's Swiss Embassy, completed in 1938, combines elements of the Turkish yalı – the wall of windows, the overhanging eaves

and oxblood-red paint – with the white stilts so beloved of Le Corbusier

Overleaf In 1810 this eighteenth-century Dutch painting of Ankara – now in the Rijksmuseum – hung in the Directorate of

Levantine Trade in Amsterdam's town hall. Ankara owed its wealth to mohair, a luxury made from the fleece of Angora goats. The

entire trade is depicted in this view: shearing, spinning, weaving, sizing, selling – and caravans setting off with their precious cargo

FLY IN THE FACE OF FASHION

<small>RATHER THAN FOLLOW THE CROWD AND DISMISS ANKARA AS
A DULL, SOULLESS MODERN CAPITAL, VISITORS SHOULD
TAKE TIME TO DISCOVER WHY THE FAMED ANGORA OF OLD,
TWICE CAPITAL IN ANCIENT TIMES, IS BACK ON THE MAP</small>

Tourists love Turkey but virtually none come to Ankara. They assume it is an artificial city, chosen as capital simply for its location and built virtually from scratch. It is indeed a new city, chosen by Atatürk for its central position and given fine, if somewhat Teutonic, government buildings during the 1920s and '30s. Since then it has suffered urban sprawl, with a current population of four million. But there is nothing new or artificial about old Ankara. This is no Turkish Brasilia.

Known as Ancyra under the Romans, as Angora in Ottoman times, Ankara was twice capital in antiquity. Today it is a neglected modern capital, still ignored by those who, when it comes to history, are in the habit of skipping adroitly from the Hittites to the new Republic. But at last a long-postponed miracle is occurring. A plethora of recent discoveries in Ulus – old Ankara – has encouraged an interest in pulling together the missing threads. The Museum of Anatolian Civilisations is no longer the sole attraction: changes in and around the ancient Citadel are now complemented by boutique hotels, one of them of outstanding quality. When planning your next trip to Turkey, why not be unfashionable and start with a few days in old Ankara before carrying on north, south, east or west? You will not be disappointed.

*Akkale, the eleventh-
century white limestone
fort built by the Seljuks
to dominate the gorge*

*of the Ankara river.
In 1402, following
the Battle of Ankara,
Tamerlane imprisoned*

*Beyazıt, the Ottoman
Sultan, inside the fort*

238 The Palace Lady's Summerhouse

*Above This fine marble
sacrificial bull from the
fifth century AD is
one of the pair at the
top of the steps in the
inner sanctum. It now
stands in a quiet corner
of the garden of the
Museum of Anatolian
Civilisations*

ROMAN ANCYRA AND OTTOMAN ANGORA

Nature has given Ankara a magnificent site from which to prosper and command. Built round an extinct volcano, the city dominates a gorge through which the Ankara river, a tributary of the Sakarya, once flowed.

From the north, Byzantine walls dominate a township of dilapidated pink brick houses and red-roofed shacks clinging in painterly disorder to the rocky escarpments rising from the valley floor. From the west, knowing eyes can pick out the line of the third-century walls built to defend Ancyra, Roman capital of the province of Galatia, spreading out across a flattening hill. From the south, the medieval Muslim, Christian and Jewish quarters of Ottoman Angora and the foundations of its seventeenth-century walls must be imagined beneath today's Ulus. Likewise the dam that once controlled the flash flooding of the now-piped river has made way for an east-west thoroughfare through the gorge.

Some three thousand years ago Ankara was a flourishing Phrygian city, which submitted to Alexander the Great before an army of nomadic Gauls appeared around 278 BC. These Celtic conquerors had lost their warlike vigour and adopted softer Anatolian ways by the time they were absorbed into the Roman Empire. Ancyra continued to prosper under the early Byzantine emperors, but the great Anatolian crossroads came under Arab, then Seljuk, then Mongol control, before the Ottoman ascendancy after 1414. Repeated assault and reconstruction brought change again and again to its ramparts and towers.

Each regime left its mark. And each was accompanied by destruction. The town in Anatolia that Atatürk chose as his capital in 1923 was a primitive place. An early new Republican on his first visit to the new capital in 1924 describes his arrival in Angora as 'through the swamp' (mosquito-infested and malarial, thanks to the confluence of Ankara's two rivers), then through 'the site of the fire' (which in 1917 destroyed half the old city), reaching 'a village of adobe huts and mud-brick houses, crooked streets either paved or of rough cobblestones'.

Other than the Roman Temple of Augustus and the fifteenth-century Hacı Bayram Mosque standing on the Phrygian acropolis, the fourth-century so-called Julian Column below them, the remains of the third-century Caracalla Baths overlooking the plain – thought to have been destroyed during the Persian occupation some five centuries later – and parts of the Roman theatre recently discovered below the Citadel's outer walls, few pre-twentieth-century monuments have survived on this combustible hillside regularly devastated by fire. All that is left of the nineteenth-century mills and tanneries is a few Ottoman buildings that have escaped the mayoral bulldozer.

The Temple of Augustus and the Hacı Bayram Mosque

To honour Caesar, the people of Galatia raised a temple of white Afyon marble on the foundations of the Moon God's former shrine. It was dedicated to 'Rome and Augustus' and, as a further touch of good citizenship, a copy of the text of Augustus's *Res Gestae Divi Augusti* – an account of his life and accomplishments that he wrote in his seventy-sixth year and circulated to the provinces – was engraved on the temple's stone walls in both Latin and Greek. On Augustus's death it was inscribed on bronze and placed in front of his mausoleum in Rome. Whereas the mausoleum was despoiled by the Goths, who left no more than a cylinder of scrubby brick, miraculously the Ankara inscription survives, albeit in need of conservation: the Monumentum Ancyranum is the most complete version in existence.

The city reached its zenith once the Roman capital had been moved from Rome to Constantinople. It became a summer resort for early Byzantine emperors escaping the heat of the capital, and was famous for its race meetings and gladiatorial contests, which were sponsored in part by the temple priesthood, as inscriptions in the temple bear witness.

The best place to understand some of the changes that were made to the temple during its long history is in the interior of the inner chamber (*cella*). Whether it had been converted into a Christian church by the mid-sixth century or was still open for Christian worship during the Crusaders' eighteen-year spell of occupation in the thirteenth century, or closed by the time the Ottoman sultan Beyazıt I was captured by the Turco-Mongol conqueror Tamerlane (Timur) during the Battle of Ankara in 1402, is anyone's guess. But twenty-five years later a shrine dedicated to the founder of the Sufi dervish sect, Hacı Bayram-ı Veli, originally known as Numan of Koyunluca, was built with reused stone against the temple/church's south face. Seljuk in style, with a wood-and-plaster *mihrab*, or prayer niche, the mosque was restored during the sixteenth century by none other than the legendary imperial Ottoman architect Sinan, before being embellished in the eighteenth century with Kütahya tiles.

The significance of Ankara's principal monument was revealed by the Flemish writer and herbalist Ogier Ghiselin de Busbecq. In Angora during his tour of Galatia in 1557, as Habsburg envoy to the court of Süleyman the Magnificent, Busbecq discovered Augustus's *Res Gestae*, long lost from the emperor's mausoleum in Rome but remembered and confirmed through the writings of the Roman historian Suetonius. Thanks to Busbecq's publication of his important discovery, the temple was frequently visited over the centuries by classical scholars. Fortunately, a plan for the temple's most dramatic reuse was averted in 1834 – one of the dervish Hacı Bayram's more prosperous descendants wished to convert the monument into a private

Below and opposite The Julian Column today and in 1884, when it was mistakenly called 'Pompey's Pillar' by the archaeologist John Henry Haynes

bathhouse attached to the mansion he had built within the temple complex.

While the mosque has remained a centre of particular devotion – one of its nearby trees is often festooned with votive rags left by those imploring cures or pregnancies – the temple building has been put to a variety of uses, even for a time as a storeroom for the infant Museum of Anatolian Civilisations. In our own time, the municipality has installed a decorative water feature, complete with illumination in coloured lights. This is not the only threat to the monument – corrosive lignite is again being burned for heating in old Ankara.

Pompeys pillar in Angora

Hay AC. 151

THE JULIAN COLUMN

The history of the Julian Column will never be known for certain. It is merely assumed that it was built in honour of Emperor Julian, who passed through Ancyra in AD361. Busbecq failed to mention it; his travelling companion, Dernschwam, was the first to describe the high base and flutes parallel to the ground. Thereafter all travellers mention it: Tournefort in 1701 said that the Turks believed the column to be the tombstone of a girl, which was why it was called Belkıs; in 1740 Pococke related it to an inscription in the city walls honouring Julian; Mordtmann in 1859 mentioned a marble column with a Corinthian capital. Intriguingly, John Henry Haynes, the American archaeologist, photographed it as 'Pompey's Pillar' in 1884.

In 1934, by then leaning dangerously in its original position beside what is now the İş Bank, it was dismantled and moved northwards. Today the monumental white-grey limestone column stands on a platform of andesite blocks in Hükümet (Government) Square.

Texier had given the number of drums as fifteen, but photographs show that, after the 1934 move, one was lost. It was not the only loss. The presence of a stork's nest on top of the column and concrete poured in 1934 onto the abacus plate make it impossible to search for any trace of a statue. Given that statues on monumental columns were usually made of bronze, it can be assumed that there used to be a bronze statue of an emperor on the top of this one. But was it Julian?

THE CARACALLA BATHS

The remains of the so-called Caracalla Baths, connected to the Temple of Augustus by a roadway flanked by second- and third-century grey-veined marble columns with Corinthian capitals, stand on the foundations of Ancyra's earliest mound, or *höyük*. Although the existence of the city's bathhouse had been confirmed to nineteenth-century travellers by an inscription recording the generosity of a third-century temple priest, its discovery in 1925 occurred by chance, when the site was designated for the new capital's ministry of national defence. To flatten the hill, the ruins of an unidentified structure – extensive remains of arches and walls rising to some thirty feet – were

The hypocaust system used to heat the 'apodyterium', or changing room, in the Roman baths, completed in 217. The building was financed by the temple priest Tiberius Julius Justus Junianus and given to the city to celebrate Caracalla's visit

dynamited, revealing the foundations of a sizeable bathhouse. Once the rubble had been disposed of as infill for the mosquito-infested swamp below the *höyük*, the site was abandoned, the ministry being built elsewhere.

The first scientific excavation of the baths began in 1931 and continued for more than a decade. Coins established that the building dates to Emperor Caracalla, whose visit to Ancyra was suitably marked at a time when Roman citizens lavished their wealth on civic projects. Archaeological evidence shows that the baths remained in use until the eighth century, when they were destroyed by fire, leaving only the basement and first floor.

For today's visitor, all that can be seen are the baths' impressive foundations: a classical complex built around three principal rooms: *caldarium*, *tepidarium* and *frigidarium*. The impressive *palaestra* (wrestling court) is surrounded by a portico with 128 marble columns (thirty-two on each side). Not a surprise to those who know how cold Ankara winters can be is the number of furnaces – eighteen in all – that were required to keep the *caldarium* hot during the cold months.

KALEİÇİ: THE TOWN WITHIN THE CITADEL WALLS

During an administrative reshuffle in 1522, the Citadel, or Kaleiçi, was separated from the Ottoman town. Until the First World War it continued to be the Christian quarter, where some of the konaks of Armenian merchants, who dealt initially in mohair and later in cotton, still survive. The ones most in need of urgent restoration are those built on the south-facing walls, best seen from the extension of the At Pazarı (Horse Market).

The rectangular Citadel, surrounded by seven gates and forty turrets, fifteen of them in the inner bailey, is a complex of inner and outer fortifications built within and around the cone of the volcano.

Perhaps unique in Anatolia, the Citadel continues to function as intended, providing shelter for a goodly section of the city's shifting populations. The demographic upheavals of the last decades of the nineteenth century, the First Balkan War in 1912–13, and the aftermath of the First World War affected all the ethnic communities crammed into the maze of alleys, connecting gardens and now-decaying merchant houses. But despite all this, and modern attempts to tidy it up, a village atmosphere survives.

THE SOUTH GATE

The Reverend Henry Van Lennep, an American proselytiser born into a well-known Levantine family from Izmir, whose first visit to Angora was in 1870, describes the main gate to the Citadel as 'made up of fragments of old buildings, chiefly marble [where] a broken lion stands on each side'. Surprisingly for one so observant, he missed the Persian inscription

One of the fifteen turrets of the Citadel's inner walls, where a village atmosphere survives still. The spolia are a rich resource for historians. Ancyra/Angora/Ankara has been a melting pot of incoming peoples since trade began

dated 1330 that hangs above it, declaring exemption from certain taxes in response to complaints from residents at the time when the Sufi-based urban fraternity of traders and craftsmen known as the Ahi were in charge of the city.

Over the past twenty-five years, pockets of semi-abandoned areas have been adopted by 'outsiders', who, bit by bit, have been trying to restore and convert the collapsing lath-and-plaster houses into restaurants and gift shops.

THE MAIN STREET

Van Lennep continued up 'the steep streets paved with trachyte to the open space between the upper part of the town and the fortifications of the Castle'. He remarked that 'remains of ancient art and splendor are met at every step, more so than in any town I have visited in this land... but they are only fragments... no building has resisted the destructive effects of time'. There is no mention of the dramatic right-angled dogleg approach into the inner fortifications: the American cleric was no military historian.

The splendour he is referring to is the medley of massive stone blocks bolstered with marble column drums, carved capitals, ornate pediments and decorative fragments brought in haste from the ruined city by desperate citizens following the Persians' catastrophic sack during the first quarter of the seventh century. Invasions were to wrack Anatolia during the eighth, ninth and tenth centuries. This fortification of the Citadel with any useful piece of marble, brick or stone was a response to the first of the Arab attacks following the Persian success, which had left the Byzantines defenceless and unprepared.

It would take far more time than the visitor will have to figure out which parts of which classical buildings are embedded in the walls. A key inscription near the keep announces that following the second Arab invasion, in AD859, the walls were rebuilt by the Byzantine Emperor Michael III. But it must be left to the trained epigrapher to grapple with the bulk of often half-hidden Latin and Greek inscriptions on the embedded fragments.

THE AT PAZARI, THE OLD HORSE MARKET

During the fifteenth, sixteenth and seventeenth centuries some dozen city caravanserais or *hans* – large inns with central courtyards – two of which now house outstanding museums, were built within spitting distance of each other in the old Horse Market, the At Pazarı, outside the South Gate in what was to become the heart of the Ottoman commercial district.

What induced the Ottomans to build these evidently expensive structures on the foundations of Roman Ancyra? Usually owned by charitable institutions, the *hans* were bonded warehouses, as well as lodgings patronised by visiting merchants there to buy, sell and store. They paid their dues accordingly and the owners turned a tidy profit.

Grain, leather, honey and dried fruits apart, the chief attraction was the increasingly profitable trade in a brand-new, strong, light, warm and enduringly beautiful fabric: mohair, known locally as *sof*. It was made from the long-fibred fleece of the Angora goat and became the major livelihood of Ankara in the fourteenth century, making the fortunes of its clothiers and the fraternity of craftsmen and traders known as the Ahi.

NEW LIFE FOR THE CARAVANSERAIS

Ankara's status as the important trading city it once was is best demonstrated by the size and function of the enchanting (and newly restored) seventeenth-century pink-brick Çukurhan on the west side of the At Pazarı, directly opposite the South Gate, the main gate into the Citadel. On a prime site within metres of Roman Ancyra's third-century wall and standing on the Roman water pipe supplying the lower town, it remained in continuous use from the seventeenth century until the building caught fire in 1950, destroying the interior, the contents and the livelihoods of a hundred or more shopkeepers. Patched and propped up, it limped on, harbouring traders in wool and grain for another four decades. Once the last of the struggling shopkeepers had closed his door in the late 1990s, the building was abandoned.

A decade later, a rotted, unstable ruin in danger of demolition, it was recognised as a building of enduring significance and placed on the 2007 World Monuments Fund's watch list of the 100 Most Endangered Sites in the World. It was saved by Çengelhan Inc, a company of the Rahmi M. Koç Foundation for Museology and Culture, which leased the *han* from the government on a twenty-nine-year basis.

Meticulously renovated, stone by stone, brick by brick, over a period of more than two-and-a-half years, it has now re-emerged as the well-managed Divan Çukurhan boutique hotel. Its nineteen rooms are ranged around a large courtyard, now covered in glass, allowing daylight to stream onto the warm, mottled raspberry of its brickwork.

The architecturally more important sixteenth-century Çengelhan, the leather merchants' caravanserai next to the Çukurhan, has now become a world-class institution, the Çengelhan Rahmi M. Koç Museum. Its great beauty is the unity of its form. Its exterior presents to the world a solid brick-and-stone front. But its stern structure protects an interior that is as refined as it is functional, offering in its architecture a split personality that perfectly reflects the genius of its creator... who some say is Mimar Sinan himself.

Endowed by Süleyman the Magnificent's son-in-law, the grand vizier Rüstem Pasha, and his favourite daughter, Mihrimah Sultan, an inscription

Byzantine Ankara's desperate response to the Arab invasions of the eighth, ninth and tenth centuries was to rebuild the walls with any useful piece of marble, brick or stone that could be carried up to the Citadel from the ancient classical city below

248 THE PALACE LADY'S SUMMERHOUSE

Opposite A twelve-branched bronze and silver stag made by the Hatti people of central Anatolia and dating to 2300 BC, found during the 1930s excavation of the royal tombs at Alacahöyük

Above Also from the Hatti culture, a steer in copper, bound and inlaid with silver and electrian, c 2500 BC. Both objects were used as finials for standards and are now in the Museum of Anatolian Civilisations

in the spandrel above the entrance dates it to 1522–23. Worth visiting for the building itself, the museum it has become boasts fourteen different departments, thirty-two exhibition rooms and more than twelve hundred objects covering everything from transport, aviation and agriculture to medicine. And still there is room for more exhibits in the vast stables beneath the building, which in its heyday would have accommodated the merchants' pack animals.

The only working *han* to retain its seventeenth-century form and two central gates is the Pilavoğlu Han, on nearby Hanlar Sokak (the Street of Hans). The *han* is one of Ankara's hidden jewels and offers the traditional combination of ateliers and inexpensive accommodation. The miracle is that it has never burnt down and still resounds to the sound of artisans at work in eighteen workshops around a peaceful central courtyard with limewashed adobe walls, which in summer is filled with sunshine and the scent of roses.

THE MUSEUM OF ANATOLIAN CIVILISATIONS

European Museum of the Year as long ago as 1997, the museum presents in chronological order an incomparable collection of Anatolian archaeology, from the Palaeolothic to the modern; this alone repays the effort of a visit to Ankara. It is housed in two fifteenth-century hans. Although neither building bears any inscription and both were put out of commission by the great fire of 1881, contemporary documents suggest that they were built between 1464 and 1471 by two of Mehmed the Conqueror's grand viziers to provide revenue for their charitable foundations in the new Ottoman capital, Istanbul, recently captured from the Byzantines.

It is worth examining the grand vizier Mahmud Pasha's stone *bedesten* (covered market), not just the objects displayed in it. There are ten domes above a central courtyard surrounded on two sides by vaulted arcades, originally providing shops and safe storage for the bazaar's valuables. As a classical rectangle, it could be said that it was the Ottoman answer to the Roman Forum, which it overlooks, having been built into the steep hillside below the city walls.

The square, two-storey Kurşunlu Han beside it is now the administrative section of the museum. Arcades on two sides of a central courtyard house twenty-eight rooms on the ground floor and thirty on the second, all complete with fireplaces and stabling for visitors' horses, camels and mules.

Modern visitors who take their archaeology at all seriously should be warned to time their visit to the museum carefully: the odd busload of tourists causes a little stir, but the laudable routine of visits by schoolchildren, brought in hordes to view the relics of the country's past, creates noise levels to rival any aviary.

Walking away from the At Pazarı down the picturesque streets lined with shops built among the ruins of the Roman town, two charming early mosques should not be missed. They were built when Ankara was the capital of the mohair trade and an independent city state.

The Ahi Şerafettin Mosque and Ahi Elvan Mosque were dedicated to the Ahi fraternity, or the *fütüvvet*, as they are called in an inscription in the Ahi Şerafettin Mosque. Their enchantingly decorated wooden ceilings are both supported by twelve wooden columns topped with recycled Corinthian capitals. The present Ahi Elvan Mosque is an early-fifteenth-century restoration. The Ahi Şerafettin (also known as the Aslanhane Mosque) dates to 1290; it has not been rebuilt and has a stunning *mihrab* (prayer niche) and *mimber* (pulpit), though it is currently closed for restoration. This is a reminder that, for over a century following the break-up of the Seljuk Empire, the semi-religious Ahi set up their own independent city state in Ankara, broadly comparable to a medieval mercantile republic in northern Europe.

The Ahi were one of many fraternities springing up among Türkmen settlers in medieval Anatolia. At a time when the wool trade was of immense importance they raised a uniquely valuable long-haired goat. These delicate animals, difficult to keep in damp climates, flourished on the dry plains about Ankara. Good husbandry, perhaps allied to local breeding methods, produced a singular long-horned goat with an exceptionally curly coat that was to become universally known as the Angora goat. Shorn in spring, a yearling's fleece was even finer than a two-year-old's; when spun and woven, it produced mohair, a beautiful fabric that resembled silk in its fineness but was tough and warm. The raw mohair was first washed, then home-spun on wooden spindles before being dyed, stretched and sized. The finished article was fit for sultans and commanded exceptional prices.

By the mid-fifteenth century, outsiders were moving into Angora to cash in on the new trade: silk weavers from Bursa and merchants from Venice, the Netherlands and Poland handled the international trade, shipping fabrics from Smyrna and Istanbul to Venice, Amsterdam and the Port of London. A *bedesten* (covered market) – now the Museum of Anatolian Civilisations – was built by one of Mehmed the Conqueror's grand viziers. European travellers started to visit the city. The Flemish diplomat Busbecq left the first eyewitness account of the dyeing of 'a cloth made of goat's wool', noting that 'the better sort of Turk in their old age is usually clothed with this sort of cloth. Süleyman [the Magnificent] himself used to wear wefts of it…'

By 1590 the population of Ankara was said to number 16,000; annual mohair production had reached 100,000 bolts; and there were over six hundred looms in 2,200 homes built along the narrow streets below the

Dedicated to the Ahi fraternity, the Ahi Elvan Mosque, with its twelve wooden columns, was restored in the early fifteenth century. It took its name from Ahi Elvan Mehmet Bey (1331–89)

Overleaf A Syro-Hittite relief in the Museum of Anatolian Civilisations, dating from the eighth or ninth century BC, and identifiable by the mitre-shaped headdress and fur-edged robe

Citadel and starting to cover the southern hillside. Strict enforcement of the export ban on raw, or even spun, mohair had ensured that the value added by turning it into one of the civilised world's most sought-after fabrics benefited the city alone. It seems to have been the English who first succeeded in breaching the monopoly. And then the goats themselves were successfully established in America, South Africa and Australia. By the time the spinning jenny made any cloth woven by wooden spindles uneconomic, the city of Angora was already in decline.

By the time the railway arrived in 1892, Angora had been largely superseded in all aspects of the mohair trade, even the market for the raw material. Bad harvests and malaria took their toll; frequent fires swept through the overcrowded trading quarters; unemployment inevitably led to a decline in population. Despite its strategic importance during the War of Independence – at one stage the roar of the fighting could be heard from the Citadel – Ankara was by 1923 a poor place awaiting another transformation.

The resurgence came with the transfer of the seat of government from Istanbul: not for the first but for the third time, the city became a capital.

Cornucopia Issue 47, 2012

Paris à la Turque

MUSÉE NISSIM DE CAMONDO

TREASURES OF A LOST DYNASTY

THE CAMONDO FAMILY, 'THE ROTHSCHILDS OF THE EAST', AMASSED
A FORTUNE IN TURKEY BEFORE MOVING TO PARIS IN 1869.
THERE, IN THE RUE DE MONCEAU, THEY ESTABLISHED AN EXQUISITE
COLLECTION OF EIGHTEENTH-CENTURY FRENCH ART, WHICH WAS
BEQUEATHED TO THE NATION IN 1935. TODAY THE MUSÉE NISSIM
DE CAMONDO IS ALL THAT SURVIVES OF THIS MAGNIFICENT BUT
SHORT-LIVED DYNASTY

*The nineteenth century
intrudes into the
bedroom of Nissim de
Camondo, the young
pilot in whose honour
his father, Moïse
Camondo, named the
museum. Above the
delicate Directoire bed
hangs a formal portrait
of Moïse's father, Count
Nissim de Camondo,
painted by Carolus
Duran in 1882*

*Previous pages
Turkish coffee at the
Hôtel de Lamballe,
Paris (Chapter 19)*

Every art-lover who has frequented the great galleries of Paris is familiar with the best of their Impressionist masterpieces. The more discriminating are almost as familiar with the exquisite collection of eighteenth-century work that embellishes the Nissim de Camondo Museum beside the Parc Monceau in the eighth *arrondissement*. Very few of them know that the fortune that endowed these great French national treasures originated in Istanbul.

In 1911 Isaac de Camondo left his vast collection of works of art, which included most particularly Japanese prints and Impressionist paintings – over 400 Utamaros and a glittering necklace of such jewels as Manet's *Le Fifre* and Monet's *Les Cathédrales de Rouen* – to the Louvre. Hung there for fifty years, as he had stipulated, they now adorn other great Paris galleries besides. In 1935, Isaac's cousin, Moïse de Camondo, bequeathed his house at 63 rue de Monceau to the Union Centrale des Arts Décoratifs. It was to be a memorial to his only son, killed flying a combat mission over the Western Front in 1917, at the age of twenty-five.

The contents of the Musée Nissim de Camondo were the fruit of a lifetime spent in the pursuit of perfection, collecting all that was finest of eighteenth-century French artefacts that came onto a flourishing art market. The house remains to this day as it was when Moïse died. Only the telltale fez which crowns a couple of portrait heads and a set of silver dishes bearing the

The family

Top row Founding father Abraham-Salomon Camondo (c. 1780–1873), with his daughter-in-law. He died in Paris but was given a state funeral in Istanbul

Bottom row The brothers Abraham-Béhor (1829–89) and Nissim (1830–89) moved the family to Paris in 1869. Both were ennobled by Victor-Emmanuel II

Opposite, top row Connoisseur cousins Isaac (1851–1911) and Moïse Camondo (1860–1935). Isaac's Impressionists went to the Louvre. Moïse created the Musée Nissim de Camondo

Opposite, bottom row End of the dynasty: Moïse's son Nissim (1892–1917) was killed in action. His daughter, Béatrice (1894–1945), died with her children and husband, Léon, at Auschwitz

tuğra, or imperial cipher, of Sultan Abdülmecid betray a Turkish connection; they must have come with the Camondos when they moved to Paris from Istanbul in 1869.

Known in their Constantinople days as 'the Rothschilds of the East', the Camondos were Sephardic Jews whose forebears had been expelled from Spain in 1492 and found shelter in the Ottoman Empire. The first we hear of them is when a merchant called Camondo with a price on his head fled to Trieste from Istanbul in 1782. That renegade's son was back in the Ottoman capital a mere two years later to repair the family fortune. They remained 'Jews among Jews', traders undistinguished from the rest of a 6,000-strong community, until the banking house founded in Istanbul in 1802 by Isaac Camondo began to flourish.

Isaac, one of many victims of the plague in 1832, was the first of the Camondo dynasty to be either boundlessly rich or wondrously cultivated, or both. Over the next 113 years they made their mark on Western Europe as well as Turkey, changed nationality four times and ended in tragic oblivion in Auschwitz in the closing months of the Second World War. Ill fortune and, in marked contrast to their friends and banking rivals the Rothschilds, lack of sons contributed to nemesis.

The foundations laid by Isaac were rapidly built on by his remarkable surviving brother, Abraham-Salomon. Already nearly fifty when he took sole control of the bank, Isaac Camondo et Cie, he was to live to ninety-two, dying in Paris as an Italian citizen, having started a Venetian and been for a time Austrian before becoming Italian when Venice joined the new Italy.

Pious and astute, Abraham-Salomon was both a dedicated Westerniser who became indispensable as adviser, banker and friend to Sultan Abdülmecid's great reforming viziers, the pashas Reşid, Fuat and Aali, and a modernising philanthropist to the empire's Jewish community. The curriculum at the school he founded for poor Jewish boys in the Hasköy district of Istanbul, intended to teach them Turkish and some French, led to vehement dispute with the conservative rabbis, who favoured Ladino, the dialect of the Sephardis, and strict rabbinical control. Abraham-Salomon, acknowledged head of both the Austrian and Jewish lay communities, even found himself for a time expelled from the religious community.

His great achievement may well have been his role in persuading the Ottoman government to implement the reforms of 1839, which granted the minorities equal civil rights. Abraham-Salomon enthusiastically promoted Jewish education to qualify boys for service in the Ottoman administration, but his interest was not exclusively philanthropic. The Camondos were to become the largest landowners in Istanbul: real-estate development of the old Genoese quarter of Galata became a second pillar to the family's expanding fortune. The Bosphorus steam ferries, the building of the Galata Bridge and the tramways were among the public works for which they arranged the financing. The bank's premises and the family's Galata residence at 6 rue Camondo, with its glassed-in winter garden, dated from the same period. So, too, did the Art Nouveau-style curving stairway, which led down from the house to what is now Bankalar Caddesi. This stairway is one of the few traces of the Camondo name left in modern Istanbul. These steps, known as the Camondo Merdivenleri, are still used daily as a convenient shortcut up the steep slope towards the schools round the Galata Tower.

The Camondos lived in style. Abraham-Salomon's country house was in Asia, on the heights of Çamlıca, with views down the Bosphorus to Seraglio Point and the Golden Horn so stunning that tradition has it that it was the place to which the Devil took Jesus to show him 'all the kingdoms of the world and the glory of them'. It was in the Çamlıca house, with its twenty-two rooms and vast pavilion commanding the famous view, that Abraham-Salomon entertained lavishly and sealed many of his banking deals.

Simultaneously escaping the summer heat, his grandsons Abraham-Béhor and Nissim moved to adjoining waterside summerhouses in Yeniköy, on the European side of the Bosphorus. Not for them the usual seasonal removal of furniture from the city to equip summer residences; all Camondo houses were fully provided for, and the grounds were said to be so full of flowers that the gardeners made a good second income from selling the surplus.

Yet in 1869 the family abandoned Istanbul for Paris. Why? The prime cause seems to have been the change in financial markets in the aftermath of the Crimean War. The Camondo bank had played a prominent part in financing Ottoman participation in that struggle. After the war the raising of funds for an increasingly indebted Ottoman administration shifted decisively to Paris. The attitude of the reactionary Istanbul rabbinate may have played its part. So, doubtless, did the influence of the new generation, for Abraham-Salomon was now an octogenarian. He was to die in Paris in 1873 but was buried in the family vault at Hasköy after an Ottoman state funeral. His only son seems never to have been active in business, and we know little of him other than that he fathered two sons himself. These two, Abraham-Béhor and Nissim, were by the end of the Crimean War in their thirties and playing prominent roles in the family's affairs. Though their grandfather proudly held Turkish and Austrian decorations, it was Abraham-Béhor and Nissim who were created hereditary counts by King Victor Emmanuel II of Italy.

Abraham-Béhor, in particular, inherited his grandfather's genius for business. Unlike their grandfather, however, the brothers spoke French and, from 1866, the bank's books were kept in French, rather than Italian or Hebrew as before. They investigated the options of moves to either Alexandria

'Les Camondo ou l'éclipse d'une fortune' by Nora Şeni and Sophie Le Tarnec was published by Actes Sud in 1997

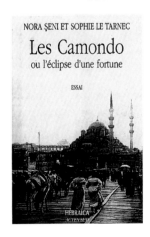

or London before deciding on Paris. It was the taller, more handsome Nissim who made the reconnaissance visits – and he who escorted the Empress Eugénie when she visited Istanbul on her way to the opening of the Suez Canal in 1869. But it was the stockier, cleverer Abraham-Béhor who handled the banking rivalries in Galata and took the key decisions.

The resourcefulness of the elder brother saw the Camondos through the chaos of the Paris Commune in 1870, when they moved to London to stay with the Sassoons. In the aftermath of the Franco-Prussian War the bank profited by funding the indemnity payments to the Germans.

The brothers were evidently inseparable. As in Istanbul, they acquired adjoining plots on rue de Monceau in Haussmann's remodelled Paris. Abraham-Béhor built a fashionable town house at No 61, while Nissim moved into the less ostentatious *hôtel* that already existed at No 63. Their joint ambition had at least three aspects: modernising the bank and giving it international scope, establishing themselves in French high society, and building collections, initially centred on Far Eastern art. They largely succeeded – despite the virulent anti-Semitism of the period. But their plans were nearly derailed disastrously in 1855, when Abraham-Béhor's son-in-law, scion of another Istanbul Jewish family and director of the bank, failed to cover his positions on the London and Paris exchanges, losing sums that in today's money would rival the losses suffered by Barings Bank in 1994. Father-in-law paid up, but the family fortunes never completely recovered.

The two devoted brothers died in 1889, each leaving one son. These first cousins, perhaps mindful of the disaster of 1885, were retrenchers rather than expansionists. Both were more interested in the arts than in business. Abraham-Béhor's son, Isaac, who acted as Turkish consul general in Paris in the 1890s, shut the Istanbul branch of the bank in 1894, and retrenched even in Paris so as to indulge to the full his love of music and his passion for collecting. He never married and it was the Louvre that benefited on his death in 1911, not least from the fruits of his patronage of the then unappreciated Impressionists. The ambitions of his cousin Moïse, Nissim's son and nine years Isaac's junior, were equally unbusinesslike. Meticulous and perfectionist, his marriage foundering, his passion was exclusively eighteenth-century France. He bought liberally, but only the best, amassing pictures, furniture, tapestries, ceramics and *objets* of every description, including panelling and wainscots.

If Moïse was reticent in business, he did not lack boldness in aesthetic matters or a clear-sighted ability to visualise the detail of a finished appearance. On his mother's death in 1910, all the buildings but the gatehouse of No 63 rue de Monceau were pulled down and all the contents of the house sold. It was unsuitable for displaying the ensemble of treasures Moïse had amassed, and he had challenged the architect René Sergent, noted for his work at Claridge's and the Savoy, to draw up plans for a completely new Neoclassical mansion to incorporate the best of his artefacts, some of which dictated the shapes of specific rooms, together with every technical sophistication and comfort of the time. Inspired by Ange-Jacques Gabriel's Petit Trianon at Versailles, Sergent's drawings satisfied even Moïse's expectations. Over the next three years the oblong parcel of land beside the Parc Monceau, with its valuable alleyway leading to the boulevard Malesherbes, was a construction site.

As with the Petit Trianon, the new, L-shaped building was raised regardless of expense, on three levels between courtyard and garden. Practical, intimate, modern, comfortable and very grand, the finishing touches to its complete success are the sweeping exterior staircases joining the main rooms with the garden, and the enchanting oval rooms that are the house's heart and focus. Whereas the great rooms catch the sun and enjoy the garden, the house is insulated from smell and sound in the service areas, and domestic life flows in and out, unseen from the boulevard Malesherbes.

Moïse moved in on the eve of the First World War, which was to shatter his world through the death in action of his only son, Nissim. Increasingly introspective in the eighteen years that remained to him, Moïse continued to embellish the house and garden, fastidiously arranging every object himself.

How long before his death in 1935 Moïse decided to leave the house as a museum to his son's memory we do not know. Nissim's surviving sister, Béatrice – who, like her husband, Léon, was a French citizen and a Christian – and their two children were already provided for. Or so it seemed, even under the Occupation. But in 1942 all four were imprisoned at Drancy. Léon and the children were shipped to Auschwitz in November 1943, Béatrice in March 1944. None survived.

Cornucopia Issue 26, 2002

Bertrand (1923–43) and Fanny (1920–43), the children of Moïse de Camondo's daughter Béatrice and Léon Reinach. The family only moved out of what is now the museum when Bertrand was born. All died at Auschwitz

Treasures of a Lost Dynasty

A homage to Neoclassicism built to display a
world-class collection of eighteenth-century art

The Hôtel Camondo
at 63 rue de Monceau,
now the Musée Nissim
de Camondo, was
built by Count Moïse
de Camondo to display
his eighteenth-century
French art collection.
René Sergent, the
French architect who
refurbished both
Claridge's and the
Savoy, modelled it on
the Petit Trianon at
Versailles. Plans were
submitted in 1912
and the house was
ready in 1914
Opposite the garden's
formal parterres

*Overleaf
The sweeping
theatrical staircase
has wrought-iron
balustrades copied
from a house in
Toulouse. Moïse
de Camondo himself
placed the lacquer
corner cabinet (one*

*of a pair, c. 1750) on
the half-landing.
The marble statue of
Venus and Eros is also
mid-eighteenth century*

Opposite The oval
room in the centre of
the house, known as
the Salon des Huet, was
designed by Sergent
around a set of pastoral
scenes by Jean-Baptiste
Huet (1745–1811).
They fit perfectly
into the panelling,
from Toulouse

Right A seventeenth-
century Gobelin
tapestry bearing
the arms of France
dominates the staircase

Left A 'duchesse brisée' chair and stool catch the afternoon sun in the Blue Drawing Room. Created by Moïse in 1923, it replaced his daughter Béatrice's apartments. She married Léon Reinach in 1919 but they lived in the house until the birth of their second child

Opposite On the bright pink walls of the Small Study hang a set of sketches by Jean-Baptiste Oudry for tapestries of Louis XV hunting. Two 'biscuit' medallions of Louis XVI hang above the eighteenth-century 'ottomane' sofa

Opposite The Porcelain Room, where Moïse ate when he was alone. His eighteenth-century Sèvres has a long history. It is part of a service given to the British envoy in Paris in 1789, sold to the Prince Regent and bought by the Rothschilds. Moïse collected fifty-four pieces. The silver dish bears the cipher of Sultan Abdülmecid

This page The size of the oval library and even its windows were dictated by the oak panelling, which came from various eighteenth-century houses in France

*Above Bankalar
Caddesi, the 'street
of banks' in Istanbul,
which the Camondos
redeveloped*

*Above right
Abraham-Béhor and
Nissim Camondo
built adjoining yalıs in
prosperous Yeniköy,
on the European shore
of the Bosphorus.
In the distance is the
Kalender Kasrı, a small
seaside palace built by
Sultan Abdülaziz*

*Opposite The
Camondo Steps in
Galata led from the
old family house down
to Bankalar Caddesi.
Almost no other trace
of the Camondo name
survives in the city*

FROM LUNACY TO DIPLOMACY

THE HÔTEL DE LAMBALLE WAS HOME TO A DOOMED PRINCESS
AND AN ASYLUM FOR MAD ARTISTS BEFORE IT BECAME TURKEY'S
EMBASSY IN PARIS. IN 1945 THE YOUNG NEVİN MENEMENCİOĞLU
CAME UPON THE ELEGANT MANSION IN THE SIXTEENTH
ARRONDISSEMENT WHEN SHE WAS SEARCHING THE CITY FOR
A BUILDING WHERE HER UNCLE, THE TURKISH AMBASSADOR,
COULD SET UP HIS MISSION

*A plaque from an
earlier Ottoman
Embassy in Paris now
displayed in the
library of the Hôtel
de Lamballe, the
Turkish Embassy in
Paris since 1945
Opposite The graceful
Neoclassical hall*

The fabled Hôtel de Lamballe, above the right bank of the Seine in the old hamlet of Passy, is as charming as any building in the city. And it surely boasts a more varied and tempestuous past than any other building in the staid sixteenth *arrondissement*. The acquisition of the Hôtel de Lamballe by the Turkish government in 1945 was something of a coup, engineered in part by a determined young woman of twenty-three named Nevin Menemencioğlu. Her uncle, Numan Menemencioğlu, Turkey's distinguished wartime foreign minister and later its forty-fourth accredited envoy to France, had arrived in the recently liberated French capital to reopen the embassy, closed in 1943 by his predecessor, Şevki Berker, who had been obliged to move to Vichy with Marshal Pétain's government. For the first year Numan Bey and his small entourage, which included his niece Nevin and her young daughter, Ayşegül, were housed in the war-weary Bristol Hotel.

It was Nevin who, scouring the city on foot for a suitable building for their needs, came quite by chance across the Hôtel de Lamballe. Lying empty, it had only recently been vacated by the Americans, who had taken it for General Eisenhower in the expectation that he would direct the invasion of Germany from Paris. On the insistence of his niece, Ambassador Menemencioğlu leased the great *hôtel* from the French government and by the end of 1945 they had moved in, with the chancery offices installed in what is now the music room. It was through his friendship with General de Gaulle that Turkish ownership of the property was won in 1951 – a unique *quid pro quo* for France's fine embassy in Ankara's Paris Caddesi.

The severely classical façade of the *hôtel* extends fully forty metres along a paved terrace overlooking gardens that once ran right down to the banks of the Seine. Most of the land had been sold in 1922, and today roads, apartment blocks and the Maison de la Radio stand between the embassy and the river. Classical grandeur still reigns in the great entrance hall, which stretches half the length of the house on the north side, but Turkish furnishings and Turkish *objets* soften the severity of the four main reception rooms that lead off it and overlook the *parterres*. Indeed, since the Second World War, a succession of ambassadors have given the place an authentically Franco-Turkish aura.

The origins of this grand stone building date from the early eighteenth century, when the Duc de Lauzan erected a two-storey house, with dormered mansard roof, on the foundations of a fifteenth-century convent. Although extensively rebuilt in the 1920s, the core of Lauzan's imposing house survives, as does the double flight of nineteen stone steps that sweeps down to the garden from the terrace. Perhaps the disreputable widower duke, who soon tired of both his new house and the new young bride for whom he had built it, frequented the summerhouse below the terrace. Scallop-shaped and paved with a mosaic of pebbles, this cave-like room still houses Lauzan's pink marble fountain, fed by one of the garden's many springs.

Nothing remains of the decorative brick of which the records speak, or of the pigeon house, chapel and orangery. The magnificent marble basin opposite the front door, now framed in ivy, is a last vestige of the Duc de Lauzan's bathhouse. The *hôtel* itself, like the eponymous avenue which skirts its garden on the southern side, owes its name to the eight-year residence of the Princesse de Lamballe, blameless (if brainless) friend of Marie Antoinette and one of the most poignant victims of the French Revolution. She acquired the Folie Lauzan, as it was then called, in 1783. She was thirty-four and had been a widow since the age of nineteen.

The Princesse de Lamballe's death was a nasty episode even by the standards of the Terror. She was diminutive, her feet so small that when a pair of her green silk slippers was found after her murder they wondered whether even Cinderella could have fitted into them. Prised from the side of the imprisoned Queen, she was lynched and her body dragged through the streets while her severed head was paraded on the point of a pike. Something of the tragedy can still, it is said, be sensed in the paved *allée* leading to the house from the handsome wrought-iron gates that open onto the rue d'Ankara. It is known as the allée Marie-Antoinette, but there is no evidence that the murder took place there.

With the Terror over, the house was sold by the dead princess's nephew to Citizen Joseph Baguenault. Thereafter it remained in that family, let and sublet until house, park and grounds were sold off in lots in 1922. During the Second Empire it had been leased as a clinic to a succession of doctors, housing residents markedly more famous, if admittedly less poignant, than the princess, whose only real distinction was the manner of her death.

Worldly and fashionable Parisians were familiar for seventy years with the clinic of the Doctors Blanche and Meuriot to which those of their number who suffered from serious nervous disorders were committed. The poet Gérard de Nerval was admitted to the clinic in 1854, only two years after his happy visit to Istanbul with Théophile Gautier. He seems to have been driven mad chiefly by the task of translating Goethe's *Faust* into French. Four years later the composer Charles Gounod was taken in while struggling with the composition of his opera *Faust*, based on Nerval's translation. And in January 1892, the writer Guy de Maupassant, reduced to final despair by recurring bouts of syphilis, was committed in a straitjacket. A year later, a month short of his forty-third birthday, he died on the upper floor of the house.

When the estate was broken up in 1922, the house was bought by the Comte de Limur and his American wife, Madeleine. A single, fateful blow of a workman's pickaxe during extensive reparations reputedly caused the collapse of the entire garden façade. Fortunately, Madame de Limur possessed a considerable fortune; undaunted, she undertook a ten-year campaign of complete reconstruction. She even added a large dining room, set functionally beside new, up-to-date kitchen facilities. Finally, she employed the then fashionable interior decorator Monsieur Sauvage to oversee the refurbishment.

The house was returned to its former glory in good time to be requisitioned by the Gestapo after the fall of Paris in 1940, before the Limurs were able to enjoy it. Although much of the valuable furniture had been removed, the Germans found a veritable treasure house, the drawing room exquisitely panelled in carved wood taken from the Tuileries Palace, where it had been Louis XV's gift to his mistress, the Marquise de Pompadour. It remains in situ; the house was neither looted nor defaced by the occupiers.

In 1972 the Turkish government erected a compact chancery building in the northwest corner of the grounds, in the lee of the hill, where the clinic's kitchen gardens had been. The music room, freed once again to fulfil its proper function, duly acquired a grand piano. But the most striking decorations of this plum-coloured room are the eight brilliantly disturbing works of the Turkish artist Fikret Muallâ. He died in Paris in 1967, knee-deep in debt, having lived three decades 'in the mouth of the lion' and parted with a painting every now and then in recognition of the help successive ambassadors afforded him.

As if to celebrate the dawn of the twenty-first century, the whole building underwent a meticulous three-year renovation that even included the statues in the garden. Only the great hall, with its huge, folding glass entrance doors, shimmering white walls of newly cleaned *pierre de France*, and freshly restored Beauvais tapestries, seems largely untouched by Turkish influence.

Being a true eighteenth-century house, it has no grand central stairway. Unobtrusively elegant, a stairwell, complete with wrought-iron banisters, is tucked away at the west end of the hall, while the milky-white marble of a sculpted goddess dominates from the eastern extremity. Doors lead off the hall into the main rooms, which might have been even grander had the Limurs not removed their best pieces when the Second World War broke out, and had the Turkish government had the funds to buy more than a proportion of the contents when it acquired the building. But it might then have sacrificed the blend of French and Turkish which is now its great charm.

The panelled drawing room has a rare collection of Ottoman pieces, as well as a good example of the paintings of the Turkish Impressionist Şevket Dağ. The Ottoman work includes a seventeenth-century embroidered panel, its silver filigree worked into the finest Bursa silk, hanging above a Dresden figure of a Janissary. A crystal *lokumluk* – sweetmeat dish – sits on a distinguished Koran stand. Here, as elsewhere, the carpets fully maintain Turkey's reputation: a particularly ravishing Hereke rug takes pride of place.

It feels entirely right that a portrait of Madame de Limur, the great benefactress of the house, who devoted a decade and much treasure to it yet never herself lived there, should be prominently hung in the drawing room. In the library, among her famous collection of books, most of which happily remain in the house, is the Turkish throne-chair specially commissioned and carved for Sultan Abdülaziz when he visited Paris in 1863 – ahead of the Empress Eugénie's celebrated stay in Istanbul on her way to the opening of the Suez Canal. No one lucky enough to be invited into the Limurs' harmonious dining room can avoid being awestruck by the four huge candelabra that were also commissioned for Sultan Abdülaziz's visit. They are the first to have been made by the celebrated Parisian silversmith Christofle.

Many stories have been written about the building of the embassies that crown the tops and cling to the slopes of Ankara's Çankaya hills. Much less is heard of the remarkable collection of Turkish embassy buildings around the world. Some are the legacy of Turkey's past, and of these the Hôtel de Lamballe is among the finest. It owes nothing to Ottoman grandeur but much to the perspicacity of the young Turkish woman who found it for her uncle in 1945. For Nevin Menemencioğlu herself, the story had a happy ending. She was based in Paris for the rest of her life, much of it as cultural attaché at the Turkish Embassy. The Hôtel de Lamballe, in which she and her uncle's successors still live and work, is a fitting memorial to her.

Cornucopia Issue 30, 2003

The garden of the Duc de Lauzan's eighteenth-century 'folie', with its elegant double staircase, once ran all the way down to the Seine

Above The fountain from the bathhouse of the Folie Lauzan

Right A portrait of Madeleine, Comtesse de Limur, who saved the house, hangs in the drawing room. The fine panelling was a gift from Louis XV to a mistress Far right The throne-chair made for the visit of Sultan Abdülaziz in 1863, the first state visit to Europe by a Turkish sovereign

The Grand Salon
is a celebration
of eighteenth-century
taste. The vases on
the ebony cabinets
belonged to Marie
Antoinette. The
Japanese lacquered
bronze bottle on
the circular table
was once Madame
de Pompadour's.
The marble bust is
by Houdon. The
Savonnerie carpet was
made in 1678 for the
Louvre's Great Gallery

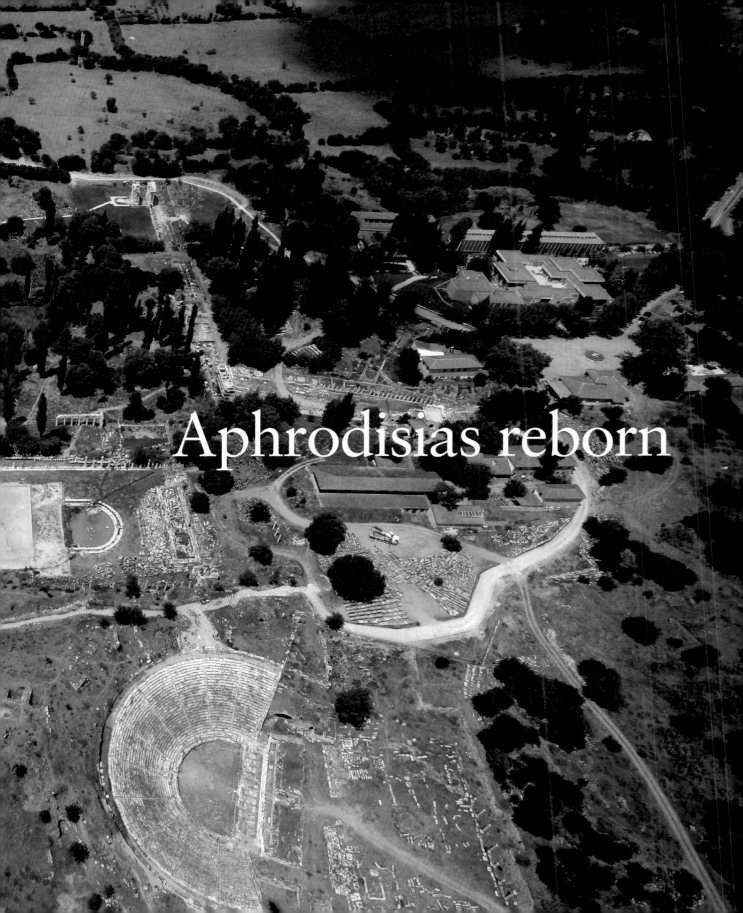

Aphrodisias reborn

EXCAVATING APHRODISIAS

CITY OF APHRODITE

ITS SCULPTORS WERE THE TOAST OF ANCIENT ROME. IT WAS
THE EMPEROR AUGUSTUS'S FAVOURITE CITY IN ASIA.
BUT FOR THE AUTHOR OF THIS BOOK, WHO HAS BEEN CLOSELY
INVOLVED WITH APHRODISIAS FOR THIRTY YEARS, IT MAY
SIMPLY BE THE MOST SEDUCTIVE CLASSICAL CITY IN
THE WORLD – AND IT IS STILL SURRENDERING ITS TREASURES

*An elite Aphrodisian
of the first century AD,
unearthed in 2005*

*Previous pages An
aerial view of the city
from the south. It was
not especially large, but
its monuments were
built on a massive scale
as a magnet for visitors.
The Theatre (right of
picture) held 8,000; the
Stadium (top) was
the largest in the
world. The giant pool
(centre) – revealed in
2016 and still being
excavated – was part of
'The Place of Palms', a
huge pleasure garden*

Aphrodisias is, they claim, the most beautiful of all the archaeological sites in western Turkey – arguably of the whole classical world. Lying some 230 kilometres east of Izmir in a valley watered by a tributary of the Upper Menderes (or Meander, ancient Maiandros), it is still relatively remote, though widening of roads, quarrying for marble and construction of new dams are changing the surrounding country.

Spectacular Graeco-Roman monuments adorn the city centre, some that have survived two millennia, others unearthed since excavations were begun in 1961, and yet others reassembled from the debris left by earthquakes. Nearly sixty years of continuous excavation is revealing the full extent of the grandeur of an inland city in the Eastern Roman Empire with a surprisingly long post-classical life which lingered into Ottoman times.

Excavation beneath the Acropolis mound during the 1960s unearthed settlements stretching back into the mists of time: Bronze Age, Chalcolithic, Neolithic. Ninoe, as the place was then known, was steeped in the tangled legends of western Asia Minor. As seat of the Carian deities and their sanctuary, from early time it attracted devotees of the fertility goddess. Sometime during the fourth or third century BC Ninoe was renamed Aphrodisias, or 'the city of Aphrodite', and the old sanctuary given some kind of temple, the vestiges of which still lie beneath the temple we see today.

The relative prosperity of the settlement and its temple was rudely interrupted during the dark days of the early first century BC when the cities of Asia Minor were caught between Roman occupier and Pontic invader from the Black Sea. Only when the sea battle of Actium in 31BC finally saw the end of the Roman Republic did Aphrodisias's loyalty to Rome bear fruit with Roman patronage and a surge of pilgrims to her temple.

Under the stability of the Roman Empire, Aphrodisias enjoyed an explosion of urban expansion. It owed much, as did the school of sculpture for which the city was to become famous throughout the Roman world, to the extensive quarries of much-prized marbles in the foothills of Babadağı (ancient Cadmus) two kilometres from the city centre. Sumptuous buildings – the late-first-century-AD Basilica was so massive that it took up three city blocks – were ornately decorated with depictions in marble of deities, emperors and local notables, as well as domestic and wild animals: the late Hellenistic city was transformed.

Seventeenth- and eighteenth-century travellers were the first to be interested by the wealth of Greek and Latin inscriptions and intrigued by the graffiti which abounded on the site. Sir Charles Fellows, setting out from Izmir in early March 1840 to record the 'beautiful city built wholly of white marble' for the London Dilettante Society, found incoming Turkomans had recently taken over the abandoned settlement that lay within walls that had encircled the Graeco-Roman city. Red-roofed lath-and-plaster houses, men, women, children, dogs, sheep and goats now huddled amongst the ruins. The fertility of the soil and the abundance of water had attracted them to settle; the village had been renamed Geyre (a modulation of ancient Caria). Of Aphrodisias's former glory the new inhabitants knew nothing.

In 1904 the Ottoman statesman and head of antiquities Osman Hamdi Bey put a stop to excavations in the Hadrianic Baths – by the French railway engineer, Paul Gaudin – and the outbreak of the Second World War interrupted excavation by an Italian archaeological team. The work of unearthing, recording, conserving and restoring the marvels now evident on the site and displayed in a purpose-built museum had to wait until 1961, when the project was put in the hands of New York University (NYU). Over the following fifty-six years just two scholars have directed the project to achieve this.

Aphrodisias is unusual in owing much of its Roman splendour to a single benefactor, one Gaius Julius Zoilos. Inscriptions confirm that, echoing the city's political aspirations and devotion to the emperors, the initial building spree was financed by this remarkable Aphrodisian, who had been enslaved, possibly by Julius Caesar himself. Inherited and freed by Octavian (later Caesar Augustus), he made a triumphant return to Aphrodisias around 38BC. The former slave in the Roman imperial service was now a city oligarch.

Appointed high priest of Aphrodite, Zoilos secured the boundaries of the goddess's sanctuary, endowed the cult and paid for a new marble temple. He was also responsible for a new stage building for the Theatre, a grand marble portico for the North Agora and much else besides. The oligarch's munificence was commemorated by a series of sculpted panels that adorned his tomb. In 1958 a magazine article on Turkey showed a photograph of Geyre villagers banking an irrigation channel with these useful panels. Professor Kenan Erim, a Turkish archaeologist at NYU excavating that summer in Italy, said that that photograph first whetted his appetite for pioneering work at Aphrodisias. The Zoilos Frieze is now displayed in the museum's main passageway, probably no more than a stone's throw from where it was unearthed.

During the 1960s, the first-century Theatre was cleared of the spoil that completely filled it, and the village houses perched on the eastern slope of the Acropolis were removed. The Hellenistic-style Theatre was found to have been considerably modified when gladiatorial fights and contests with wild beasts became fashionable under Rome. Excavation brought to light Zoilos's elaborate three-storey stage building, together with a big cache of statues now in the museum. The jewel in the crown was a pair of boxers, complete, life-size statues of athletic victors of the third century AD [page 292]. Mature and muscular in their nudity, they are bare-knuckled, with leather thongs wrapped around the full length of their arms.

On the east wall of the Zoilos stage building, the Aphrodisians later proudly inscribed an astonishing collection of documents bearing witness to their city's special relationship with Rome. These imperial letters record the grants of autonomy, immunity from taxation, and asylum rights for the shrine of Aphrodite. The inscription begins with a majestic testimonial, incised in exquisite Greek lettering, from the Emperor Augustus when he was Octavian the Triumvir, naming Aphrodisias the one city in all Asia he had selected as his own. The texts on this 'Archival Wall' suffered slight later adjustment: when the Aphrodisians converted to Christianity during the fifth century AD, the pious denizens renamed their city Stavropolis (City of the Cross) and had most visible mentions of the pagan goddess Aphrodite chiselled out.

Repair and reopening to public access of the finest, grandest and largest of the city's pair of bathhouses, the Hadrianic Baths, was completed in 2016. A surprise find during that season was a bronze coin of the early seventh century beneath restored paving in the central *caldarium*, or hot room, suggesting that the Christian citizens of mid-Byzantine Aphrodisias were still affluent enough to afford expensive repairs to keep both aqueduct and furnaces functioning in the old Roman bathhouse. It is a building of a light freshwater limestone, once splendid with marble revetment on the walls and striking for its complicated underground service corridors, complete with furnaces and water channels. The decoration of the forecourt of the *palaestra* (wrestling school), with its large piers carved with figures of Eros hunting animals

animals intertwined in scrolls of acanthus leaves, is unmistakably Aphrodisian.

When Aphrodite's Temple is surrounded by carpets of spring anemones, though greatly changed since Zoilos's day, it is much as Fellows saw it in 1840. It had been in due course converted into a church, with a massively engineered reordering of its structure to provide roof, apse, nave, aisles and narthex. When you sit on one of the fallen marble pillars, the outlines of the temple as well as the church are still evident in this once holy place.

Before entering by the West Gate, Fellows noted a 'mile of ornately sculpted marble sarcophagi lining either side of the road'. Some of these now line the pathways and ring the museum, introducing us to generations of Aphrodisian families seen through the eyes of gifted and original artists whose style of sculpture has been termed 'mannerist', even 'baroque'.

The spectacular first-century Stadium to the north of the West Gate is the finest complete example of its kind to survive from antiquity. In the AD350s city walls were hastily built against its northern line. Two curved ends and sides bowed out to form an ellipse ensure all spectators an unobstructed view of the entire field. It measures an astonishing 270 metres in length. Whilst the city had a population of some 8,000, the thirty tiers of seating are capable of accommodating 30,000 – though a notable adaptation in the east end was evidently made to accommodate gladiatorial fights and contests with wild animals following the city's decline. No ancient building at Aphrodisias escapes a share of telltale graffiti. In the Stadium, not only graffiti but cuttings for awnings, masons' marks and inscriptions for reserved seats, which include women's names, survive: a book on its own.

The Aphrodisians were notably keen on ostentatious gateways, particularly when embellishing their city's main thoroughfare running north-south through the city centre: the Tetrapylon Street. The monumental Tetrapylon is the most northerly monument revealed so far – a gateway leading westward into the holy precinct of the Temple of Aphrodite. It is of astonishing grandeur. Some could say it is overly grand. Whatever is said, this remarkable gateway with its four rows of four columns of mixed marbles simply defines religious and public space. Further south, the Propylon, at the entrance into the Sebasteion, a temple complex dedicated to the emperors and Aphrodite, lacks the elaborate decoration and the grey marble barley-sugar columns of the Tetrapylon; for all that, it boasted life-size statues of Roman nobility. Rebuilding of the Propylon's main structure was completed in 2016, less eye-catching but no less interesting than the 1990 reassembly (anastylosis) of the Tetrapylon itself.

The Sebasteion was the latest in architectural fashion in the first century – an almost Modernist, exhibitionist temple complex – dedicated to both Aphrodite and the Julio-Claudian emperors. It was paid for by two families and only discovered in 1979 beneath a line of cottages in Geyre. In the last decade, enough of it has been rebuilt, incorporating casts of sculpted panels of gods and emperors, to give an understanding of the lost temple and the precinct's ancient splendour as well as the Aphrodisians' dedication to the emperors – more so than to Aphrodite herself.

It is hoped that anastylosis of the imposing Agora Gate that leads from the Tetrapylon Street into the vast pleasure garden known as 'the South Agora' may follow. A verse inscription naming this complex 'The Place of Palms', found on a piece of fallen masonry belonging to the Agora Gate, gives its correct name. Excavation over the past five years has uncovered a grand urban park of a kind known to have been fashionable in imperial Rome; it is western Turkey's most unusual ancient complex. Its construction saw a massive engineering project paid for by local grandees and involved cutting back the theatre hill and supporting it with a massive twenty-metre-tall retaining wall to create enough flat space for a complex measuring 230 by 60 metres with some 500 metres of colonnaded porticoes around it. The bizarre sixth-century repairs to some of the columns' Ionic capitals might, however, have made an imperial architect blush. These long porticoes enabled Aphrodisians to stroll down avenues of palms – deep trenches revealed plantings for Cretan date palms (*Phoenix theophrasti*). The huge, waist-deep, artificially raised pool (175 metres long, 25 metres wide) had semicircular ends with fountains and double seating that allowed viewing either way.

Graffiti abound in Aphrodisias. The Place of Palms is no exception. In 2016, along with an unexpectedly intense find of post-antique medieval coins, broken marbles and one beautiful fragment of a Julio-Claudian male portrait, the most outstanding find was a sixth-century graffito on the pool edge commemorating one 'Kolotron, chief of the gold workers', accompanied by engraved busts of champion athletes, one wearing an elaborate victor's crown and the other – a much larger bust – of a thick-necked boxer or wrestler with a single lock of hair emerging from his otherwise clean-shaven head, hairstyle of the professional late-Roman heavy athlete. The graffitist himself is well known from other inscriptions in both Theatre and Stadium.

The first surprise during the 2016 excavation of the Tetrapylon Street came south of the Sebasteion's Propylon: a possibly mid-Byzantine bathhouse built partly across the street, unusual in itself and evidence of the city's adaptation in the face of contemporary stress. The second surprise was a large, veiled female portrait head, clearly of the early imperial period, discovered amongst fallen rubble north of the Propylon. It has an ideal Augustan physiognomy, with the tight 'melon' hairstyle of a beautiful young woman. Careful mounting of the head on a surviving statue found earlier nearby showed that the two belonged together. The statue was identified from the inscription on its base as 'Aemilia

Lepida, daughter of Marcus Lepidus'. Aemilia's statue once belonged to the famous statue display on the Propylon, which honoured more than fifteen princes and princesses of the extended Julio-Claudian family, all the way back to Aineias and Aphrodite. The Aphrodisians were of course not at all concerned about the scandalous hot gossip surrounding Aemilia's unhappy fate, and preserved the statue that honoured her on the Propylon until the seventh century.

Well born, the daughter of an aristocrat of long lineage – the powerful Tiberian senator Marcus Lepidus – Aemilia was married in AD23 to Drusus Caesar, who, with his brother, was designated imperial successor to the suspicious Tiberius Caesar. Seven years later both brothers were arrested on charges of treason, imprisoned and subsequently disposed of. Like her husband – whom, according to Tacitus, 'she had pursued with ceaseless accusations' – Aemilia also met her end in the high drama of Palatine politics. She remained unpunished, infamous as she was, for as long as her father lived but subsequently fell victim to the informers for 'adultery with a slave'. Tacitus adds 'there was no question about her guilt, so without an attempt at defence she put an end to her life'.

Each season's work by the archaeologists at Aphrodisias produces surprises and new treasures. Aemilia's beauty personifies all the emotions that Aphrodisias evokes in those bewitched by this ancient city. Striking male beauty had been unearthed in 2005: a miraculously well-preserved late-Antonine portrait head, this time of a young man of the local elite [page 286]. It was found on the floor of an important chamber at the south end of the Basilica. Such spectacular discoveries are but a part of the complex project pursued under the direction of Professor Bert Smith, of Oxford and New York Universities, who succeeded Kenan Erim as director in 1991.

Aphrodisias remains remarkably untouched by the intrusions of the twenty-first century. The heady spoils of over half a century of excavations are safely housed in the museum and its garden – ornately carved sarcophagi, the finest statuary by generations of local craftsmen, trial pieces from the sculpture workshop; and a whole new gallery has been added to display the seventy and more sculpted reliefs, in their original sequence, from the Sebasteion's north and south buildings. The teams of local villagers who have worked for decades with the architects and conservators are now highly skilled artisans – the new generation of Aphrodisians are conserving the artworks of their forebears.

Aphrodisias is smaller than Ephesus, less showy than Pergamum, less ancient than Sardis, yet it yields to none for addictive charm, a charm which is all to do with its atmosphere: millennial sanctity coupled with the splendour of ancient architecture and the finest marble statuary, in a site excavated with

Mature and muscular, statues of Piseas (top) and Candidianus, champion boxers on the international circuit, stood either side of the Theatre stage in late-Roman times. Both have partly shaved heads and are naked except for leather thongs round their arms

A poignant carving of Aion (Eternity) from the sarcophagus of Gaius Julius Zoilos, a former slave who became a great benefactor

subtle expertise. The site is still studded with vines, pomegranates, figs and mature stands of poplar. When the sun goes down and the moisture rises, red squirrels still chase each other's tails about the great plane tree with its roots entwined amongst the ruins of the Sebasteion's lost temple. Octavian the Triumvir rightly declared that, of all the cities in Asia, Aphrodisias was the one to be preferred.

Cornucopia Issue 56, 2017

*The Aphrodisians loved
ostentatious gateways
Above and right The heavily
carved second-century
Tetrapylon (four gates),
entrance to the sanctuary
of Aphrodite, dominated
the main street. It was
reconstructed in 1991
Top The Propylon,
gateway to the Sebasteion,
was not reassembled until
2016. Now plain, it was
once filled with statues,
including that of Aemilia
Lepida, overleaf*

The head of 'Aemilia
Lepida, daughter of
Marcus Lepidus' was
the great sculpture
discovery of 2016.
Aemilia, a famed
beauty, here seen with

a 'melon' hairstyle and
veil, was married to
a son of the Emperor
Germanicus. She took
her own life in the
high drama of Palatine
politics in AD36

Opposite Aemilia's
beautiful head has been
reunited with her body.
The statue once stood on
the Propylon, the gateway
to the grand Sebasteion
temple complex

ACKNOWLEDGEMENTS

The author is much indebted to the many friends in Turkey, France and Britain who helped over the articles published in *Cornucopia*. Immeasurable thanks are due to the ambassadors accredited to Turkey in the 1990s and early 2000s, whose embassies and consulates are featured, especially Dr Ekkehard Eickhoff, Susie Nemazee and Sir Peter Westmacott, and Dimitrios and Evelyne Macris; to the descendants of Kıbrıslı Mehmet Emin Pasha and Hekimbaşı Salih Efendi; to Selahattin and Ayşe Beyazıt, owners of the the Çürüksulu Mehmet Pasha Yalı; to Sevim Saka and her daughter Ayşe Bermek, owners of the Ahmet Vefik Pasha Library; to the late Zeki Kuneralp and to Sinan Kuneralp (grandson and great-grandson of Zeki Pasha) and Rukiye Kuneralp; to the Germen family; to Suna Mardin, owner of the Ratip Efendi Yalı; to Nedret and Mark Butler, owners of Sumahan on the Water, to Murat and Nina Köprülü, owners of the Ethem Pertev Yalı; to all the Hemşinli, notably the Yücel family; to Sema Menteşeoğlu and Ömer Oflaz, who introduced me to 'the Lake'; to Dr Mine Sofuoğlu of Ankara's Çengelhan Rahmi M. Koç Museum; to Prof Dr Zeynep Önen of VEKAM, and to Alageyik Apaydın and the late Osman Okyar, who plied me with information on old Ankara; to Prof Bert Smith, director of excavations at Aphrodisias, Trevor Proudfoot, director of the Cliveden Conservation Workshop, Dr Julia Lenaghan of the Ashmolean Museum, Oxford, and Dr Thomas Kaefer and Dr Gerhard Paul, senior anastylosis architects at Aphrodisias; to the late Arlette Mellaart for sharing her knowledge of the Bosphorus; to Prof Paolo Girardelli, for his advice on Istanbul's Italian architects; to Marie-Noël de Gary, formerly of the Musée Nissim de Camondo; to Uluç Özülker, Turkish ambassador to Paris, and his wife Selma Hanım; to Necla Erad, Atom and Naile Damalı, Polat and İclal Gülkan, Gerda Pensoy, Karaca and Zeynep Taşkent, and Sema Rabb for letting me stay with them, lending me their drivers or enthusiastically coming on these outings.

Thanks to Clive Crook for the book's design, to Fritz von der Schulenburg, Simon Upton, Jürgen Frank, Brian McKee, Cemal Emden and Jean-Marie del Moral for their magnificent photographs, and to Susana Raby, Hilary Stafford-Clark and Tony Barrell for invaluable editing.

Gratitude goes above all to Laurence and Linda Kelly and Mollie Norwich for proposing the project and for their continuing enthusiasm; and to John and Berrin Scott for their unfailing support in completing the book. Thanks are also due to John Julius Norwich for his generous foreword, and to Timothy Daunt, for his enouragement in the writing of these articles over a some twenty-five years.

PICTURE CREDITS

CORNUCOPIA ARTICLES

The chapters in this book first appeared as articles in *Cornucopia Magazine*.

Chapters

1 'Palaces of Diplomacy I', No 5, 1993
Photographs: Fritz von der Schulenburg
2 'Boating with Billy', No 52, 2015
Photographs: Fritz von der Schulenburg and Simon Upton
3 'Palaces of Diplomacy II', No 6, 1994
Photographs: Fritz von der Schulenburg
4 'The Jewel Box', No 7, 1994
5 'The Vizier's Retreat', No 8, 1995
6 'A Room for the Books', No 9, 1995
7 'Water's Edge', No 10, 1993
8 'The Great Yalı of Zeki Pasha', No 17, 1999
9 'Some Enchanted Evenings', No 18, 1999
Chaps 4–9 photographs: Simon Upton
10 'The House that Came out of the Blue', No 21, 2000
Photographs: Jean-Marie del Moral
11 'In the Spirit's Wake', No 34, 2005
Photographs: Jürgen Frank
12 'The Palace Lady's Summerhouse', No 36, 2006
Photographs: Fritz von der Schulenburg
13 'Country Houses that Ride the Storm', No 12, 1997
Photographs: Simon Upton
14 'Reflections on Water', No 20, 2000
Photographs: Fritz von der Schulenburg
15 'Sublime Portals', No 43, 2010
Photographs: Cemal Emden
16 'A Brave New World', No 39, 2008
17 'Fly in the Face of Fashion', No 47, 2012
Chaps 16–17 photographs: Fritz von der Schulenburg
18 'Treasures of a Lost Dynasty', No 26, 2002
19 'From Lunacy to Diplomacy', No 30, 2002
Chaps 18–19 photographs: by Jean-Marie del Moral
20 'Aphrodite's City', No 56, 2017
Photographs courtesy of Aphrodisias Excavations and Prof. R.R.R. Smith

GLOSSARY

AŞIBOYA Traditional red iron-oxide and linseed-oil paint often described as oxblood red
AUSPICIOUS EVENT Mahmud II's disbandment of the Janissary corps, 1826
BAILO Venetian envoy
BEDESTEN Covered market
BEY Title of a gentleman, used after the name (see *Hanım*)
CAPITULATIONS Treaty detailing rights, privileges and obligations granted by the Ottoman Sultan to European trading partners
DİVAN Council of ministers
DRAGOMAN Interpreter
FİRMAN Sultan's edict generally bearing his *tuğra*
GRAND VIZIER (Turkish *sadrazam*) Prime minister
GAZİ Popular title for Atatürk; used since early Ottoman times for victorious generals
HALİÇ The Golden Horn
HAMAM Turkish bath
HAN Caravanserai, from the Turkish *kervansaray*
HANIM Lady, placed after the first name when used as a title (see *Bey*)
HAREM Women's, or family, quarters of an Ottoman house (see *Selamlık*)
HÖYÜK Ancient mound
İSKELE Landing stage
İSTİKLÂL CADDESİ 'Independence Avenue', in Beyoğlu, formerly Grand' Rue de Pera
KAPLICA Thermal springs
KHEDIVE Turkish *Hidiv*, Ottoman viceroy of Egypt
KONAK Mansion
KÖŞK Origin of word 'kiosk'. Typically Ottoman summerhouse or garden pavilion; can also be a large residential building
LODOS South wind
MİHRAB Prayer niche
MİMBER Mosque pulpit
PASHA An honorary title awarded to senior Ottoman officers and dignitaries
PHANARIOTS Greeks living near the Orthodox Patriarchate in Fener on the Golden Horn
SELAMLIK Men's quarters or reception rooms (see Harem)
SELSEBİL Cascade fountain
SİPAHİ Landed Ottoman cavalry officer
SOFA Central hall
TANZİMAT Mid-19th century reform movement
TUĞRA Sultan's cipher
USTA Master craftsman
VIZIER Ottoman minister (see Grand vizier)
VOIVODE Title of princes of Wallachia and Moldavia
YALI Waterside residence

INDEX

Abbas Hilmi II, Khedive of Egypt 41, 47, 49, 109 172, 181; Khediva Mother, Princess Emine Necibe İlhami 32–33, 35, 41, 47; Princess Atiye (daughter) 73, 118

Abdülaziz 39, 89, 128, 274, 280

Abdülhamid II 22, 45, 46, 47, 50, 80, 89, 98, 100, 115, 120, 177, 197, 232

Abdülmecid I 17, 36, 38, 45, 73, 89, 91, 128, 260, 273

Aggiman, J.N. 220, 223

Afif Pasha Yalı, Yeniköy 39

Akkoyunlu tribe 169

Ahi fraternity 245, 246, 250–251

Ahi Elvan Mosque 250–251

Ahi Şerafettin Mosque 250

Ahmed III 35

Ahmed Vefik Pasha 79, 80, 81, 84; Library 78–85

Ahmet of Tiflis 185

Albanians 72, 118, 230

Aleppo 68–69, 70, 72

Ali Rıza Pasha (Menteşe) konak and family 169, 170, 173, 177, 180–181

Almanköy, Ankara 227, 228–229

Amcazade Hüseyin Pasha Yalı (see Köprülü Yalı)

Anadoluhisarı (village) 88, 97, 102, 139

Anadolu Hisarı (fortress) 35, 69

American Civil War 172

American Peace Corps 172

And, Cenap 117

Angora goat 233–235, 246, 250

Ankara 6, 7, 11, 18, 60, 73 101, 109, 117, 158, 186 192–253, 278, 280, 298; Ankara Garı (station) 192–193, 195, 196

Aphrodisias 7, 139, 284–297, 298

Aphrodite 287–292, 294

Armenians, 11, 35, 128, 155, 243; Patriarch 13

Art Deco 49, 195, 200, 203, 224, 230

Art Nouveau 39, 47, 49 137, 138, 261

Artvin bullfighting 157

Atatürk, Mustafa Kemal Pasha (Gazi) 18, 60, 116, 17, 158, 195, 206, 220, 236, 239, 223, 227

Atatürk Orman Çiftliği 226

Augustus, Emperor 240, 287, 289; *Res Gestae Divi Augusti* 240; Temple of 238, 239, 240, 242, 250

Auschwitz 258, 260, 263

Auspicious Event 16, 299

Austrian Embassy: Istanbul 13, 41, 46–47, 50–51; Ankara 216–217

Ayaz Pasha 72

Ayazpaşa (district) 60, 72

Ayder 157, 158

Aydın 98

Baghdad railway 195

Baguenault, Joseph 279

Bankalar Caddesi, Istanbul 99, 261, 274

Barry, Sir Charles 16, 20

Baştımar family 101, 102

Bebek 32–33, 35, 41, 47, 49, 115, 121

Bedriye Hanım (Milona) 101, 102, 105

Beekeeping 151, 157, 171

Belger, Prof Nihat Reşat 116

Belgian Embassy 220–221

Belgrade Forest 42, 49

Berker, Şevki 277

Bernard, Dr Karl Ambros 89

Bezm-î Âlem Valide Sultan 127–128

Beyazıt, Selahattin and Ayşe 57, 61, 298

Beyazıt I 237, 240

Beykoz, cricket pitch 49; opaline glass 61, 64–65

Beylerbeyi Palace 36, 38–39

Beyoğlu (see Pera)

Bibesco, Marthe, Princess 60

Bilgişin family (see Dirvana)

Birgi, Muharrem Nuri 56–67, 84

Bobet, Louison 198

Bouligny, Don Juan de 43

Bozok, Salih 205–206

British Embassy; Pera 12 13, 14, 15–18; Tarabya 39, 41, 45, 52, 212; Ankara 205–212, 230

Bruck, Baron Karl von 14

Burnaby, Captain Fred 185

Bursa 185, 250, 280

Busbecq, Ogier Ghiselin de 240, 241, 250

Butler, Nedret and Mark 127, 129–131, 139, 298

Büyükada (also see Princes Islands) 99, 100

Büyükdere 39, 41–45, 49, 54

Byzantines 12, 18, 46, 58, 72, 136, 140, 184, 185, 239, 240, 245, 246, 249, 289

Camondo family 256–275

Camondo Steps 261, 274

Canning, Sir Stratford 16, 18, 20, 44, 45

Cansever, Turgut 58, 61, 84

Caracalla Baths 239, 242, 243

Caria 169, 287, 288

Catherine the Great 13, 37, 70, 218

Caunus 171, 172, 174

Cemile Sultan 73, 91

Cenani (Ercan), Tevfik and Nadire 128–131

Chambrun, Charles de 198

Charles III of Spain 43, 54

Chasse, Patrick 140, 142

Christie, Agatha 58

Christoph & Unmack 227, 228

Cicero affair 230

Cingria, Alphonse 46

Clavijo, González de 155, 158

Committee of Union and Progress, 73, 100, 116

Corpi, Ignazio 17, 18, 30

Crimea 153, 154, 156, 158

Crimean War 18, 261

Currie, Sir Philip 22

Cyprus 71, 76

Çamlıhemşin 150–165

Çengelhan Rahmi M. Koç
Museum 246, 298

Çengelköy 36, 118, 126–133

Çukurhan (Divan
Çukurhan Hotel) 246

Çürüksulu Mehmet Pasha
59–60, 64; Belkıs Hanım
(daughter) 57, 60, 61;
Yalı (Muharrem Nuri
Birgi Yalı) 56–67

Dağ, Şevket 280

Dalaman 167, 172, 181

Dalyan 167, 171, 172

Darius 69, 97

D'Aronco, Raimondo 39,
47, 49, 52–53

Demetrius, Patriarch 43

Dernschwam, Hanz 241

Disraeli, Benjamin 15

Dirvana family (See Kıbrıslı
Mehmet Emin Pasha)

Divriği, Great Mosque and
Hospital 7, 182–193

Doğançay, Fethi 117

Dolmabahçe 16, 17, 36, 101

Dominioni, Caccia 213

Dörpfeld, Dr Wilhelm 45

Dragoyannis family 45

Drancy 263

Drusus Caesar 292

Dunand, Jean (laquer
mural) 202–203, 204

Duran, Carolus 256–257

Dutch Embassy, Pera
10–11, 12–13, 14,
18–19, 28

Earthquakes 14, 26, 41,
46, 47, 49, 59, 98, 99,
129, 167, 171, 173, 287

Ecevit, Bülent 110

Edin, Rıfat 140

Edirne 42, 70

Egli, Ernst 232–233

Egypt 12, 44

Egyptian Embassy (see
Khediva Mother's
Palace)

Egyptians 32–33, 35, 41,
47, 49, 60, 73, 76, 102,
108, 109, 110, 118, 136,
171–172, 181, 299

Eisenhower, General 277

Elgin, Lord 43, 44

Elizabeth I 12

Elizabeth II 205, 212

English High School,
Istanbul 101

Enver Pasha 73, 116

Ephesus 7, 169, 292

Erdebil, Bazaars of 185

Erim, Prof Kenan 7, 139,
289, 292

Erzincan 183, 184

Ertegün, Mehmet Münir
232

Ertegün, Mica 140, 146

Ethem Pertev (Eczacı)
38, 137, 140; Yalı
134–147, 298

Eugénie, Empress of France
39, 262, 280

Evliya Çelebi 185, 186

Esvapçıbaşı Sabit Efendi
116

Euphrates 183, 184

Faisal II of Iraq 107, 109,
110–111

Fane, Violet (Mrs Singleton)
see Sir Philip Currie)

Fazıl Ahmet (Aykaç) 76

Fazile (İbrahim), Princess
106–107, 109, 110–111

Fellows, Sir Charles
167, 169, 170, 288, 290

Fener (see Phanariot)

Fethi Ahmed Pasha Yalı 35

Fevziye, Empress of Iran 109

Fires 12, 13, 14, 15, 16, 25,
28, 39, 42, 43, 45, 49,
59, 80, 138, 212, 249

First Balkan War 243

First World War 46, 47,
73, 76, 128, 156, 169,
195, 205, 220, 223, 226,
230, 243, 263

Flora and gardens 12, 16,
42, 46, 54, 60, 69, 88,
89, 108, 138, 140, 152,
155, 156, 157, 158,
168, 172, 204, 213,
216–217, 261, 291

Fossati brothers 14, 18, 26

Franco-Prussian War 262

François I of France 12, 15

Franz Josef I of Austria
46–47, 50

French Embassy, Pera
12, 14, 18–19, 24–25;
Tarabya 39, 41, 44–45;
Ankara 198–205

Galata 11, 12, 17, 260,
261, 262, 274–275;
Galata Bridge 58

Galatia, Roman province of
196, 239, 240

Galatasaray 12; hamam
61; Imperial College of
Medicine 16, 88, 89, 90

Gautier, Théophile 44, 279

Gebze 140

Gencer, Leyla 91

George V 210

German Embassy:
Ayazpaşa 11 17, 18;
Tarabya 39, 41, 46;
Ankara 226–230

Germanicus, Emperor 296

Germen Yalı 114–125

Golden Horn 11, 12, 16, 22,
35, 43, 58, 62, 261, 299

Goltz Pasha 98, 197

Gounod, Charles 279

Grand National Assembly,
Ankara 101, 116, 195

Grand' Rue de Pera (İstiklâl
Caddesi) 11, 12, 13, 18,
99, 299

Greek Orthodox Patriarch
of Jerusalem 41, 46

Greeks 11, 35, 41, 43, 98,
102, 109, 170, 196, 299

Göbbels, Hubert 17

Gunther, Wladyslaw 223

Gutschow, Konstanty 227

Gülhane Decree (see
Tanzimat)

Güneşin, Mürşide 138–139

Gürer, Heidemaria 217

Habsburgs 35, 41, 43, 46,
47, 50–51, 216, 217, 240

Hacı Bayram Mosque
238–239, 240

Haghia Sophia 6, 18, 58

Hamlin, Dr Cyrus 80

Hanzade Sultan 100, 109,
110–111

Haroun al-Rashid 84

Haussmann, Baron 262

Haydar Emre & Cie 216

Haydarpaşa Station 212

Haynes, John Henry
240–241, 242

Hayri Kaptan 138
Hekimbaşı Salih Efendi
  37–38, 87–92, 298;
  Yalı 37–38, 86–95
Henri IV of France 15
Hemşin (see Çamlıhemşin)
Hill, Derek 56–57
Hitler, Adolph 227
Hittites 195, 236, 250,
  252–253
Hobart Pasha 212
Holzmeister, Clemens
  216, 217
Hornby, (Emelia) Lady 17
Hungarian Embassy 230
Hussein, King of Jordan 110
Ignatiev, General Nikolai
  44, 49
Iraq 107, 109, 110, 197, 205
Iraqi Revolution 110
Italian Embassy: Pera 11, 13,
  18, 28–29; Tarabya 39,
  41, 49, 52–53; Ankara
  204, 206, 212, 213–215
Izmir 101, 102, 117, 154, 155,
  158, 170, 243, 287, 288
Iwanicki, Karol 223
Janissaries 13, 16, 42,
  280, 299
Jason and the Argonauts
  39, 108, 151
Julian, Emperor 241–242
Julian Column 239, 240–242
Julius Caesar 288
Joukowsky, Martha 139
Kaçkar Mts 151, 156–157
Kandilli 7, 36, 60, 91, 116
Kanlıca 38, 88, 128,
  135, 138, 140
Karlowitz, Treaty of 35
Kaslowsky family 77

Kavalalı Mehmed Ali
  Pasha 108, 118
Khediva Mother (see
  Abbas Hilmi II)
Khediva Mother's Palace
  32–33, 35, 41, 47, 49
Khurram Shah of Ahlat 185
Kıbrıslı Mehmet Emin Pasha
  68–72; Yalı 37, 68–77
Kılıç Ali 206
Knox-Helm, Alexander
  205, 206, 208
Koç, Rahmi M. 36 (also
  see Çengelhan)
Komili family 77
Konaklar Mahallesi 152
Konya 72, 183, 184
Köprülü family 35, 135,
  136, 139, 140, 298
Köprülü (Amcazade
  Hüseyin Pasha) Yalı
  34–35, 72, 139
Köyceğiz 148–149, 151,
  166–181
Krencker, Daniel 239
Krippel, Heinrich 194–195
Kuneralp, Zeki 100, 298
Kuzguncuk 35
Lamballe, Hôtel de 276–283
Lamballe, Princesse de 7,
  278
Laprade, Albert 198, 204
Lasciac, Antonio 47
Laurecisque, Pierre 15, 25
Lausanne, Treaty of 196,
  205, 232
Lauzan, Duc de 278, 280
Layard, Henry Austin 80
Le Corbusier 36, 233
Leiden University 79,
  80–81, 298

Leleu, Jules 203, 204
Le Nôtre, André 204
Lennep, The Reverend
  Henry Van 243–245
Leoni, Giacomo 17
Lepida, Aemilia 292,
  294, 296–297
Le Tarnec, Sophie 261
Limur, Comte and Comtesse
  de 279, 280–281
Lindsay, Sir Ronald 206
London Dilettante Society
  288
Loraine, Sir Percy 212
Loti, Pierre 73
Louis-Philippe of France 15
Leishman, John G. A. 17, 18
Louvre 257, 258, 262, 282
Löwenhielm, Carl Gustaf
  8–9, 11
Mahmud II 98, 108, 127,
  299
Mahmud Nedim Pasha 128
Malatya 183, 184, 186
Manzikert, Battle of 184
Marmara Island 220
Marmara University 39, 45
Mardin family 107–110, 298
Marie Antoinette 7, 278, 282
Martin, Henri 232
Maupassant, Guy de 279
Mehmed the Conqueror
  (Fatih Sultan Mehmed II)
  79, 88, 97, 249, 250
Mehmed V Reşad 100, 115
  121; wives 116
Mehmed VI Vahdettin 100,
  101, 195, 196; Princess
  Sabiha (daughter) 100
Mehmet Ali, Prince 110
Memmo, Andrea 13

Menemenci, Refika 101, 105
Menemencioğlu, Ethem 60
Menemencioğlu, Nevin and
  Numan 277, 280
Mengujek (Menguçlu)
  dynasty 184
Menteşeoğlu family
  168–170, 174, 177, 298
Mevlâna 184
Michael III, Emperor 245
Mihrimah Sultan 246
Mitterrand, President 18, 25
Mohair 233, 243, 246,
  250, 251
Moltke, Field Marshal
  Helmuth von 46
Mongeri, Giulio 230
Monte Carlo 110, 169
Mordtmann, J.H. 242
Mosul 206
Muallâ, Fikret 279
Musée des Colonies 204
Musée Nissim de Camondo
  256–275
Museum of Anatolian
  Civilisations, Ankara
  236, 239, 241, 248–249
Mussolini, Benito 213, 214
Mustafa Reşid Pasha 71, 260
Nadolny, Rudolf 227, 230
Napoleon III 39
Napoleon Bonaparte 44
Neoclassical style 14, 39,
  72, 84, 98, 117, 223,
  224, 226, 261, 277, 285
Nerval, Gérard de 15, 279
Neslişah Sultan 100, 109
Nicolson, Nigel 107
Nightingale, Florence 17,
  18, 20
Noailles, Comtesse de 60

Notre Dame de Sion, Sisters 46; School 101
Orient Express 58, 220
Ortaköy 101, 116
Ostrorog Yalı 36, 60
Öztürk, Hüseyin 139
Palin, Nils Gustaf 11, 14, 15
Pallavicini, Count 47
Papen, Franz von 216, 227
Pardoe, Julia 38, 69, 88
Paris 7, 59, 60, 71, 76, 80, 83, 99, 109, 116, 140, 169, 204, 254–285, 298
Paulician Christians 184
Pera (Beyoğlu) 8–31, 41, 44, 45, 47, 99, 212
Pera House 15–17, 20–23
Pera Museum 22–23
Perugia 170, 177
Petit Trianon (Versailles) 198, 204, 263, 264
Pferschy, Othmar 192–193, 195, 298
Phanariots 43, 44, 45, 299
Philipp Holzmann AG 227
Phrygians 239
Pilavoğlu Han, Ankara 249
Pococke, Edward 241–242
Polish Embassy 222–226
Pompadour, Mme de 279, 282
Pope John XXIII 213
Princes Islands 42, 99, 212
Ratip, Ebubekir 108–112
Ratıp Efendi Yalı 106–113
Reinach, Léon and Béatrice 258–259 263, 270
Rhodes 100, 169
Rıza Tevfik (Bölükbaşı) 76
Robert College 17, 80
Rome 240, 287–291

Roncalli, Monsignor (see Pope John XXIII)
Roussin, Admiral 14–15
Rumelihisarı (village) 76, 79, 80, 97, 98, 100, 102
Rumeli Hisarı (fortress) 69, 79, 80, 88, 90, 142
Russian Embassy: Pera 13, 14, 18–19, 26–27; Büyükdere 41, 44, 48, 49; Ankara 218–219, 223
Rüstem Pasha 58, 246
Sadullah Pasha Yalı 36–37
Saffet Pasha Yalı 138
St Petersburg 12, 14, 18, 70, 109
Sait Halim Pasha Yalı 39
Sakıp Sabancı Museum 4–5, 7, 39, 298
Saka family 84, 298
Schede, Martin 239
Schliemann, Heinrich 45
Sébastiani, Horace-François Bastien 44
Second World War 47, 57, 60, 76, 100, 101, 138, 154, 186, 204, 206, 211, 216, 226, 227, 232, 260, 278, 280, 288
Selim II 71
Selim III 44, 58, 169
Seljuks 169, 170, 183–186, 237, 239, 240, 250, 291
Sergent, René 262–264, 269
Simeryol railway line 186
Sinan, Mimar 42, 240, 246
Sivas 183, 186, 195
Smith, Thomas 16, 20
Smith, Prof RRR 7, 292, 298
Sokollu Mehmed Pasha 58
Spanish Embassy,

Büyükdere 39, 41 43, 54
Stark, Freya 57, 87, 91, 94, 167
Stratford de Redcliffe, Lord (see Canning)
Suetonius 240
Suez Canal 39, 262, 280
Sumahan on the Water 126–133, 139
Surich, Comrade 218
Süleyman the Magnificent 42, 58, 72, 240, 246
Swedish Embassy, Pera 8–9, 11, 12, 14–15
Sweet Waters of Asia 69
Swiss Embassy 232–233
Şeni, Nora 261
Tacitus 292
Tamerlane 155, 237, 240
Tanzimat 38, 71, 136, 299
Tarabya 15, 39, 41–46, 49, 52–53, 212, 226
Tehran 80, 154
Texier, Charles 15, 242
Tırnakçızade family 59
Tiberius Caesar 292
Tiberius Julius Justus Junianus 242
Topkapı Palace 8–9, 11, 12, 57, 115, 186
Tophane 12, 88, 100
Trabzon 101, 151, 158
Trade 11, 18, 59, 101, 151, 153, 156, 157, 172, 184, 186, 245, 246, 249, 250, 251, 260, 299
Tugay, Emine (Fuat)136
Tunalı family 117
Turco-Russian War 98, 156
Turkish Embassy, Paris (see Hôtel de Lamballe)

Umberto, King of Italy 110
Union Centrale des Arts Décoratifs 257
Ürgüplü, Hayri 110
Üsküdar 57, 61, 62, 69, 115, 212
Valens, Emperor 42
Vallaury, Alexandre 39, 79, 81–83, 99
Vaniköy 114–125
Venice 12, 13, 14, 28–29, 37 58, 250, 260
Victor Emmanuel II 261
Victoria, Queen 15, 20, 36
Vlora family 118
War of Independence 116, 196, 197, 251
Wilhelm I, Kaiser 39, 45
Wilhelm II, Kaiser 18, 46
Wood, Building with 39, 70, 72, 99, 117, 140, 151, 153, 173, 220, 273
Wortley Montagu, Lady Mary 42
Yakup Kadri (Karaosmanoğlu) 204
Yahya Kemal (Beyatlı) 76
Yalova Spa 116
Yemen 58
Yeniköy 39, 40–41, 46, 49, 50–51, 87, 106–113, 118, 261, 274
Yıldız Palace 45, 121
Ypsilanti, Prince Alexander 44
Yutkevich, Sergei 218
Zeki Pasha Yalı 96–105
Zilkale 158
Zoilos, Gaius Julius 288, 289, 290, 293
Zonaro, Fausto 22–23